# SAILING DIRECTIONS EAST AND NORTH COASTS OF IRELAND

*First published 1930, East Coast*
*Second Edition, 1946, do.*
*Third Edition, 1956, East and North Coasts*
*Fourth Edition, 1965, do.*
*Fifth Edition, 1970, do.*
*Sixth Edition, 1979, do.*
*Seventh Edition, 1991, do.*
*Eighth Edition, 1995, do.*
*Ninth Edition, 1999, do.*
© Irish Cruising Club Publications Ltd.

The Irish Cruising Club Publications also publishes a companion volume *South and West Coasts of Ireland - Sailing Directions*. Both volumes are available from booksellers and chandlers. In the U.K. (excluding Northern Ireland and all overseas areas) copies may be obtained from the agents Imray, Laurie, Norie & Wilson Ltd., Wych House, The Broadway, St. Ives, Huntingdon, Cambridgeshire PE17 4BT, England, Telephone 44 (0) 1480-462114 and in Ireland they may be obtained from Arthur Orr, Evergreen, 11 Old Holywood Road, Belfast BT4 2HJ Northern Ireland Telephone 44 (0) 1232-763601.

Plans - © *Irish Cruising Club Publications Ltd.*
The plans contained in these Sailing Directions are not to be used for navigation. They are included to assist the user to more readily relate to the text and should always be used with the latest up to date navigational charts.

Printed by W. & G. Baird Ltd., Greystone Press, Antrim.

ISBN No. 0 9501717 8 6

# SAILING DIRECTIONS

## for the

# EAST AND NORTH COASTS OF IRELAND

Compiled by Members of the Club, together with information
supplied by many other yachtsmen who have enjoyed the Irish Coast
With a foreword by Sandy Taggart, Honorary Member of the Irish
Cruising Club and distinguished past Hon. Sec. of the Clyde Cruising Club.

*"What joy to sail the crested sea and watch the waves beat white upon the Irish shore."*

# Foreword

When invited to write this foreword I reflected upon the time I first purchased a copy of the Irish Cruising Club Sailing Directions and was astonished at the fact that it was almost 50 years ago. Various editions have been purchased since then and it is worthy of note how the Sailing Directions have developed in so many ways over the years to the latest edition now presented to you. They must rank with the best publications of their type available to cruising people.

The main element of success of such publications is that they are prepared by cruising sailors not exclusively for their own use but for the use of like minded people who enjoy cruising in interesting and challenging waters. Also where fellow cruisers meet in many of the snug havens covered by this publication, experiences are exchanged and friendships established.

A great deal of hard work goes into the production, maintenance and updating of such a definitive work and it is appropriate that an expression of appreciation should be made for all the voluntary hours put in and contributions of information submitted by so many.

Recent editions of the Sailing Directions have been greatly enhanced by excellent aerial colour photography. This not only gives a view from another dimension while actually cruising but also provides great enjoyment when cruise planning or recounting to friends the joys of cruising in Irish waters. The warmth of the legendary Irish welcome and hospitality exudes from every one.

The charts are also clear with prominent type, much needed as the cruising years have rolled by and there is excellent detail in the body of the text of many other anchorages, harbours and havens not covered by chart or photograph. Just the right sort of precise information to set the mind at rest when on a cruising adventure in strange waters.

The Irish Cruising Club is to be congratulated on the production of this latest edition of the East and North Coasts Sailing Directions to Ireland which has certainly set a new high standard.

Thank you for the great honour in asking me to write this piece and for the fellowship and friendship of fellow members and all other cruising folk that I have enjoyed over the years.


February 1999

SANDY TAGGART
*Honorary Member*

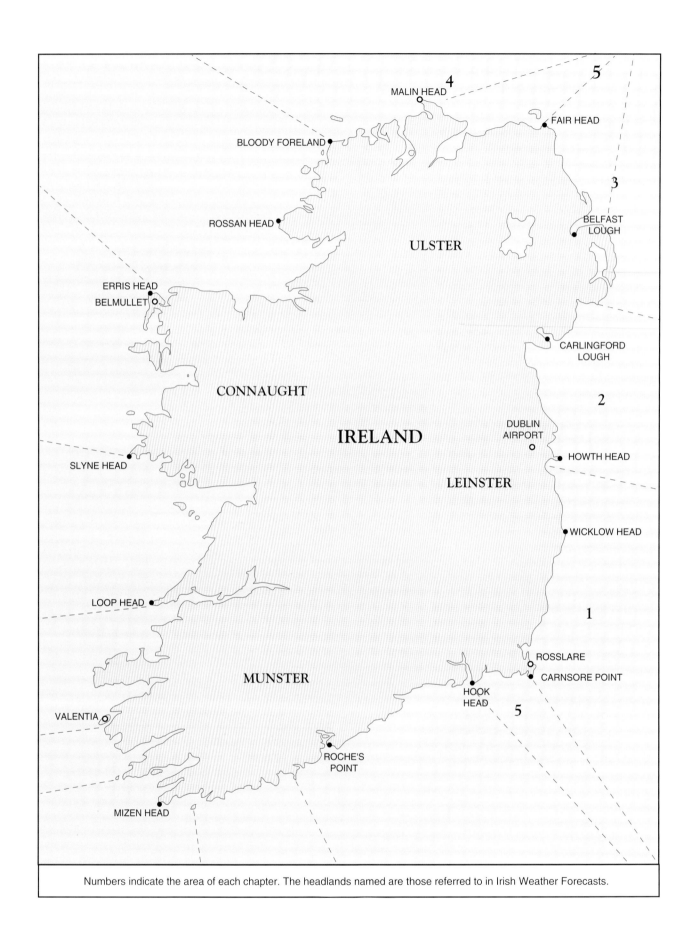

4

MALIN HEAD ●

5

FAIR HEAD ●

BLOODY FORELAND ●

3

BELFAST
LOUGH ●

ULSTER

ROSSAN HEAD ●

ERRIS HEAD ●
BELMULLET ○

CARLINGFORD
LOUGH

CONNAUGHT

2

IRELAND

DUBLIN
AIRPORT ○

SLYNE HEAD ●

HOWTH HEAD ●

LEINSTER

WICKLOW HEAD ●

LOOP HEAD ●

1

MUNSTER

ROSSLARE ○

CARNSORE POINT ●

VALENTIA ○

HOOK
HEAD ●

5

ROCHE'S
POINT ●

MIZEN HEAD ●

Numbers indicate the area of each chapter. The headlands named are those referred to in Irish Weather Forecasts.

# CONTENTS

# APPENDICES

# EAST AND NORTH COASTS

# CARNSORE POINT
## to
# BLOODY FORELAND

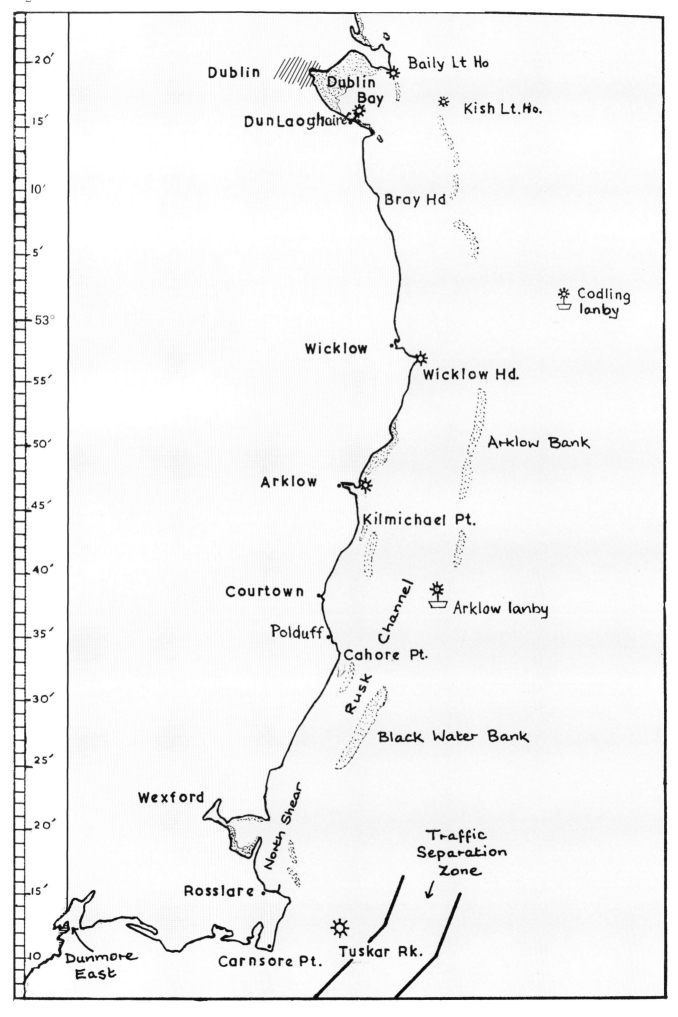

# Chapter 1

## CARNSORE POINT TO DUBLIN BAY

**Charts** (*see Appendix 1*)
The two charts required are 1787 and 1468 and only these are normally used. The smaller scale charts 1410 and 1411 would be adequate for passage making. They include the W coast of Wales and the Isle of Man and 1411 covers as far N as Larne. A Traffic Separation Zone is in operation off Tuskar Rock. (*See chart 1787*).

**General**
This part of the coast is fronted by a series of banks at varying distances from the shore. There are no very attractive anchorages. Rosslare provides shelter in S winds. Arklow and Wicklow are safe harbours and useful stopping places. Dun Laoghaire is a major yachting centre.

**Tides**
The flood tide runs Northerly into and up St George's Channel while the tide is rising at Dover and the ebb runs out Southerly for the other 6 hours approximately. The stream turns more or less simultaneously everywhere outside the banks but the time of HW, which is roughly −0500 Dover at Carnsore Point, becomes progressively later between this and Dublin Bay where it is +0020 Dover. Inshore the stream turns earlier than in the open sea. It flows across the sandbanks, the flood setting onto their inner side and the ebb onto their outer side. A description of local tidal streams is given where necessary.

**Approaching the Irish Sea from the West**
The area W of Carnsore Point is described in the Club's *South and West Coasts of Ireland – Sailing Directions*. In calm, clear weather yachts usually take the short route through Saltee Sound, close round Carnsore Point, then up to Greenore Point and either in to Rosslare or N inside the banks. However, if there was any possibility of fog, yachts would be well advised to keep outside the Coningbeg LV and the Tuskar Rock.

**Approaching the Irish Sea from the South**
The SE corner of Ireland is always a potentially dangerous landfall for yachts coming from Land's End, owing to the combination of outlying rocks and cross tides. It is difficult to estimate the tidal set off the Bristol Channel, and as Ireland is approached the streams become stronger. In poor visibility it would be dangerous to come in W of the Tuskar. If the bearings of its radio beacon can be taken the landfall is simplified. While the Tuskar is not an ideal landfall it is much better than the Smalls off the Welsh coast. Yachts bound from Land's End to Dublin whose direct course passes close to the Smalls should nevertheless aim to pass close to the Tuskar. Yachtsmen not pressed for time might prefer to sail from the Scillies to Dunmore East, which has the advantage of avoiding the shipping lanes.

**If bound for Rosslare from the South**, a yacht need not leave the Tuskar to port. Instead leave South Rock buoy fairly close to starboard and proceed 330° towards South Long buoy at the entrance to South Shear. Take care that a strong ebb tide flowing SSW does not set you near The Bailies. Traffic Separation Lanes are shown on chart 1787. The inshore lane is for SW-going ships and passes 2M SE of the Tuskar. Yachts bound round the Tuskar should therefore keep within 2M of it, where nothing larger than coasters should be encountered. A yacht which must cross the lanes should do so as quickly as possible at right angles.

## DIRECTIONS

### TUSKAR TO DUBLIN BAY
The normal route is outside the Blackwater bank, inside the South Arklow Lanby Buoy and from there past Wicklow Head. In foggy conditions it would be safer to keep well outside the banks and the Codling Lanby Buoy, setting a course to pass E of the Kish Light and when this light is sighted, it is then safe to approach Dublin Bay. The danger in being too close outside the banks is that the ebb sets obliquely across them from seaward. Conversely, if sailing inside the banks the flood setting onto their inner side must be avoided.

**Bound South from Dublin Bay**, a yacht should first make for Wicklow Head. After passing W of Arklow Bank, Arklow Lanby buoy may be used to depart for the English Channel, a course 180° from it leading between Cape Cornwall Bank and Seven Stones. Alternatively, after passing Horseshoe buoy (off Wicklow Head), a course 190° from it leads to the Tuskar, the usual departure point. If bound for the South of Ireland an inshore route may be preferred passing outside Glassgorman banks, through the Rusk channel towards Rosslare and finally close round Greenore Point and Carnsore Point. This passage should not be attempted at night.

## CARNSORE POINT

Carnsore Point, the SE extremity of Ireland, is a clay cliff 16m high with rocky shelves below it and a depth of 18m 3 cables off. In clear weather its position may be judged by Forth Mountain, just SW of Wexford, which is 225m high and often visible from 20M offshore. In rough weather with wind against tide there is quite a dangerous race off the point around the times of local HW and LW.

**Tuskar Rock**, 6M ENE of Carnsore Point, is 5m high with a tall lighthouse and a radio mast. It is foul for 1 cable on its N and W sides but steepto on its E side. At 2 cables SW of it there is a rock awash. About 6 cables SSW of it is South Rock, 2·4m deep, 7·5 cables S of which is a S Card. buoy showing Q (6) + LFl.15s. Gipsy Rock, 2m deep, lies 2 cables NNW of the Tuskar. Tuskar lighthouse is white, Q (2) 7·5s33m24M Horn (4) 45sRC. Racon.

### Tidal stream

Outside the rock the tide runs about NE from −0530 Dover till HW Dover and then SW for 6 hours at 2·5 kn. Yachts should give the Tuskar a good berth, particularly in light weather, for as well as the tide setting onto the rock there is probably an eddy running back towards it on the other side.

**Fundale Rock** is the end of a reef running SE from Crossfintan Point. It is 0·5M offshore and 1M NE of Carnsore Point. It dries at half tide and till recently was marked by a perch which has broken down. Off Fundale Rock there is a Porthand Can Light Buoy Fl (2) R 10s. Should the buoy have gone, Black Rock open of Carnsore Point leads SE of the rock. **Collough Rock**, 0·5 of a cable wide and awash at its N edge, is not marked and lies about 1·75M NE of Carnsore Point and 0·5M E of Crossfintan Point. **Black Rock** just open of Carnsore Point leads SE of it. Ballytrent House in line with **Whilkeen Rock** and bearing 340° leads close NE of it. Whilkeen Rock lies 8 cables N by W of Collough Rock. It is at the outer end of a reef extending 4 cables out from the shore. It often cannot be spotted near HW and is awash at HWS. Ballytrent House bearing 330° leads close NE of it and Carne pier bearing 240° leads close SE of it. **The Bailies** is an irregular bank of rocks and coarse ground 9m to 10m deep in places. It is situated halfway between the Tuskar and the coast W of it. The tidal streams crossing it cause heavy overfalls which are frequently dangerous, although on approach it may not appear so. The area should be avoided, which fortunately is not difficult as the channels E and W of it are both over 1M wide.

## ST MARGARET'S BAY

St. Margaret's Bay, between Whilkeen Rock and Carne pier 0·5M SW of it, provides shelter in winds between SW and NNW. Approaching from Carnsore Point pass close to Fundale buoy and from it steer N, which leads between the offshore rocks and Collough Rock. When Carne pier bears WNW, turn in steering NW. Coming from N, having cleared Whilkeen Rock by 2 cables, steer towards the pier. Anchor 2 or 3 cables NE of the pier in 3m to 4 m – sand. It is a useful and comfortable anchorage in strong NW wind, to which Rosslare is dangerously exposed. The pier dries and yachts should not consider mooring alongside. Also, rocks extend 20m beyond the pier head.
   Carne Pier Fl.R.3s4M.

### Facilities (CARNE)
- There is a small shop here, also a restaurant.
- Visitors may use fishermen's moorings when not in use.
- Supermarket at Lady's Island, 3M from Pier. Electrical repairs 1M.
- Pubs and restaurants within 5 miles.
- Cab hire adjacent to pier.

## GREENORE POINT

Greenore Point, the SE end of Rosslare Bay, is 18m high with clay cliffs. It is surrounded by dangers. Carrick Rock extends 3·5 cables ENE of the point and is marked by a red mast. There is a dangerous unmarked wreck, the remains of a steamer, 6·5 cables E of the point where the depth is only about 3m. Splaugh Rock covers a large area 6 to 7·5 cables SE of Greenore Point. Part of it would be dry at LAT and all of it is less than 2m deep. The red buoy marking it, Fl.R 6s, is 8 cables ENE of **Splaugh Rock**. Calmines (locally called The Cawmeens) is a shoal patch which dries along part of its outer edge about 4 cables offshore and which extends 0·5M NW of Carrick Rock. A red buoy, Fl.R. 2s, marking its NE side is 1·6M and 106° from Rosslare Lt. The red sector of Rosslare light covers it.

5

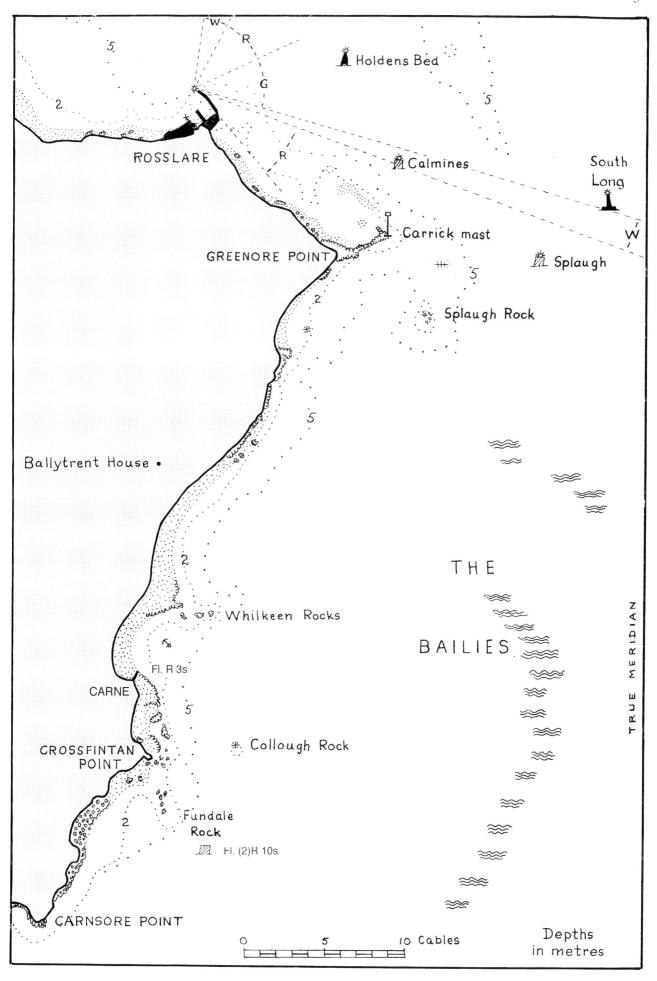

W
R
G
R
Holdens Bed

ROSSLARE

Calmines

South
Long

Carrick mast

GREENORE POINT

Splaugh

2

5

Splaugh Rock

Ballytrent House •

5

THE

2

BAILIES

Whilkeen Rocks

Fl. R 3s

CARNE

5

CROSSFINTAN
POINT

Collough Rock

Fundale
Rock

2

Fl. (2)R 10s

CARNSORE POINT

0          5          10 Cables

Depths
in metres

TRUE MERIDIAN

## Directions
### CARNSORE POINT TO ROSSLARE

This passage should not be attempted at night. Keep a sharp lookout for lobster pots. In rough onshore weather it is better to sail outside Collough Rock (*see above*) and outside or 1 cable W of Splaugh buoy, but avoid The Bailies by keeping Splaugh buoy bearing NE when within 2M of it. Going S this means heading for Carnsore Point till Ballytrent House is abeam and then turning S till Black Rock appears outside Carnsore Point. The normal and shortest route is from 1·5 cables off Carnsore Point to Fundale buoy, then N to pass between Collough Rock and Crossfintan Point. When the latter comes abeam steer towards Greenore Point, about 016°. This should lead outside Whilkeen Rock, but if it cannot be seen before Carna pier bears 240° head out a bit. When Ballytrent House comes abeam alter course to 030° to leave Carrick mast about 1·5 cables to port, then steer for Calmines buoy and after leaving it to port head for Rosslare Pier and do not go S of the straight course to the pier.

**Bound South from Rosslare pier**, after rounding Carrick mast steer SW till 0·5M off the shore, then continue at this distance off and when past Ballytrent House if Whilkeen Rock cannot be seen take bearings to clear it (*see above*). When past it steer for the furthest land and when E of Carna pier get Fundale buoy bearing S and steer for it. If beating, it is simplest to pass outside Collough Rock but do not tack out too far as it is best to keep well away from The Bailies. Careful pilotage is essential beating past Splaugh Rock. Splaugh buoy bearing 050° leads 1 cable SE of it. Rosslare Pier Lighthouse in line with Carrick Mast leads 1·75 cables NE of it but only about 60m SW of the dangerous wreck, so keep the lighthouse slightly open left of the mast. To pass NE of the wreck keep Calmines buoy bearing 325° or less, or Carrick mast 280° or less. In Northerly or Southerly winds it is simpler to beat inside Splaugh Rock and the wreck. Rosslare Pier visible outside Greenore Point leads only 0·5 of a cable SW of the rock so keep it closed. On the other tack keep between 1 and 3 cables away from Carrick mast. Avoid the rock 2 cables offshore 0·5M SSW of Greenore Point. Closer to the point it is safe to tack 1·5 cables offshore.

### SOUTH SHEAR

South Shear, the channel between Holdens Bed (*see below*) on the N and Greenore Point foreshore and rocks, is 0·5M wide and leads into South Bay and Rosslare Harbour. It is entered between Splaugh buoy and South Long buoy and from nearer the latter it is a direct course in to Rosslare leaving Calmines buoy close to port and Holden's Bed buoy some distance to starboard. At night the white sector of Rosslare light leads in. Coming in from the Tuskar allowance must be made for the strong cross tide. It is unwise to attempt entry in poor visibility unless you have facilities for establishing the course made good.

## Tidal streams

Inshore of the Tuskar the flood usually starts at +0500 Dover and runs NNE at up to 2·5 kn at springs. The ebb starts at −0200 Dover and runs SSW at up to 3·25 kn at springs. Unfortunately, in this area the time of change, direction and rate is apt to vary a lot. At the South Shear the ingoing stream averages 1 kn running from −0600 Dover for 3 hours, the outgoing stream averaging 2 kn for 9 hours from −0300 Dover. Inshore of Long Bank the Northerly stream ceases at −0200 Dover and the Southerly stream ceases at −0400 Dover. In Rosslare Bay the streams are weak generally Northerly from 0500 Dover to −0100 Dover.

## Banks and buoys

The following banks are between Greenore Point and Cahore Point. Being mostly of sand their positions and depths tend to alter and it is therefore important to avoid them:

**Holdens Bed**, NE of the South Shear channel, has a least depth of 5·8m. Close N of it **Long Bank** starts with a least depth of 2·8m near its centre extending N for 4M. The following buoys mark these banks: **South Long**, S Card VQ (6) + LFl.10s, Whis. is off the SE end of Holdens Bed. S. Holdens Buoy Fl.(2) G 6s is due S of the Bed. W Holdens Buoy Fl.(3) G10s lies SW of Holdens Bed. **West Long** QG lies W of the shallow parts of Long Bank. **North Long**, N Card. Q, Whis. lies off the N point of Long Bank. Barham Shoals, 8m deep, extend N of North Long buoy.

**Lucifer Bank**, least depth 3·5m, lies 1·5M E of Long Bank. Lucifer buoy, E Card VQ(3)5s, is moored well E of the S end of the bank which is called New Ground.

**Blackwater Bank** N of Lucifer Bank is 8M long. Its S part has a least depth of 2m and its N part, called Moneyweights Bank, dries for about 0·5M. The following buoys mark it: South Blackwater, S Card Q (6) + LFl.15s, Whis. is between it and Lucifer Bank. SE Blackwater, red, Fl.R 10s, is off the E side of its S part. East Blackwater, E Card Q (3)10s Whis. is off the E side of its N part. West Blackwater, Fl.G. 6s. in position 52° 25′·83 N 06° 13′·50 W is off the W side of its S part. No 1 Rusk, green, unlit, is off the W side of its N part. North Blackwater, N Card Q is off its N end.

**Rusk Bank** has a least depth of 2·4m. Its S part is separated from Moneyweights Bank by 0·5M wide Rusk Channel. Its N part extends 1M towards Cahore Point. It is marked by 3 red buoys on its E side: No. 2 Rusk Fl.(3)R. 10s, No. 4 Rusk (unlit) and No. 6 Rusk Fl.R. 3s. near its N tip. The No. 1 Rusk Buoy (unlit) lies approximately ·5M E of the No. 2 Rusk, and along with the latter buoy, marks the S entrance to the Rusk Channel.

**The Ram**, between Rusk Bank and Cahore Point, has a least depth of 1·4m near the shore but less water has been reported on a number of occasions in the last few years.

## ROSSLARE HARBOUR *(BA Chart 1772)*

HW – 0500 Dover. Rise 2·5 – 1·4/0·8 – 0·0M. Rosslare Europort is a very busy roll-on, roll-off Port, and in 1998 was the busiest Passenger Port on the island of Ireland. Shipping Traffic consists of Conventional Vessels [speed up to 22 knots] and Fast Ferries [speed up to 40 knots]. In June/July/August approximately 80 ships visit the Port each week. Yachts should call ROSSLARE HARBOUR on VHF Channel 12 (or telephone 053 57921/087 2320251) when approaching the Port. Yachts may lie alongside fishing boats or the Pier to the SW of the Port (depth is 3·7m at chart datum). Yachts should not anchor within 5 cables N and E or 3 cables W of the NE Breakwater, or in the approaches to the Port. The area NW of Ballygeary Light, marked with an anchor on the plan, could be fully occupied with lobster pots. A better anchorage would be further to the NW in winds between WSW and SE. Any anchorage or berth alongside will be uncomfortable in moderate winds from WNW to ENE, and dangerous when winds freshen between W and ESE. If this happens, leave without delay, at night putting to sea through the South Shear. Rosslare Harbour is still a valuable anchorage/berth for yachts bound S and held up by head winds.

**Facilities:** Engine & Electrical Repair Facilities [Rosslare Ship Repairs Telephone 053-33194] Fuel, Water and Provisions are available in plentiful supply locally. Water is available on Ro-Ro Quays. Fuel and Gas from local Garages. There is a good supermarket in the village, which will assist in deliveries. Four good hotels, about 100 B&Bs and many good restaurants and pubs within 3 miles of the village. There are frequent bus/rail connections to all major towns in Ireland. Car Hire, Taxi Service and Tourist Office, are readily accessible in the main Terminal Building.

**Lights:** From a Red Tower at the end of the NE Breakwater, elevation 15m Occ WRG 5s 13–10M. It shows Red over Foul Ground from Greenore Point. White sector along the South Shear, 286° to 291°. Green over S part of Holden's Bed. Red over the N part where Holden's bed is shallowest. White over the North Shear, 188° to 208°. Green over South Bay. On the NE end of the reclaimed land to the SW of the Port there is Ballygeary Light Occ WR 1.7s 7m 4M, Red shore to 152°, White (intensified) 152° to 200° (48°), White (unintensified) 200° to 205° (5°). A Green Conical Buoy QG ROSSLARE 3 is positioned to the NW of the Port at 52°15·36′N 6°20·45′W, to mark the dredged area [7·5m].

**LIFEBOAT** *(See Appendix 7)*

*Rosslare Harbour from S.*

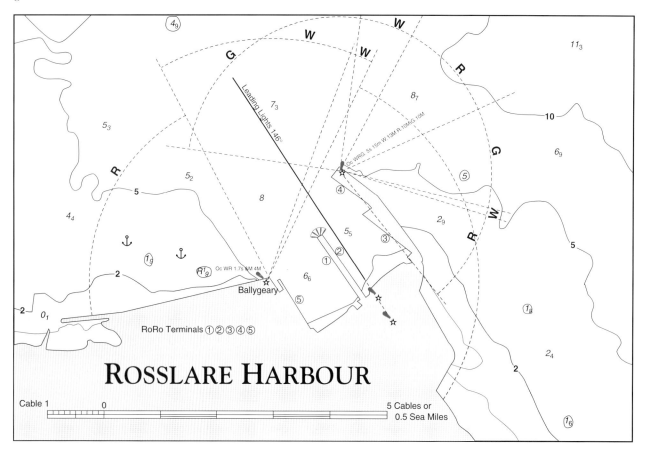

## ROSSLARE HARBOUR

**WEXFORD HARBOUR**

On the bar HWS −0330 Dover and HWN +0630 Dover; at the quay 1 hour later. Rise: 1·7-1·4/0·5-0·4m. There is a safe sheltered anchorage off Wexford town quays. The port is no longer used commercially, only by local fishing boats. Approximately 20 orange buoys are laid by members of the Wexford Harbour Boat Club. Steering 263° from the North Long Buoy for a distance of approx. 2M will bring a yacht to the off-lying landfall buoy which is the beginning of the marked channel laid by the Boat Club. In strong wind between S and E the sea breaks on the bar and it is dangerous to go anywhere near it. Slaney wreck, 1·25M SE of Raven Point, is no longer a serious danger. Advice regarding the state of the channel, and possibly a pilot to guide you in, may be obtained from the following: Wexford Harbour Boat Club, Telephone 053-22039 also on VHF 16, or Seamus Fenlon: 053-46566.

### Anchorage

Having entered between the training walls, a yacht should leave the island (ballast bank) to starboard. It is convenient to berth alongside the wooden quays or beside the mussel boats berthed there (but see below). Alternatively, a yacht may anchor on the E side between the ballast bank and the bridge. On the W side it is shoal for about 1·5 cables below the bridge, and there is a covered rock there. There are 4 visitor courtesy moorings directly N of the ballast bank.

Motor yachts may pass below the central arch of the bridge, clearance 5·7m, and beyond it should leave the 1m high Black Rock 0·5 of a cable to port till it bears S, so as to avoid the unmarked and submerged Kilcock Rock, which lies 1 cable N of Black Rock. There is convenient anchorage in 3m off the Wexford Harbour Boat Club clubhouse and slip on the S shore just W of the abutment of a previous bridge. The river Slaney is navigable as far as Enniscorthy.

It is not currently (1999) possible to berth at the Quays due to harbour works, but visiting yachts may tie up outside the Mussel Boats at the new berth on the E side of the river.

**Facilities:** Fuel and fresh water along the quays. Good shops (6 day week), hotels, banks,. close to quay. Swimming pool, caravan park at Ferrybank (end of bridge) also garage, hospital, launderette and restaurants. Showers at Wexford Harbour Boat Club where visitors are welcome. Engine repairs – William Furlong Telephone 053-35179. Trains to Dublin and Cork. Local buses. National Heritage Park 3 km and Wildlife Bird Sanctuary 3 km.

## ROSSLARE BAY TO CAHORE POINT

The passage inside the banks should be used with caution at night as two of the buoys in the Rusk Channel are unlit. S of this channel and N of the entrance to Wexford there is plenty of space and the coast is a sandy beach free of dangers. For 6M N of Blackwater

*Wexford Harbour from NW.*

Head it is backed by a clay cliff up to 50m high. Do not forget that the tide flows obliquely across the banks, the flood setting on their inner sides and the ebb on the outer sides.

### Directions
Pass not more than 1M W of West Long and North Long buoys, then leave West Blackwater buoy to starboard and pass between No 1 and No 2 Rusk buoys into the Rusk channel. No 4 Rusk buoy should be left close to port as the E side of the channel is reported to be shoaling. Pass out between No 6 Rusk and North Blackwater buoy.

### Tidal streams
Between Wexford and Cahore Point the NNE stream starts at +0430 Dover and the SSW stream at −0200 Dover, maximum speed about 2 kn.

### The Sluice
If you prefer to sail along the coast keep reasonably close inshore when inside the Rusk Bank. Watch out for No 6 Rusk buoy and when it bears 050° turn out and keep it bearing between 050° and 060° which leads between the shallow N end of Rusk Bank and the 1·4m deep Ram. A direct course from No 6 Rusk buoy to Cahore Point leads just N of the Ram. Small yachts using echosounders sometimes sail close along the shore inside the Ram where the depth is about 2m but this cannot be recommended. Less water has been reported by a number of members in this area, so great care should be taken.

*Courtown Harbour.*

*The narrow entrance to Courtown Harbour is regularly dredged by crane.*

the ebb tide does not carry the yacht inside a line joining the 2 buoys.

## ARKLOW BANK

Arklow Bank is a dangerous narrow ridge mostly shallow and awash in places. It is 12M long, its S end 5M E of Glassgorman Bank, and its N end 4M E of the N point of Brittas Bay. Yachts should keep away from it, especially in calm weather, fog or darkness. As on all the banks off this coast, the flood turns towards it near its inner side and flows NE across it, the ebb crossing it SW.

It is marked by the following buoys (Note that there are none on the W side):

**Arklow Lanby**, a red pillar 12m high, Fl.(2)W 12s15M. Horn: Mo(A) 30s, Racon. It is 1·5M SSE of the S of the bank.

**South Arklow**, S Card V Q (6) + LFl.10s, is at the S end.

**No 1 Arklow**, red, Fl.(3)R.10s, is 1M E of the bank and 4M NNE of the S Card.

**No 2 Arklow**, red, Fl.R.6s, is 1M E of the bank and 6M N of No 1.

**North Arklow**, N Card Q. Whis. is off the N end.

**Arklow Head Quarry**, 1M S of Arklow harbour has a jetty with a 3m high stone mole extending seaward 2 cables S of it. Yachts should not go near this. Light Oc.R.10s9M, is shown from the jetty and a QY on mole.

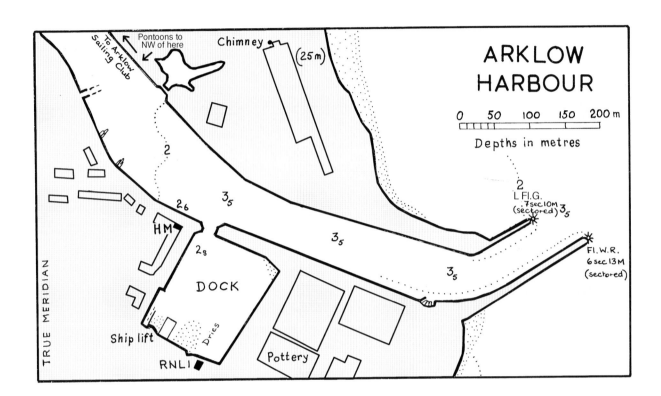

ARKLOW HARBOUR

0    50    100    150    200 m

Depths in metres

## ARKLOW HARBOUR

HW −0200 Dover. Rise (HW): 1·7-1·4/1·2-0·8. This is a river port with busy commercial quays and a sheltered dock used by fishing boats and yachts. It is a safe place to leave a yacht. Pontoons are now provided on N bank of river to the N of basin entrance where yachts may lie alongside.

### Directions

Arklow Harbour may be identified by a 25m high factory with a 44m high chimney which stands on the shore close N of the piers. The piers are apt to blanket the wind and yachts must enter under power except in modest winds between N and E. The entrance is unsafe after 5 or 6 hours of a F6 from N through E to SW, or sooner with a stronger wind. In F5 N wind there can be a nasty sea but in summer it is usually possible to enter with care and full control. Enter midway between the piers. Careful allowance must be made for the ebb tide which sets SE across the entrance. Proceed in near midchannel till the 14m wide dock entrance opens to port, turn in and steer for the middle part of the SE side of the dock, berthing

alongside it or another vessel. River banks are lit by quartz halogen lights.

### Approaches and entrance

The bar, the channel to 12m away from the piers, and the quays on the N side are kept dredged to not less than 3·5m. There is 2·6m alongside the old low quay beyond the dock entrance. Do not go beyond this as the next piece of new quay dries alongside and the river beyond it is shallow with obstructions. The entrance and much of the dock is 2·8m deep, the bottom is very soft mud. At LWS it dries on both sides of the ship lift, and in the E corner. Care should be taken in leaving a boat in the dock as it is used by large fishing vessels – consult the HM – Telephone 0402-32466, Fax 0402-31068 VHF Ch. 16, 14.

### Lights

S pierhead: Fl.WR 6s11m13M W from 223° to 350°, R elsewhere.
N pierhead LFl.G 7s7m10M.

*Arklow Harbour from S.*

**Facilities:** Water hydrant near NW side of dock. On the SE side water cans may be filled, with permission, in the pottery. Nearest petrol 0·5M at N end of road bridge. Diesel delivered aboard. The syncrolift in the Dock, operated by Arklow Slipway Ltd. Phone 0402-33233, Fax 0402-33234, may be used to lift out a yacht for temporary repairs. Arklow Sailing Club, a single storey building, is situated up stream next to the office of Arklow Shipping on the NE side of the river. There is a landing quay that itself has a rocky bottom at only 1m LWS. With permission from the A.S.C. the 3 or 4 moorings can be used on a 24 hour basis by visiting yachts. Showers and WC available at the clubhouse when open – most evenings, later on Wednesdays and at weekends. There is a hardware store some 50 yards up stream from the dock entrance which stocks much useful chandlery Telephone 0402-31274, Arklow Sailing Club, Hon. Sec. Telephone 0402-39914. All supplies and services in the town. EC Wed. Tourist information from Bord Failte in the town. For after hours fuel or groceries a 24-hour service station is located about 100 yards north of the bridge on the Dublin Road. Harbour dues for yachts are £7 per calendar week, or part thereof.

## ARKLOW TO WICKLOW HEAD

The first 5 M NE of Arklow is a sandy beach terminating at Mizen Head, a rocky point 10m high with a rock about 2m high just off it. Beyond this is Brittas Bay, 2·25M long, N of which is one third of 1M of rocky cliff with caravans parked above it. As far as this a yacht may safely approach within 3 or 4 cables of the shore but off the next 1·25M long unnamed bay, the S end of which is called Jack's Hole, there is a dangerous unmarked rocky shoal called Wolf Rock. It lies 0·5M off the shore of the N half of the bay and covers an area extending from 2·5 to 4·5 cables S of Ardmore Point. Part of it dries about 1m, which means it is awash at about threequarter flood. The normal course from Mizen Head to Horseshoe buoy, 025°, leads clear of Wolf Rock but if for instance a yacht is beating it is vital not to tack in towards the N part of this bay. Towards the S end of the bay there is a row of white chalets and a hotel. Ardmore Point, 15m high with steep grassy sides, has no buildings on it. At night keep Wicklow Head light bearing not more than 010°.

## HORSESHOE SHOAL

Horseshoe Shoal, a bank of stones 0·5m deep in

*Wicklow Head, with Denis Doyle's* Moonduster *sailing past on her way to winning the Round Ireland Race.*

places, lies S of Wicklow Head and yachts should pass to seaward of its Red Can Buoy, Fl R 3s, which lies 1·25 M SSE of Wicklow Head. The unmarked passage inside the bank cannot be recommended.

### Anchorages

In offshore winds temporary anchorage out of the tide (especially the flood) may be had: (1) 2 to 3 cables NNW of Mizen Head in 1·5 to 3·5m, (2) In Jack's Hole not more than 1 cable N of the point in 1·5m or (3) a shade further out if greater depth required.

### WICKLOW HEAD

Wicklow Head is 71m high and has 2 disused lighthouses on its summit. Light: Fl.(3)15s37m 23M is shown from a white tower on the outer slope of the Head. The bottom is uneven with 7m to 9m in places

up to 1·5M off the Head. The spring tide there reaches 4 kn so in fresh winds it can be extremely rough. Along the coast between Wicklow Head and Wicklow Harbour the tide always runs SE, a weak eddy during the flood and the ebb reaching 3kn. There is a sewage outfall buoy, Fl.(4)Y 10s approximately 7 cables 036° from East Pier Light.

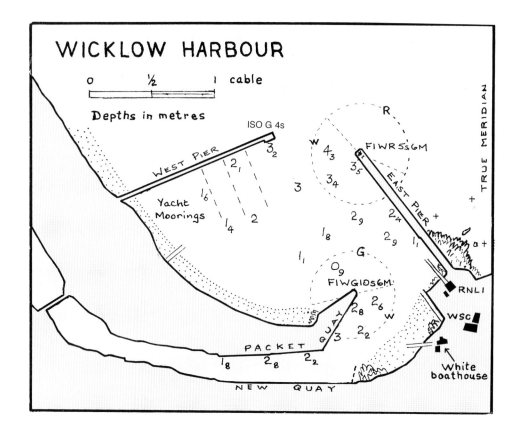

## WICKLOW HARBOUR

HW −0010 Dover. Rise (HW): 2·7-2·3m. This is an artificial harbour at the mouth of the River Vartry, 1·5M NW of Wicklow Head. It provides safe shelter alongside in the river and is always accessible. The E pier quay and the packet quay are used by large coasters.

**The outer harbour** is open to the NE so a yacht anchored there may roll, but in offshore winds it is comfortable. Anchor halfway between the ends of the W pier and the packet quay outside the yacht club moorings, (one of which may be made available) but clear of turning circle. Nearer the packet quay it starts getting shallow. A small yacht might anchor between the moorings and the W pier. It is often convenient to berth alongside the E pier. Dredging takes place at regular 6 year intervals.

**Inner harbour:** To enter, steer from between the outer piers towards the white boathouse and when the face of the packet quay opens turn sharp to starboard. To avoid the shallows on the SE side do not allow the front of the RNLI boathouse to close. The S side of the river is dredged and the quays rebuilt. This side is intended to be used by fishing boats and yachts. If it is not available a yacht might go alongside the packet quay but should not be left there unattended without obtaining permission at the Harbour office, Telephone 0404-67455, which is in the middle of that pier. Yachts are often left alongside the inner end of the packet quay.

### Lights

W Pier Head, on a green metal column, Iso.G. 4s.5m6M. E Pier Head, from a white lighthouse, Fl WR 5s11m6M. R from 136° through S to 293°, W 293° to 136°. Packet quay, Light on a metal column, Fl.WG 10s5m6M. G from 076° through E to 256°, W 256° to 076°.

**Facilities:** Repairs to hulls and engines. Fuel available in town. Water tap at WSC and N and S quays. Normal requirements in Wicklow town, EC Thur, Tourist Information Office. Showers at Sailing Club. Launderette in town. Train to Dublin. Airport 40M. Small harbour dues. Lifeboat. Good pubs, restaurants and entertainment available in town. (*see Appendix 7*).

## WICKLOW TO DUBLIN BAY

### Offshore banks and buoys

There is an almost continuous line of banks between 5M and 6M off this coast. The depths are mostly 3m to 5m, but 2m or less in a few places. In calm weather a yacht may cross the deeper parts of the banks with extreme caution but otherwise they should be avoided. The flood sets NE across and between them and the ebb SW. India Bank, 5M NE of Wicklow Head, has a least depth of 3·5m. Extending N of it is South Ridge with 5m. South India buoy, S Card Q (6) + LFl.15s, lies off the S end. North India buoy, N Card V.Q, lies off the N end of South Ridge.

*Wicklow Harbour from S.*

## Tidal Streams and Races

Yachtsmen should note that the tidal streams run up to 4 kn in the following locations which should be avoided in wind against tide conditions:

1. Between Bray Bank and Codling Bank
2. Between the South Codling Buoy and the North India Buoy
3. Up to 0·5M of the W side of the India Bank
4. Off the Horseshoe Buoy Wicklow Head.

## CODLING BANK

Codling Bank is crescent-shaped and stretches from 3M NNE to 5M N of South Ridge. Its rocky bottom is covered with narrow ridges of gravel and large boulders. There is a ridge 4m deep on its N edge and not far from the E end of this a ridge with a least depth of 2·6m runs SE. It is subject to heavy overfalls and yachts should keep clear of it.

**Bray and Kish Banks** extend 9·5M N from a 0·75M gap N of Codling Bank. Bray Bank's least depth is 4m. On the N part of Kish Bank there is as little as 1·6m.

## Buoys and Lights

Codling Lanby, a red pillar 12m high, Fl.W 4s12m 15M, Horn 20s, Racon lies 6·5M ESE of the bank. South Codling, S Card VQ (6) + LFl.10s, lies off the SE end of the bank. West Codling, green, Fl.G 10s, lies off the SW corner of the bank. East Codling, red, Fl.(4)R 10s, lies off the NE of the bank. East Kish, red, Fl.(2)R 10s, lies 0·5M E off the bank where the N half starts getting shallow. North Kish, N Card VQ, lies close off the N end of the bank. Kish Bank Lighthouse, 31m high, is a white tower with a red band and a helicopter platform on top. Light: Fl.(2)20s29m22M, Horn (2)30s, it is 0·5M NE of the N end of the bank. Bennett Bank, 3M N of Kish Bank, does not concern yachts, being 10m deep. Its buoy is S Card Q (6) + LFl.15s, Whis.

## COAST FROM WICKLOW TO DUBLIN BAY

Except for a short rocky stretch at Greystones, there is a beach all the way from Wicklow Harbour to Bray Head. Much of it is steep-to but it is simplest to advise yachts not to go closer than 1 cable except when rounding Six Mile Point, which requires a berth of 2 cables. There are 2 small shoals which yachts usually ignore. Moulditch Bank (3·8m) is 1M SE by E of Greystones with a red buoy, Fl.R.10s. Breaches Shoal (5m) is 3M SSE of the Moulditch and has a red buoy Fl.(2)R 6s. In rough onshore conditions it is better to sail E of these buoys. A special Can Light Buoy with Top Mark, Fl.Y, 5s. has been placed in position 53°08'·38N 06°02'·44W marking an outfall off Greystones.

## Rocks

Cable Rock, which dries 2m, lies 0·5 of a cable off the S end of Bray Head. Periwinkle and Crab Rocks are drying reefs which extend almost 1 cable off the N and NW part of the head. Between Bray Head and Killiney there are extensive sandy beaches with several rocks, some of which dry. This coast should therefore be given a berth of at least 3 cables until close to the entrance to Dalkey Sound.

## Buoys

**In Killiney Bay** there are 2 outfall Yellow Buoys in position (1) 1·9M N of Bray Head and (2) 1·3M S of Dalkey Island.

*Greystones Harbour from S.*

## GREYSTONES HARBOUR

Greystones Harbour, 2M S of Bray Head is small and shallow with a ruined breakwater. In summer it is full of small boats. In settled conditions a yacht can anchor temporarily in 3·5 m N of the mouth of the harbour which is convenient for dinghy landing.

Yachts can lie afloat at all states of tide at the "Old Kish Base", at eastern side of entrance to harbour.

**Facilities:** Good supermarkets, shops, banks, pubs, restaurants, medical doctors and fuel, all available close to harbour.

## BRAY HARBOUR

One M North of Bray Head. Pier Heads not lit. Yellow buoy (Fl. (4) Y. 10s.) marks pipeline head 1·2m to NE of entrance. The Harbour is tidal and is useable 3 hours from H.W. At LWS it dries out to entrance.

H.W. Bray is Dublin – 6 mins. Harbour contains large selection of Bilge Keelers, Drop Keelers and small craft, all moored fore and aft. Suitable for visitors prepared to dry out on a mooring, or alongside the S. Pier (exposed to NE winds) or at one of three landing ladders on N Pier (fendering difficult as wooden piles are far apart). When entering Harbour, keep close to S. Pier for best water.

### Bray Sailing Club:

Welcomes visiting yachts and has showers, bar and telephone. Open weekends April to November, all of July and Wednesday and Friday evenings all year round. Phone 01-2860272 to arrange moorings, etc.

### Anchorages

Good shelter may be had from winds between SW and NW by anchoring about 50m off the Harbour, in good sandy holding ground. Unlit racing marks are laid off-shore in summer months.

### Facilities

All stores, services and repairs, including sail repairs, are available in or near the town. Also pubs, restaurants, evening entertainment, golf, tennis, fishing, snooker, cinema and night clubs. Excellent transport facilities. *(Also see Appendix 14)*.

## DALKEY ISLAND

Dalkey Island, at the S end of Dublin Bay, is 24m high with a Martello Tower. Three cables outside it is the Muglins, a rock on which there is a white conical beacon with a red band. Muglins Light, Fl.W.5s14m11M. The Muglins is clear all round except for one rock close W of it, over which there is one m at LW.

## DALKEY SOUND

Dalkey Sound runs inside Dalkey Island and the line of rocks stretching 3·5 cables NNW of it. There is a clear passage through the sound keeping within 1 cable of the steep-to shore, and this is the normal entrance to Dublin Bay for yachts coming up the coast. The tide runs strongly through the sound. It turns about 2 hours before HW and LW at springs, later at neaps. If the tide is foul it is better to use Muglins Sound unless motoring or running before a fresh breeze through the sound. Winds between S and NW are usually calm or fluky in places. The flood tide through the sound is an inshore branch of the tide sweeping round Killiney Bay but a yacht approaching from the S first meets the main flood running abeam of her course out of the bay and S of Dalkey Island towards the Muglins. In light conditions if this has not been adequately anticipated one can of course go through the Muglins Sound instead. During Skiff Regattas, lines of buoys are laid across Dalkey Sound off Coliemore Harbour. It is safe to pass between these buoys.

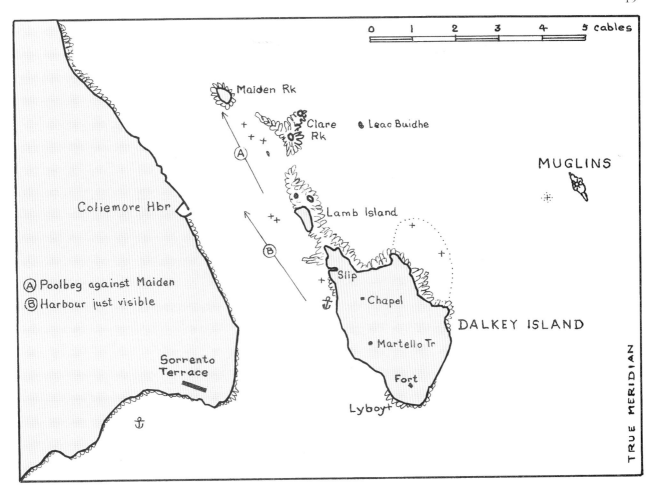

*Dalkey Sound from SW.*

## Dangers

The dangers are all on the island side. A reef extends along the shore from opposite the fort to halfway towards the Martello Tower. Its outer point is Lyboy Rock, 0·4m deep and 50m from the shore. Close S of the landing steps there is a small rock which dries at LAT. N of the steps a narrow reef runs out ending with a 0·6m deep rock 70m offshore. There is another rock with 0·6m about 90m W of Lamb Islet. A rock which dries at half tide lies 80m SW of Clare Rock with other drying rocks inside it. Between it and Maiden Rock there are rocks with 0·5m depth.

Beating through the sound you may tack quite close to the shore but should avoid the above rocks as follows. Keep 80m off Dalkey Island between its S end and the Martello Tower. Between abreast of the chapel and a line from Coliemore harbour to The Muglins, begin to tack immediately the top of Dun Laoghaire pier shows outside the coast (323°). NW of this keep the red Poolbeg lighthouse (Liffey entrance) to the left of Maiden Rock (bearing not less than 331°). Give the SW of Maiden Rock a berth of 30m. Its NW end needs a berth of 45m. Near HW a yacht which can ignore the nondrying rocks between Lamb Islet and Maiden Rock should keep the Martello Tower open to the right of Lamb Islet to avoid the halftide rock off Clare Rock.

## MUGLINS SOUND

Muglins Sound is an alternative approach to Dublin Bay. There are some rocks which must be avoided but the channel between them has a least width of 1.5 cables.

### Rocks

About 120m NNE of the NNE point of Dalkey Island there is a rock with 0·4m over it. SE of this and N of the E point of the island there is a rock with 1·6m. Almost 1 cable E of Clare Rock is Leac Buidhe Rock which just dries. It lies where the E end of Sorrento Terrace shows over the grassy top of Lamb Islet. On the S wall of the Liffey there is a pair of very high chimneys. The lefthand chimney in line with the outer edge of Dun Laoghaire pier leads clear of all the rocks on this side. The same chimney in line with Dun Laoghaire E pier lighthouse leads clear of the rocks off Dalkey Island but would lead over Leac Buidhe. About 90m W of the Muglins, where the beacon is in line with the NW end of the landing quay, there is a rock with 1m over it. Below half tide most yachts should keep clear of it. The tide runs N or S between the E side of Dalkey Island and the Muglins.

### BURFORD BANK

Burford Bank lies 1M outside Dublin Bay. It is narrow and runs N and S with a buoy off each end which lie 2·5 M apart. The least depth on the bank is 4·6m so yachts need only avoid it in rough weather.

**Buoys:** S Card V Q. (6) + LFl.10s Whis. N Card Q. Whis.

### DUBLIN BAY

Dublin Bay is W of a line from the Muglins to The Baily, the SE point of the Hill of Howth. Shipping has right of way over yachts within the bay. VHF Coastal Station Call 16 Work 67, 65, 83.

### Lights

**Baily lighthouse**, a conspicuous granite tower, shows Fl.W 15s. 41m26M. RC. There are no offshore dangers in the bay. The S shore is steep-to for about 1M from Sorrento Point, the entrance to Dalkey Sound, to a Martello Tower. Between this tower and Sandycove Point, 0·5M further in keep 1 cable offshore. In Scotsman's Bay between this point and the E pier of Dun Laoghaire Harbour keep 2 cables offshore. Beyond the harbour keep its E pier open of its W pier and do not let the red **Poolbeg lighthouse** at the Liffey entrance bear more than 005°. On the N side of the bay keep the Poolbeg bearing more than 235° and on the Howth shore keep outside the bay between Drumleck Point with a beacon on it and Lions Head, 4 cables NNW of **The Baily**.

### Buoys

Yachts may pass any side of the buoys within the bay except that in onshore near gale conditions Rosbeg Bank, least depth 4·6m, should be avoided by keeping E of a line between The Baily and Rosbeg East E Card buoy Q(3)10s about 7 cables SSE of The Baily and Rosbeg South Card Q(6) + LFl.15s, bearing 204° 1·80M from the Baily. There are a number of unlit cone racing buoys SW of a line from the Muglins to Poolbeg lighthouse.

### Tidal streams

The flood, entering on both sides of Dalkey Island, sweeps round the shores of Dublin Bay and rejoins the main stream outside Rosbeg Bank. Along the S shore the tide turns about −0310 local HW and LW. Off the N shore the tide runs to seaward for 9 hours from local HW +0315 to −0015 next HW and then runs in from The Baily for about 3·5 hours. There is not much stream in the middle of the bay but just outside the bay the tide flows at up to 3·25 kn at springs, the N going flood starting at LW and the S going ebb at HW Dublin Bar.

### BULLOCH HARBOUR

Bulloch Harbour, 1M SE of Dun Laoghaire, is of little interest to yachts as it dries out and is packed with small boats. Should a yacht need to be taken in, do so near HW and, to avoid those rocks in the approach which dry at neaps, enter keeping a black and white post with a black board on top in line with the left edge of the lower notice "Danger Slow" (both on the shore side of the entrance). When 10m from the entrance turn sharp to starboard to open it before turning in. At HWS there is 2·7m in the N corner, at the crane and 2m further along the quay.

**Facilities:** There is a yacht chandlery and a new two tonne electric crane has been installed.

### Anchorages

Dun Laoghaire Harbour is a major yachting centre and High Speed Ferryport. It provides ideal anchorages for visiting yachts to the N of the yacht moorings in the centre of the harbour. It may not be

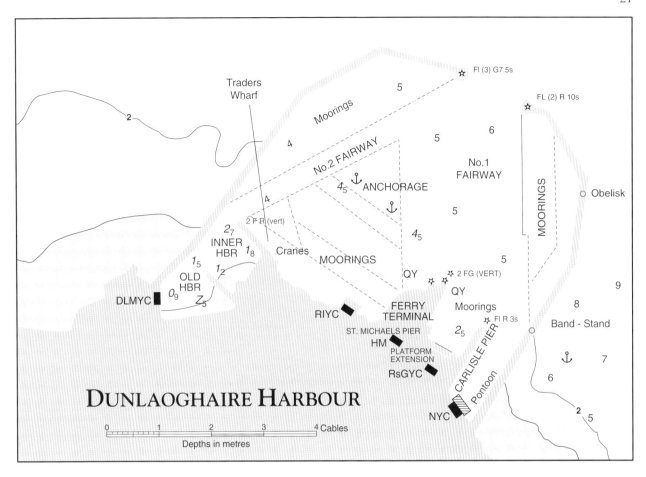

Traders Wharf

Fl (3) G7.5s

FL (2) R 10s

Moorings

5

5

6

No.2 FAIRWAY

4

5

No.1 FAIRWAY

2

4

4

4₅ ⚓ ANCHORAGE

5

⚓

MOORINGS

Obelisk

2 F R (vert)

4₅

5

INNER HBR 1₈

2₇

Cranes

MOORINGS

5

1₅

1₂

OLD HBR

QY

2 FG (VERT)

QY

9

DLMYC 0₉ Z₅

Moorings

8

RIYC

FERRY TERMINAL

Band - Stand

ST. MICHAELS PIER

Fl R 3s

HM

2₅

PLATFORM EXTENSION

6

⚓ 7

RsGYC

DUNLAOGHAIRE HARBOUR

NYC

Pontoon

2₅

0    1    2    3    4 Cables

Depths in metres

---

necessary to anchor as any one of the 4 Yacht Clubs may be able to provide the visitor with a mooring. However, some people might like to try one of the following places: off Bellingham, a tiny harbour with a red boathouse behind it, 4 cables NW of Drumleck Point, the S tip of Howth. Anchor not less than 1 cable off the harbour in 3 to 5m, well sheltered in winds from NW to ENE, slightly tiderode. In Scotsmans Bay just 1 cable SE of the bandstand on Dun Laoghaire E Pier. Depth about 6m, well sheltered in winds from SSE to WNW. In Dalkey Sound (*see above*) fairly close to Dalkey Island near the white waterfountain SE of the landing place. Depth about 4m, well sheltered in all except S winds, much quieter than Dun Laoghaire in NE swell, tiderode.

## DUN LAOGHAIRE HARBOUR

HW +0030 Dover. Rise: 4·1-3·4/1·5-0·6m. Port operations VHF Call 16 Work 14, Telephone 012801130. This large harbour is alongside the town on the S side of Dublin Bay. It has suitable depths for sailing yachts except in the old harbour and the S half of the inner harbour. Much of the main harbour and all of the old and inner harbours are occupied by yacht moorings. Four yacht clubs have premises alongside the harbour. There is a floating pontoon at the National Yacht Club for 4 visiting yachts to take on fuel, water and stores. It is 60ft long. The spring tidal range is about 3·5m. Contact Boatman on VHF Channel M to

get clearance. Royal Irish YC Telephone 01-2842194; Royal St. George YC Telephone 01-2801208, VHF 37, and National YC Telephone 01-2841483 – all have permanent secretaries who should be contacted on arrival if you wish to use their facilities, which include bars, meals, showers. Visitors are expected to conform to a reasonable standard of dress when using the club premises. Enquire about visitors' moorings. Ferry service during normal day time and evening racing.

**Caution**

When passing through the harbour entrance keep a bit away from the pierheads. There are drying boulders 8 m off the E side and fishing lines are often cast off the W pier. Avoid entering or leaving at the same time as the High Speed ferries because when they are under way it is obligatory to keep clear of the fairway and the harbour mouth. The ferries berth at the terminal at St. Michael's Pier and fishing boats use the inner harbour. Anchorage is prohibited in the fairways. Mariners should take care not to sail closer than 15m off the Retaining Wall of St. Michael's Terminal as the wall armouring shoals outwards to the sea bed. Yachts, when lying alongside club pontoon, should tend their lines carefully when HSS Ferry is manoeuvering and creating wash in the harbour. Boats may moor for short periods to the pontoons off the Royal St. George Yacht Club.

*Dun Laoghaire from S with Poolbeg Lt. (top centre).*

## DUN LAOGHAIRE TRAFFIC REGULATIONS N.T.M. NO. 3 OF 1995

All visiting yachts, (locally based yachts are excluded) are required to inform Dun Laoghaire Harbour C/S "Harbour Office" by VHF on channel 16 or Working channel 14 ETA at the breakwater at least 2 hours in advance of arrival and also to notify their ETD at least 1 hour in advance. Two high intensity quick flashing Yellow signal Lights are displayed both by night and by day when traffic with large power driven vessels is taking place or imminent. This signal light is shown from the seaward end of St. Michael's Terminal. When large vessels are moving in the harbour fairway and/or the above signal is displayed all yachts are to keep the main fairway clear; ie keep clear of, or keep to the sides of, the main fairway to allow a free and unhindered passage for the large power driven vessels.

## MAIN FAIRWAY LIMITS

**Eastern limit** runs from a line drawn from the Band Stand on the East Pier to the East Pier Head Light, with an extension running at a tangent to the pierhead at the Northernmost section of the area.

**Western limit** runs from a point on the new HSS RoRo Berth Retaining Wall, 50m from the Western extreme of the berths ramp mounting in a 354° direction to the West Pier, where Front and Rear transit marks consisting of black and white triangular shapes, on the lower and upper levels of the pier, indicate the Western limit of the Main Fairway.

## Anchorage

The anchorage area is shown on the plan. It is best to anchor just outside the yacht moorings clear of No. 1 Fairway. Visiting yachts are often allocated moorings by the club boatmen. In the unlikely event of a NE gale in summer the anchorage becomes untenable. Winds between N and E can make it uncomfortable on board and in fine anticyclonic weather there is often an unpleasant roll. The Royal St George YC moorings off the E pier are the least affected in these conditions. This club also has a couple of moorings E of the W ferry pier, close inshore, the best place for a visitor if one of them is free. Yachts sometimes berth at the shoreward face of Traders Wharf but a big swell in the harbour gets in there too. In such conditions someone should remain on board. The seaward side of Traders Wharf is foul.

**Facilities:** Yachts arriving from outside the European Union are required to clear Customs. If a Customs Officer does not come on board, clearance may be obtained by visiting their office at St. Michael's Ferry Terminal. Visitors should report the arrival of their yacht at the Harbour Office. Yachtsmen are often offered temporary honorary membership by the local yacht clubs and may then use their slips for landing and hauling out dinghies. Club boatmen can advise about visitors' requirements. Royal St. George YC Telephone 01-2801208; Royal Irish YC Telephone 01-2842194; and National YC Telephone 01 - 2805725; Boathouse 01-2841483; all have electrically operated cranes to lift 5 tonnes, and a drying out dock. Visitors' moorings are also available, together with such club

*National Yacht Club, Dun Laoghaire.*

facilities as showers, meals, bar, etc. on contacting the Hon. Sec. Water and diesel can be supplied by pipe alongside the Yacht Clubs. In the old harbour yachts can be dried out alongside at LW. Apply to the HM for the use of these facilities. There are shipwrights, yacht chandlers and a sailmaker not far from the harbour. All stores are available in the town. Very good rail connections to centre of Dublin every 15 minutes. Shopping Centre late closing Thursday and Friday.

## Lights
E Pier Head, 12m Granite Tower, Red Lantern, Fl.(2) R 10s. 16m17M Horn (1) 30s, or bell 6s. W Pier Head, 9m Granite Tower, Green Lantern Fl.(3)G 7·5s11m7M vis 188° to 062° (234°).
Carlisle Pier Fl.R.3s9m1M.
St. Michael's Pier 2 FG (vert). Traders Wharf 2 FR (vert)7m1M. Port operations – VHF. Call 14, 16, Work 14.

## DUBLIN
HW +0035 Dover. Rise: 4·13·4/1·50·6m. The busy commercial port in the River Liffey has little to attract yachts and no special provision for them. It provides better shelter than Dun Laoghaire in strong NE wind. There are no anchorages for yachts, which usually berth near the inner end of the S quays, 3·25M from the entrance. It is unwise to leave a yacht unattended there owing to theft and vandalism. A lifting bridge operates across the river.

## Directions
A traffic separation scheme is due to be implemented before the summer of 1999. This will involve separation lanes north and south of the Burford Bank. New editions of Admiralty Chart No. 1415 Dublin Bay will be issued. This is a national scheme approved by the Dept. of the Marine and to which Rule 10 of the Collision Regulations will apply.

The entrance is between Poolbeg and Bull Lighthouses in the middle of Dublin Bay. Yachts should show that they are taking care to keep out of the way of ships. A circular traffic separation zone, marked by a spherical buoy with a radius of 100m (0·05M) is centered on 53°19'·9 N 6°04'·58 W. Yachts may pass either side of the buoys outside but after entering should remain within the dredged channel which is marked by red buoys on the S side and by green buoys and beacons on the N side. There is no difficulty in proceeding as far as the Toll Bridge, which is about 2·75M from the harbour entrance, except to keep clear of the traffic. Further in beyond the Toll Bridge, northerly and southerly winds are fluky and it is better to motor if possible. Small boats sailing should keep out of the fairway channel and preferably proceed under motor. This obviously precludes sailing within the Harbour area as the port is now extremely busy with commercial traffic.

**The Toll Bridge** has a lifting span with a width of 31m and a vertical clearance of 2·2m (HWS) when closed.

*The Royal Irish Yacht Club, Dun Laoghaire – believed to be the world's oldest purpose-designed yacht club building.*

The bridge transit traffic is controlled by following signals:

| Signal | Meaning |
| --- | --- |
| 3 Red Vertical Lts. | Stop |
| 3 Green vertical Lts. | Proceed |
| 3 Red Flashing Vertical Lts. | Emergency. Stop or divert. |

A yacht wishing to proceed up the river should contact Dublin Port Radio on Channel 12 and notify the Harbour Master of its intentions. A vessel requiring to transit the bridge should arrange a time in advance with the Harbour Master's office or through Dublin Port Radio. The bridge operator will man the control cabin about 20 minutes before the scheduled time of transit. Communications can be established with the bridge operator, call sign 'Eastlink' on VHF channel 12 or 13. The bridge will not be opened during peak traffic times.

## Lights
**Approaches to Dublin Port:** Fairway Buoys **No. 1** G Fl. (3) G. **No. 3** G IQ.G. **No. 4** R IQR. S Card Q (6) + LFl. 15s.

**At the entrance: Poolbeg**, a red tower 20m high with a white building behind it, Oc.(2)R 20s20m15M.

Horn(2)60s. **N Bull Lighthouse** Fl.(3)G 10s15m15M. **The S side of the channel to Dublin** is marked by red lights and the **N side** by green lights.(*See chart 1447.*) Facilities: The city has three yacht chandlers (*see Appendix 13*), and stores and service of all kinds are available.

## ENTRANCE TO INLAND WATERWAYS
**GRAND CANAL – Leading to the Shannon river and the west coast of Ireland via Limerick and the south coast of Ireland via the Barrow river and the Waterford estuary.**

The Grand Canal is entered through the dock on the S side of the river Liffey, W of the lifting bridge and can be entered 2 hours either side of high water and enables boats drawing 1m to reach the Shannon, maximum size of boat 18·5m × 4m. In dry weather the depths are somewhat reduced. Headroom: 2·6m over a width of 2·4m on curved arches. It is no longer used commercially. It is advisable to contact the office of Public Works, Waterways Division, 51 St Stephen's Green, Dublin 2, Telephone 01-6613111, or Dock Master at Ringsend, telephone 01-6689466, if planning to make a passage through the canal.

# Chapter 2

## HILL OF HOWTH TO ST JOHN'S POINT

*Baily Light House.*                                                                            *Permission of Commissioners of Irish Lights.*

*St. John's Point Light House.*                    *Permission of Commissioners of Irish Lights.*

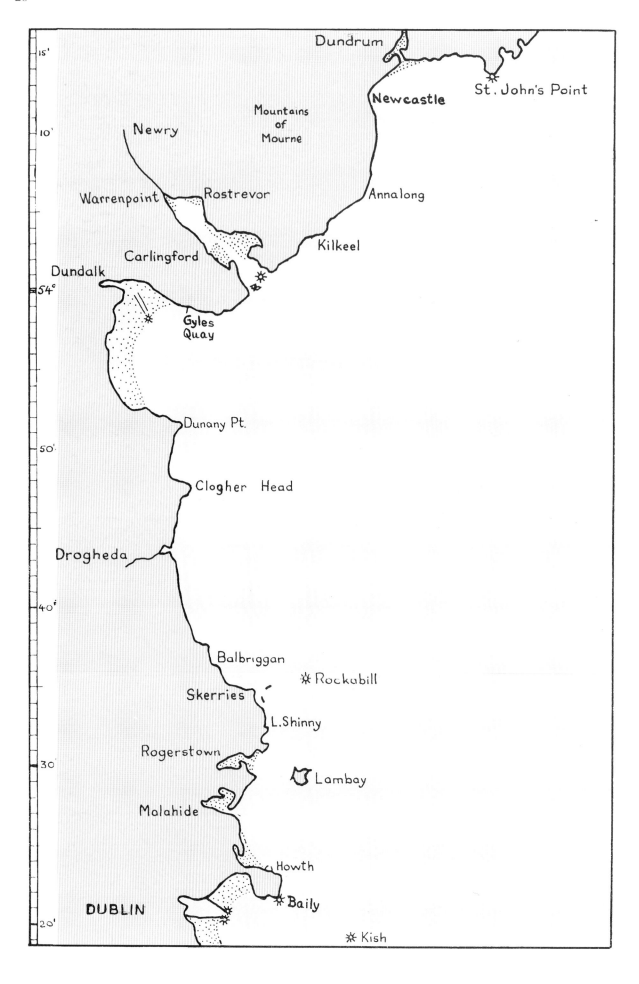

# Chapter 2

## HILL OF HOWTH TO
## ST JOHN'S POINT

**Charts**

This coast is covered by Charts 44, 2800. Carlingford Lough is the only larger scale one likely to be required by visitors. (*See Appendix 1*).

**General**

Yachts making a direct passage between Dun Laoghaire and the North of Ireland will normally bypass the coast described in this chapter and need

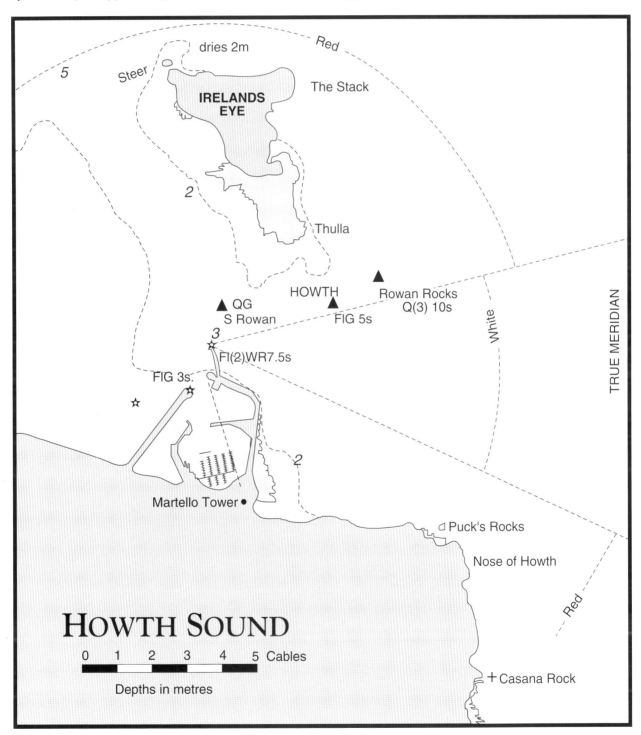

dries 2m

Red

Steer

5

IRELANDS EYE

The Stack

2

Thulla

HOWTH

▲ Rowan Rocks
Q(3) 10s

▲ QG
S Rowan

▲
FIG 5s

White

TRUE MERIDIAN

3
☆
Fl(2)WR7.5s

FIG 3s.
☆

☆

2

Martello Tower •

◁ Puck's Rocks

Nose of Howth

Red

# HOWTH SOUND

0    1    2    3    4    5 Cables

Depths in metres

+ Casana Rock

28

*Howth Harbour and Marina from NW.*

only note that the course from the Baily to St John's Point is 015°, 54M. Those wishing to shorten the passage can anchor at Loughshinny in winds from SSW through to NNW, at Skerries or Port Oriel in SE to W winds. In Loughshinny take care to anchor clear of the moored crab and lobster cages. The only really attractive inlet on this coast is Carlingford Lough.

**Tides**

HW everywhere along this coast is close to HW Dover. Between Dublin Bay and Anglesea the main flood runs N while the tide is rising at Dover. Out towards the Isle of Man it turns E to fill Liverpool Bay. The ebb runs in the opposite direction for the other 6 hours. Along the coast the tides run fairly strongly S of Rockabill but become weaker further N, particularly offshore. The streams are negligible S of St John's Point, SE of which the floods from N and S meet. It is best, sailing N or S, to aim to pass St John's Point at HW, though this usually involves some adverse tide at Rockabill unless you stop somewhere in between. After leaving the River Liffey, the area to the N is very shallow, so yachts of medium draft and over should make for the Baily Lt. Inside the North Bull Lt. there is an anchorage for shallow draft craft off the Clontarf Yacht and Boat Club, with bar, shower facilities and fuel close by. A regular boatman is available, and watch is kept on VHF – Channel M c/s "Tarf base".

**Coast**

The E side of Hill of Howth is steep-to except close in 2 to 6 cables N of the Baily Fl.15s 41m 26M Racon, and at Casana Rock which is 4 cables S of the Nose and must be given a berth of 50m. Just NW of the Nose there is a rock which dries about 50m outside Puck's Rocks. A berth of 1 cable clears it. There are loose boulders off the E pier of Howth harbour.

**IRELAND'S EYE**

Ireland's Eye, 1M N of Howth, is a rocky island 97m high.

**Dangers**

There are two reefs running out from Thulla, the islet at its SE end. Do not pass between the islet and the buoys marking them, Rowan Rocks E Card buoy, Q (3)10s, marking N Rowan rock and a green buoy, Q G, marking S Rowan rock. The NE corner of the island is a prominent high pillarshaped rock called The Stack. Keep outside a line from the E Card. buoy to The Stack to avoid a drying rock 1 cable NE of Thulla. There are drying rocks in the bay SSW of The Stack. At the NW corner of Ireland's Eye there is an islet, The Steer, close N of the Martello tower. The N coast of the island is steepto except for a rock which dries 2m about 100m NE of The Steer. There is also a sunken rock close W of The Steer. On the W side of the island the water is shoal with a sandy bottom and a few projecting ledges.

## Howth Sound

Approaching from seaward Rowan Rocks buoy must be to starboard and Nose of Howth given a berth of 1 cable. Watch out for lobster pot buoys between The Nose and harbour. After leaving S Rowan green buoy to starboard, turn NW and when the Martello tower above the root of the E pier comes in line with the outer end of that pier (160°), keep on this transit to pass through the sound till abeam of the NW end of Ireland's Eye. Craft drawing 6 ft or more should not attempt entry to the Sound at low water in strong easterly gales with swell running.

## HOWTH HARBOUR

HW +0025 Dover. Rise 4·13·4/1·20·5m. This has always been an active fishing port and yachting centre. Its marina is shown on the sketch plan.

## Directions

Approaching from the E give the pier a berth of 200m. Do not turn until the harbour is well open, entering nearer to W pier head. The Marina entrance is clearly marked with green and red markers. It is important to keep between these poles as the harbour dries on either side at low water. Once inside the Marina basin, keep to the Marina side of the orange buoys to stay in the fairway. Fishing vessels must be given right of way on entering or leaving harbour. Contact the Marina Office Telephone 01-8392777 or Howth Yacht Club C/s Howth Marina (24 hour watch) on VHF 80 for a berth. Visitor's berths are limited in season. Anchorages may be found west of the West Pier. Fishing dock not available to leisure craft without special permission from HM. Channel and Marina dredged to 2·8m MLWS. Howth YC, HM, and Marina

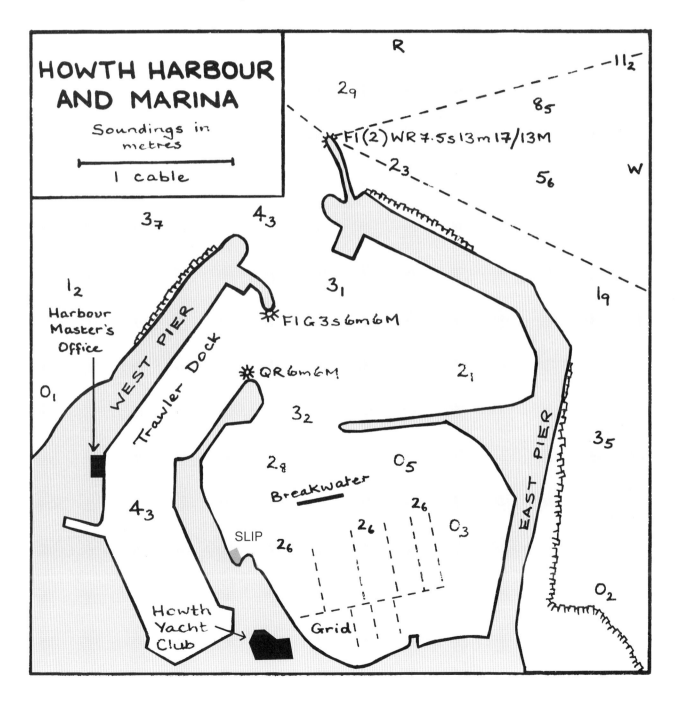

*Howth Harbour and Marina from S with Ireland's Eye and Lambay Island in the distance.*

*Howth Yacht Club has most facilities, including a 7 tonne crane.*

Office as shown on plan. Marina charge (1999) 35p per ft. per day, 35p per ft. per day × 7 per week with 1 day free. Winter storage rate October to April (5·5 months) £15 per ft. E-mail:admin@hyc.iol.ie.

**Facilities:** Visitors' mooring and/or alongside berths are available in the harbour and marina. Showers, meals and bar in Howth Yacht Club whose fulltime secretary will advise. Fuel, water and electricity in marina. All repairs and chandlery, crane 7 tonnes capacity, drying out pad and divers, slipway, groceries, laundry. Calor Gas available from harbour hardware 2 minutes walk from Yacht Club. Rapid rail service (DART) to Dublin every 15 minutes, taxis, Dublin Airport 20 minutes by car. Pubs with traditional Irish Music and excellent restaurants to suit all pockets. EC Sat.

## Lights

E pier Light Tower Fl.(2) WR 7·5s13m W12M R9M W 256° to 295° (39°). R 295° to 256° (321°). W Pier Light Fl. G 3s6m6M. Trawler breakwater head QR 6m6M.

## Inshore Tidal Streams

(Times refer to local HW and LW). At the Baily the stream coming out of Dublin Bay causes overfalls, quite nasty at times, where it meets the main stream. Close inshore on the E side of Howth Hill the stream turns N −0130 LW and S −0115 HW and runs at 2 kn. This stream divides at Ireland's Eye, one part running N and on through Lambay Sound, and the other part passing up Howth Sound where the flood begins −0130 LW and the ebb −0130 HW, running at 2 kn. This latter flood stream slackens in pace beyond Ireland's Eye and after filling Baldoyle, Malahide and Rogerstown inlets joins the stream passing through Lambay Sound where it attains a rate of 2·5 kn.

## Lights

Dublin Airport Control tower at 53° 26′N, 6° 15′W, some 4M N of Dublin and the same distance inland, shows Aero Al WG 4s, elev 95m.

## MALAHIDE

HW +0020 Dover. Rise: 4·5-3·3/1·7-0·3m. This estuary 4M N of Howth is a safe and quiet anchorage for yachts drawing up to 2m. The bar outside the entrance is 0·3m deep and there are sandbanks on either side of it. The entrance is not lighted and should not be approached after dark or in thick weather. In daylight strangers can enter easily at half flood. The flood stream runs up to 3 kn at springs and the ebb may run 3·5 kn.

## MALAHIDE MARINA

A Marina with 350 serviced pontoon berths and linear berthage for vessels up to 75 metres in length. Petrol and diesel can be obtained in the Hoist Bay, at the northern side of the Marina, with a fully serviced boatyard, including a 30-ton travel hoist with mast crane. The Marina Office is staffed 24 hours a day.

Visitors should call "Malahide Marina" on CH 37(M1) or 80, or tel 845 4129.

Marina charges 1999: Daily £1.50 per meter, minimum charge £10. Short stay (max 5 hours) £5.00. Weekly £7.70 per metre. Monthly £28.00 per metre.

**Facilities:** Toilets, showers, refuse disposal, boatyard, 30-ton travel hoist, hardstanding, fuel (diesel and petrol), water, chandlery, restaurant. Dublin International Airport 15 minutes by car. Dublin city centre 25 minutes by rail. Numerous shops, hardware, restaurants and pubs 5 minutes walk from Marina.

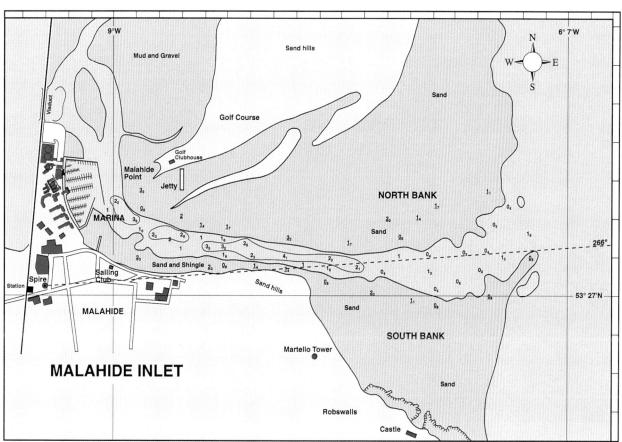

MALAHIDE INLET

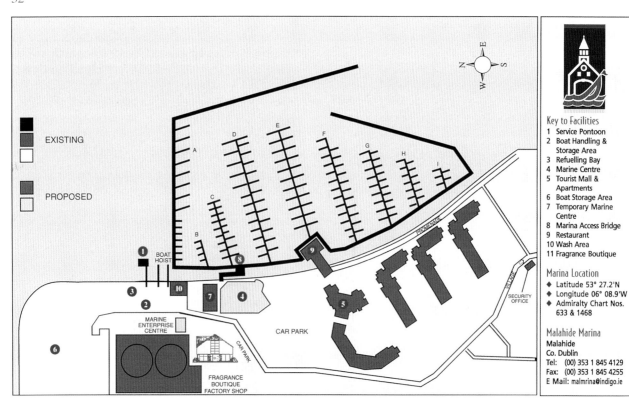

EXISTING

PROPOSED

Key to Facilities
1 Service Pontoon
2 Boat Handling & Storage Area
3 Refuelling Bay
4 Marine Centre
5 Tourist Mall & Apartments
6 Boat Storage Area
7 Temporary Marine Centre
8 Marina Access Bridge
9 Restaurant
10 Wash Area
11 Fragrance Boutique

Marina Location
◆ Latitude 53° 27.2'N
◆ Longitude 06° 08.9'W
◆ Admiralty Chart Nos. 633 & 1468

Malahide Marina
Malahide
Co. Dublin
Tel:   (00) 353 1 845 4129
Fax:  (00) 353 1 845 4255
E Mail: malmrina@indigo.ie

BOAT HOIST

MARINE ENTERPRISE CENTRE

CAR PARK

CAR PARK

FRAGRANCE BOUTIQUE FACTORY SHOP

SECURITY OFFICE

*Malahide from NW.*

## MALAHIDE YACHT CLUB

### Channel Buoys

The channel is marked with a safe water mark at the entrance to the estuary with red and green buoys up to the marina entrance also marked: Red Green Lights/Daymarks mark the breakwaters. They are moored near the edge of the narrow channel rather than on the banks and may therefore be passed fairly close. These buoys may under normal circumstances be considered reliable. They are maintained by the Malahide Yacht Club and their positions are altered after any major change around the bar or in the channel.

### Caution

In view of the foregoing, it is advisable for visitors not accustomed to the area to contact the Marina Office (01-8454129 or VHF 37) for the latest information in this regard.

### Directions

The bar has 2·4m 2 hours each side of HW. Although the channel at the entrance and inside is very narrow, the banks on either hand are clearly defined at halftide as they are fairly steep-to. There is a slipway and concrete landing stage which is accessible at most states of the tide. The deepest channel is close to the N of the line of moored yachts all the way up to the marina. The river is extremely full of moorings and yachts are advised not to anchor further in than 3 or 4 cables to seaward of the Grand Hotel and even there it is advisable to rig a tripping line.

**Facilities:** Visiting yachtsmen are welcome to use the facilities of Malahide Yacht Club which is open at weekends and most evenings during summer. Otherwise every facility is available in the village centre within a few hundred yards of the slip: Good shops, several hotels, pubs, a wide range of good restaurants, dry cleaning and launderette, fuel from a garage, gas from a hardware, doctors and dentists, frequent bus and train service to Dublin.

A comprehensive repair service is available. Moorings may be available on application to MYC boatman who is on duty at weekends and any evening when tides permit racing. A local boatman, (William Hatch), runs a ferry service and may have moorings available. He also looks after boats left at anchorage or in an emergency.

## LAMBAY ISLAND

This island lies 6M N of Howth and 2M offshore. It is private property above the HW mark and is a bird sanctuary.

The harbour is under the jurisdiction of the Office of Public Works, and dries out.

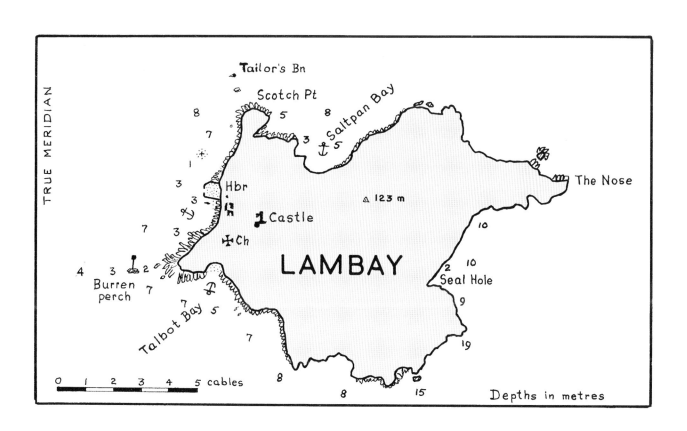

*The small harbour at Lambay almost dries at low water.*

**Rocks**

There are no offshore dangers except for 3 rocks on the W side. Burrin Rocks are 2 cables W of the W point of the island with a reef in between. They are dry at LW and are marked by a starboard hand minor beacon. A ledge extending W of the rocks is marked by the tide flowing across it but it has adequate depth for yachts if the perch is given a berth of 30m. Do not go between the perch and the point. Tailor's Rocks extend 1·5 cables NNW of Scotch Point, the NW corner of the island. They are marked by a green conical lighted buoy Q. FL. painted with the letters "TR" moored 0·2M due N. They dry and should be given a berth of at least 1 cable. There is an unmarked rock with 1·2m over it 1 cable N of the harbour and 1 cable off the shore, so it is best to keep at least 1·5 cables off the shore between the harbour and Scotch Point and 1 cable W of the Taylor buoy. About 60m S of the outer part of the harbour there is a small rock which dries 0·8m.

**Anchorages**

All on sand in about 3 or 4m. Saltpan Bay (Swallow Cove on old charts) gives excellent shelter in S winds when it is often quite free from swell and relatively calm. It can in fact be used in winds between SE and W. It is a very useful stopping place for a yacht beating S. Talbot's Bay gives shelter from N and NE wind but there is often an uncomfortable swell there. On the W side of the island anchor SW of the harbour where there is good shelter between E and S winds. It is open to a fetch of 2M or 3M from the W and is of course exposed to winds from the N.

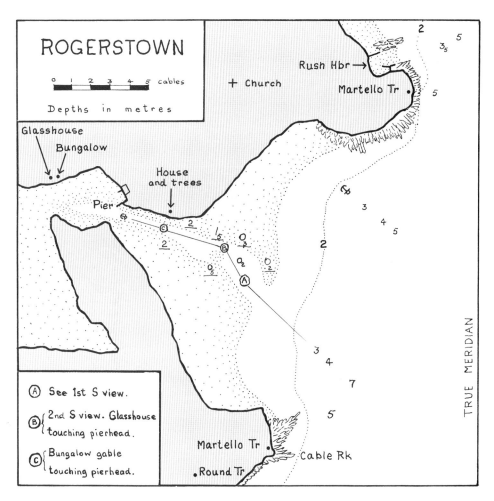

ROGERSTOWN

0 1 2 3 4 5 cables

Depths in metres

Glasshouse
Bungalow
House and trees
Pier
+ Church
Rush Hbr →
Martello Tr
Martello Tr
Round Tr
Cable Rk

Ⓐ See 1st S view.

Ⓑ { 2nd S view. Glasshouse touching pierhead.

Ⓒ { Bungalow gable touching pierhead.

TRUE MERIDIAN

## ROGERSTOWN INLET

This sheltered creek in the bay facing Lambay Island is entered across a bar of sand and gravel which almost dries and tends to vary in position. It should therefore be entered only in modest weather and at least 1 hour before HW as there is the possibility of accidental grounding. Most of the local boats are shallow draught and moored W of the pier, with some deeper draught boats moored E of the pier. There is some space E of it for visiting yachts drawing not more than 1·7m to anchor or they may avail of a vacant mooring for a few hours. The S end of Rogerstown Bay is Portrane Point where there is a Martello tower, a round tower, a new water tower and a clock tower.

Rush Sailing Club has built a new clubhouse at Rogerstown, where showers are available at weekends. During the sailing season, the members lay 4 porthand and 4 starboardhand markers to assist entry to the Estuary.

### Rocks

Cable Rock off this point covers at HW.

### Directions

Approaching the entrance keep the whole of Howth Head well open of Portrane Point. Enter steering 313° towards the most easterly house on the N shore of the channel – this house has trees close around it.

When the round tower bears 194° (see transit) alter course to 330° till the round tower bears 188° (see transit) when the glasshouse should be just clear of the end of the pier (about 292°). Alter course to 275° till abeam of the house with trees, then alter course again and steer towards the end of the pier which should be in line with the gable of the cottage to the right of the glasshouse. (There is an inconspicuous cottage in between them.) Anchor downstream of the pier and of any yacht moored there, 2m, sand and mud. The channel is narrow and the ebb can reach 4 kn at springs so it might be wise to moor. It is best to land on the sand E of the pier. The Rush Sailing Club slip N of the pier is inaccessible at LW. The pier dries and the end of its W side is occupied by the Lambay ferry. Water at inner end of pier.

**Facilities:** Nearest facilities 1·5M away at Rush, where basic supplies and services are available.

### Coastal anchorages

On the N side of Rogerstown Bay it is usually quite comfortable to anchor in NW wind, but it is not suitable for landing. Off Rush Harbour it is possible to anchor temporarily in offshore wind and quiet conditions and convenient for landing by dinghy. However the nearest shops and garages are 0·5M away. The harbour dries at half tide so can only be used by small shallow draught yachts.

*Rogerstown Inlet from S.*

## LOUGHSHINNY

Loughshinny is a cove about 1·5M N of Rush point. Near its S point there is a Martello tower and on the N side a pier SE of which is a perch. Much of the cove is shallow but there is a limited area over 2m deep in the centre where there is good shelter in winds between SSW and NNW. In SW to S wind it may be comfortable but in NW to N wind a yacht is usually rolling. It is not a safe harbour in strong NE to S winds.

To avoid the reefs on both sides of the entrance, steer W halfway between the perch and the S point. Anchor as soon as the pierhead bears N, when the inner end of the quay will appear beyond it. Take care to anchor clear of the crab and lobster cages. The pier dries at LW, otherwise landing is convenient.

**Facilities:** A very small shop with phone, water from a house.

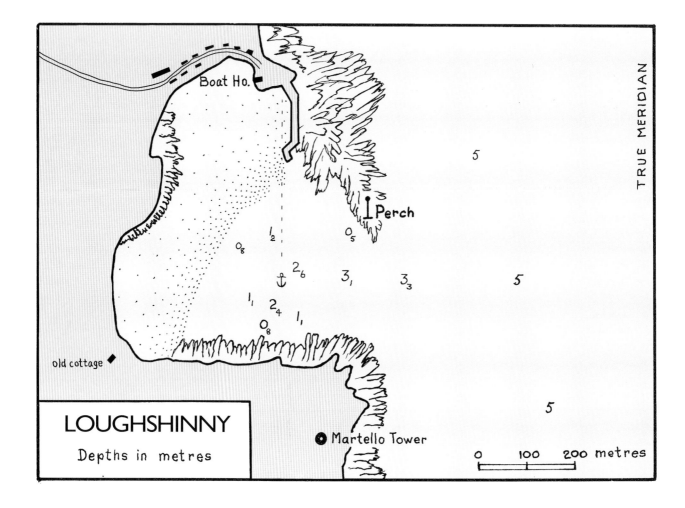

*Loughshinny from SW.*

## SKERRIES ISLANDS
Red Island is joined to the mainland. Shenicks Island and Colt Island are almost joined to the beach at LW. St Patrick's Island is very foul but there is a good passage inside it with a least depth of 3m. Passing between Colt Island and St Patrick's Island, sailing S, keep the Martello tower on Shenick's in line with the top of Pope's Hall Hill bearing 188°. To pass between St Patrick's and Shenick's keep the middle of Colt Island bearing 325°.

## SKERRIES BAY
This bay has good holding and is well sheltered in winds between W and E by S. It is completely exposed to the N quarter and strong wind between NE and ESE makes it pretty rough. Yachts are moored there in summer. The pier dries except for the outer 60m, which has less than 1m. It is used by fishing boats but their owners have no objection to yachts berthing alongside them, provided they are prepared to cast off, sometimes at short notice, when the boats put to sea. Light, on the pierhead, shows Oc R 6s between 103° and 154°.

## Directions
Approaching from the E take care to avoid the reefs. Keep well clear of the Skerries and Red Islands and pass N of Cross Rock red buoy, Fl.R 10s. This buoy is difficult to see against shore lights. Do not turn into the bay till the pierhead bears less than 154°. Anchor outside the moored yachts in 3 or 4m. Alternatively, if space is free, anchor E of the moorings and about 1 cable away from the pier which should be bearing 090° or more. Land at the pier or on the slip just N of it.

**Facilities:** There is a sailing club with showers and a bar, and most facilities are available in Skerries. Good restaurants. EC Thurs. There is an excellent seafood restaurant on the pier. Anyone requiring moorings for the night should telephone 01-8490113 in advance of arrival. General enquiries should be made to the sailing club's boatman.

## ROCKABILL LIGHTHOUSE
Rockabill lies about 2·5M E by N of St Patrick's Island. It consists of two 9 m high rocks, close together and steep-to. Light, from a white tower with black band 32m high, Fl WR 12s45m W22M R18M Horn (4) 60s, W from 178° through W to 329°, R 329° to 178°.

## Tidal streams
Tidal streams between Rockabill and Skerries run NNW and SSE, 6 hours each way starting at LW and HW Dover, but inshore the ebb starts at −0030 Dover and runs for 7 hours, speed at springs 1·5 kn, faster between the islands.

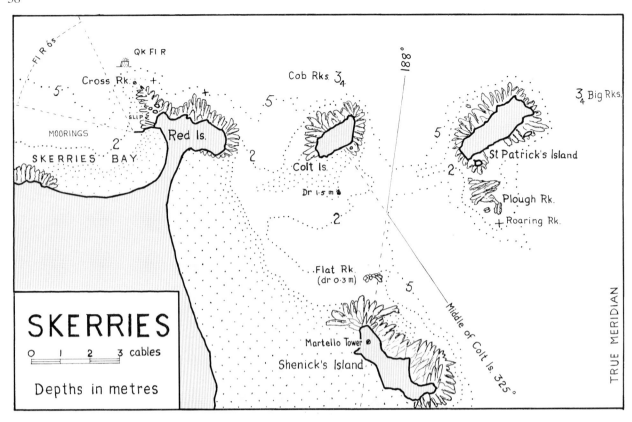

*Approach to Skerries from SE with Shenick's Island to the left and Colt Island to the right.*

*Skerries Bay from SE.*

## BALBRIGGAN

HW + 0015 Dover. Rise (HW): 4·4/3·6m. This small
artificial harbour is 3M NW of Skerries. It dries out
completely and is well sheltered. It is used by local
yachts as well as by many trawlers and is attractive
for visitors who are happy to dry out alongside. The
harbour has been recently dredged and generally
overhauled, making it quite a pleasant place to
overnight. However, it is advisable to be security con-
scious when leaving a boat unattended.

### Lights

Pierhead light from a white tower on the N corner of
the pier, Fl.(3) WRG 20s10M W from 193° to 288°, R
over the Skerries, G over Cardy Rocks.

### Directions

You cannot anchor near the harbour at LW as it is
shallow for 4 cables offshore. The depth at HWS
alongside the quays is about 3·5m so a yacht drawing
1·5m could normally enter 2 hours before HW.
Approach steering between W and SW towards the
middle of the beach just N of the harbour and when
the inner pier opens up bear round for the entrance.
Go in nearer the N pierhead and steer SE till on line
between an old capstan on the pier near the lighthouse and the entrance to the inner harbour, then go
through the outer harbour keeping on this line. From
the inner harbour entrance steer to pass halfway
between the N corner of the pub and the NW quay,
then bear round towards the SE quay and go alongside there.

**Facilities:** The main street with shops and good
restaurants quite close. EC Thur. Beside the slip there
is a building with restaurant, bars, saunas, and a swimming pool. water, fuel and gas available. Engine
repairs: J. Kennedy at Balrothery Telephone
01-8411496, or M. Redden at Skerries Telephone
01-8491462.

## BALBRIGGAN TO RIVER BOYNE

The coast between Balbriggan and the River Boyne
is lowlying and unwelcoming to the yachtsman. In
particular keep well clear of Cardy Rocks about 1M
N of Balbriggan which extend eastwards, dry at half
tide and are marked by a red perch. Gormanstown
Aerodrome borders the coast about 1M N of the
Cardies. It can be recognised by a conspicuous radio
mast (height 150 ft) lit during darkness by 3 vertical
red lights and some lower level red lights, visible at
sea for a considerable distance.

### Caution

Between March and October Army firing exercises may
be carried out from Gormanstown at intermittent times.
Red flags are flown outside the coastal railway line
when the exercises occur. Careful watch is maintained
by army authorities for sea traffic. Range 10M centred
on 53° 38′ 41″N and 06° 13′ 41″W, radial boundaries bearing 015° and 122° from firing point. Further information obtainable from E coast Garda barracks Telephone
01-8412102. Platen cement works chimney (153 ft) situated about 5M from coast and 2M SW of Drogheda,
has an aero beacon Q Fl. R and 2 FR 11M. This beacon
is in line of River Boyne leading lights (248°).

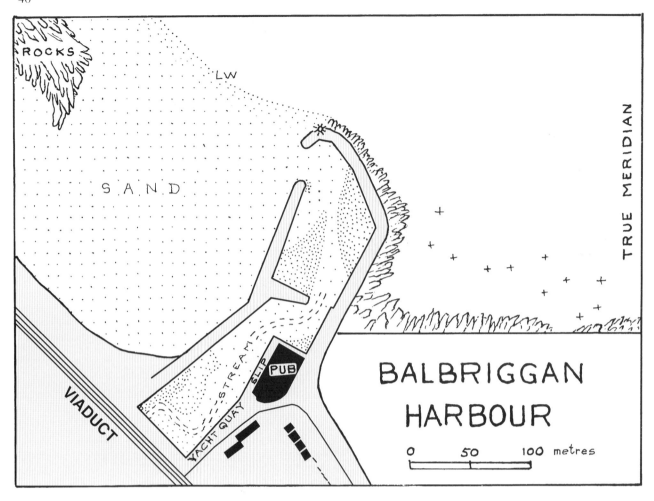

ROCKS

LW

SAND

TRUE MERIDIAN

VIADUCT

YACHT QUAY

STREAM

SLIP

PUB

BALBRIGGAN
HARBOUR

0    50    100 metres

*Balbriggan Harbour from SE.*

*Balbriggan Harbour—entrance.*

*Balbriggan Harbour—inner basin.*

## RIVER BOYNE

HW at the mouth +0015 Dover. Rise (HW): 5·4/4·1 m. The Boyne enters the sea about 9M N of Skerries and at suitable rise of tide gives access to the busy commercial port of Drogheda 4M inland. The navigable channel is between 50m and 75m wide upstream of the part shown on the plan and it is approximately in the middle between the training walls which confine the river all the way to Drogheda. There is nowhere suitable for anchoring, nor is there any special berth for yachts in Drogheda. However, they are not unwelcome there and it is a well sheltered place to spend a night. Chart 1431 is essential to help identify the lights if entering in the dark.

### Lights and Daymarks

**Leading lights** in large white lanterns. Front Light Oc.W 12s 8m 15M, vis 203 degrees to 293 degrees (90 degrees). Rear Light Oc.W 12s 12m 17M, vis 246 degrees to 252 degrees. Leading line 248 degrees. **North Light,** Fl.R 4s 7m 15M, vis 282 degrees to 288 degrees. **Aleria Beacon,** QG, is a large stone structure located on the end of the north-training wall. **Lyons Light,** Fl (3) R 5s, is a steel beacon on the end of the S training wall. **South Bull,** Fl R 2s, is a large stone beacon halfway along the S training wall. All lights and marks are fixed beacons showing Fl.R on south bank and Fl. G on north bank up to Drogheda.

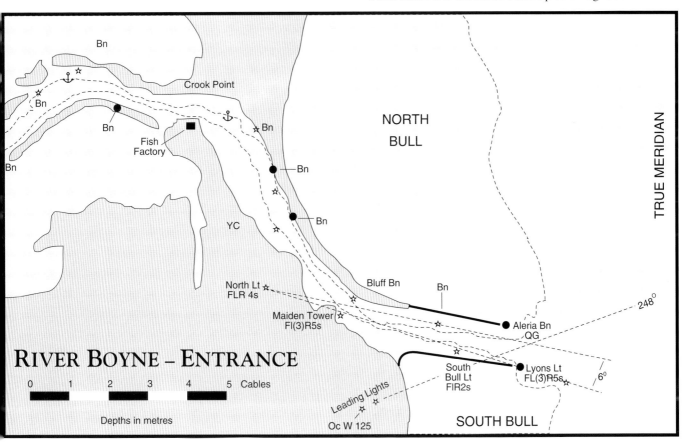

Bn

Crook Point

Bn

Bn

Fish Factory

Bn

Bn

Bn

YC

Bn

NORTH BULL

TRUE MERIDIAN

North Lt
FLR 4s

Bluff Bn

Bn

248°

Maiden Tower
Fl(3)R5s

Aleria Bn
QG

# RIVER BOYNE – ENTRANCE

South
Bull Lt
FlR2s

Lyons Lt
FL(3)R5s

6°

0    1    2    3    4    5 Cables

Leading Lights

Depths in metres

Oc W 125

SOUTH BULL

*River Boyne entrance from SE.*

*Boyne River Mouth—¼ mile ENE. Lead in lights (arrowed) nearly in line.*

*Drogheda from SE.*

**The Beacons** are large, built of stone, and taper slightly to a rounded top. **Maiden Tower** is an old narrow square stone tower 21m high. Light Beacon Fl.(3) R 5s.

**Directions**

The bar off the entrance is about 0·6m at chart datum. When calculating what time to enter Drogheda consideration must be given to weather conditions and barometric pressure. Northerly winds cut the tide, southerly winds increase the tides. Low barometric pressure increases the tides, high barometric pressure cuts the tides. When entering the channel maintain the leading line of 248 degrees. As you approach the actual entrance with the **North light** opening on your starboard bow you may enter the channel and maintain a centre channel line course all the way to Drogheda. It is advisable to use your engine in the channel. Strong flood and ebb tides can be expected, especially ebb when there has been heavy or prolonged rainfall. When approaching from the south avoid a large rock approximately 1 cable east of **Lyons Light.** This rock is visible on big spring ebbs. With winds from the northeast to the southeast and ebb tide a large steep sea and swell may be expected on the bar and extreme caution must be exercised if entering during such condition. Adequate underkeel allowance must be considered for the fall.

**Anchorages**

It is not advisable to anchor in river. Commercial shipping moves into and out of the river 3 hours before high water and up to 2 hours after high water. When really necessary, however, anchoring is possible for short periods, i.e., from 2 hours after high water until 3 hours before the next high water. The only possible anchorages are shown on the plan and are close in to the N bank about 3 cables E of the old fish factory (situated on the S bank) and again further up the river at the bend about 2·5 cables W of Crook Point beacon (The Hole). A concrete pumphouse will be seen between Crook Point and The Hole. Moor with 2 anchors. Use a riding light at night and maintain a VHF radio watch on CH. 11, the port operational channel. Apart from commercial shipping, there is a risk of damage from trawlers or interfering with salmon fishers.

**DROGHEDA**

Railway viaduct 27m clearance above HWS. Berthing above viaduct on N side. Mooring alongside dredger is no longer possible. There are 518m of Public Quays. The quay upriver of this area is protected by gabions not visible at high water and should not be used for yacht moorings. HM, will readily advise. Telephone: Office N Quay 041-9838378 Home 041-983885, Mobile 086-2547827.

**Facilities:** No specific yacht facilities. Shopping, water, fuel, convenient to quays. Port Control VHF Ch. 11. Check with Harbour Master for tidal information and any shipping movements. Hotels and

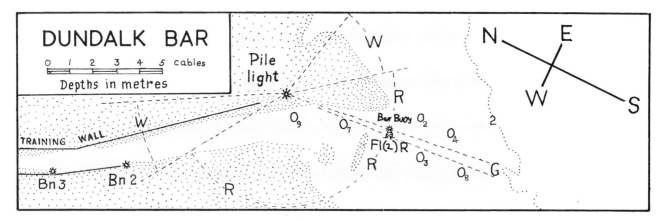

closer approach occulting G light as described under lights above. When No 2 beacon comes abeam to port, turn into channel. Leave Nos 2, 4, 6, 8 and 10 beacons close to port hand. After passing 10 steer midchannel between 5 (now lit) and 12. Leave 7, 9, 9A and 11 close to starboard. Leave 16 and 18 close to port hand. Between 16 and 18 steer midchannel, passing sewerage works to port. Leave 18 fine to port hand then hug the S bank until clear of "Towers" (1 cable W of 18). Head for mid channel between oil depot on S bank and beacon 15. Berth dries to soft mud. Ask for advice. Harbour Offices on quay and in Quay Street close by

Telephone: Office 04-234096. Radio watch available, VHF Ch. 16/14, 2 hours before HW and 2 hours after HW otherwise only when commercial shipping entering or leaving. Pilot boatman's Telephone 042-35644; available unless on holiday.

**Facilities:** Quay available for drying out at Ballurgan Point (N bank). Water and diesel available on pier. Shops open Thurs. and Fri. until 9 p.m. Small shops open until 11 p.m. All repairs except sails. Dundalk is on the main NS rail link, with hotels, pubs, buses, taxis. No harbour dues.

*Dundalk from SE.*

## CARLINGFORD LOUGH

HW +0015 Dover. Rise: 4·8-4·3/1·8-0·7m. This lough is the most picturesque inlet on the E coast and well worth a visit. It is 8M long and its upper part lies between the wooded lower slopes of the Mountains of Mourne and the steep barren Carlingford Mountain. This makes its position very conspicuous from seaward. The mouth of the lough is encumbered with rocky shoals, access being through a buoyed channel with 6·3m least depth. Inside there is complete shelter from swell but no really snug anchorage. In the upper part, with 5·4m least depth in channel, there is a very large area suitable for anchoring but nowhere sheltered in strong NW wind except Warrenpoint and Carlingford Marina which is cradled between the mountains of Mourne to the N and E and Slieve Foy to the S and W. There are 6 small towns, Greenore, Carlingford and Omeath on the Republic shore and Warrenpoint, Rostrevor and Greencastle on the Northern Ireland side. It is necessary to have chart 2800 and keeping in the buoyed channel, the anchorages may be reached safely. The border between the Republic of Ireland and Northern Ireland lies at the top end of Carlingford Lough on the port side. Yachts arriving from outside the European Union should contact the Customs Authorities at the next port of call after passing this frontier. Flag Quebec should be flown close up at the yard and courtesy ensigns as appropriate. If the Customs are not easily available, report to the nearest Police Station (Northern Ireland) or Garda Station (Republic of Ireland) for clearance to proceed. Yachts registered in the European Union arriving from an EU country are not required to report to Customs.

### Dangers in the approach

Ballagan Spit with detached rocks at its outer end extends 0·75M, ESE from Ballagan Point, the SW side of the entrance. The Breast and Morgan Pladdy, with depths of 1·8m and 1·3m respectively, lie between Ballagan Spit and Cranfield Point. Nelly Pladdy, a dangerous unmarked rock which rarely uncovers, lies about 2·5 cables SE of Cranfield Point. Hellyhunter Rock, 1·4m deep, lies about 1·25M SE of Cranfield Point and is marked by a S Card. buoy 0·5M S of it.

### Lights

Carlingford Safe Water spherical buoy, LFl.10s, whistle, is 3M SSE of Cranfield Point. **Hellyhunter** S Card buoy Q (6) + LFl.15s Whis Racon "K". **Haulbowline Lighthouse** a grey tower 34m high shows Fl.(3) W 10s17M. At 11m below the main light FR shows from 196° to 208° indicating the turning point in the fairway. Horn 30s when visibility is bad in the entrance. **Leading lights** on pile structures in line 310° 26′ show Oc. 3sW11M Vis 295° to 325° (30° ARC.).

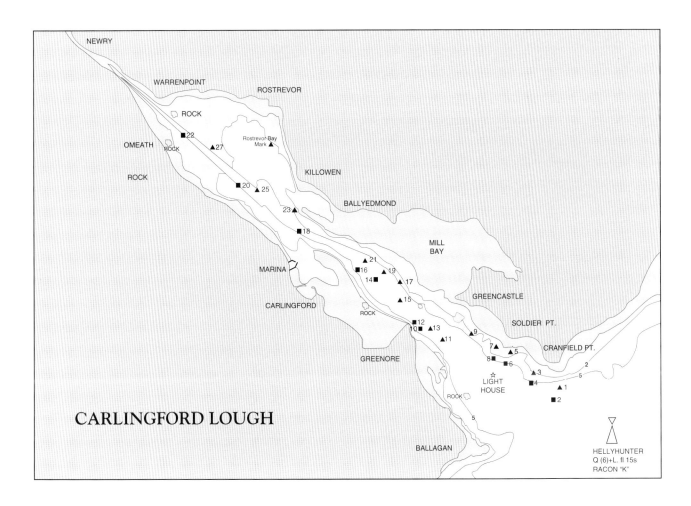

CARLINGFORD LOUGH

*Carlingford Harbour from SE with Marina to the North.*

*Carlingford entrance from SE.*

**Caution**

A yacht with reasonable power might enter against the ebb. However, with onshore wind and ebb the entrance becomes dangerous and should on no account be approached. With strong onshore winds there is an element of danger even with the flood. In light conditions the wind or the engine must be reliable enough to take the yacht clear of any dangers on which the strong tides might set her.

**Tidal Streams**

The flood starts about −0500 Dover and the ebb +0020 Dover. 1Me outside the entrance the streams are not felt. They reach a rate of 3·5 kn in the buoyed approach channel, 4·5 kn just E of the lighthouse, 1·5 kn between the entrance and Greenore, 5 kn off Greenore, 2·5 kn between Stalka and Watson Rocks and 1·5 kn off Carlingford. They are only just perceptible off Rostrevor. From abreast the lighthouse to No 5 buoy the flood tends to set N. There is a S-going eddy during the flood along the E side of Block House Island. Otherwise the flood follows the channels normally, as does the ebb.

**Directions**

From the N, or from the Carlingford buoy, pass S of the Hellyhunter buoy, where the line of the leading light beacons will be picked up. Coming from the S the offshore dangers must be given a safe berth. After passing Imogene buoy abeam to Port, set course 033° to clear Ballagan Spit and therafter pick up the leading lights about 0·5M N of the Hellyhunter Buoy. Enter the lough between the buoys with the leading lights in line 310° 26′ till the lighthouse is past abeam, then alter course to port and head for Greenore Point which has buildings and a plantation of pine. Leave odd numbered buoys to starboard and even num-

bered red buoys to port. Without chart 2800 it is best to remain in the buoyed channel as there are some dangerous rocks outside it. With head wind it is better to motor but if necessary it is possible to beat in. This involves short tacks where there are dangers on both sides, as between buoys 1, 3, 5 and 7 on Starboard Hand and 2, 4, 6 and 8 on the Port Hand but do not tack too far outside the buoys in clear areas lest the tide sweep you onto a rock before you get back. As the entrance channel is only 80m wide, yachts should keep well clear of commercial traffic in this area.

**GREENCASTLE**

Greencastle on the N shore is the nearest anchorage to the entrance and as sheltered as any other in the lough. However, it is the only one whose approaches are not buoyed, and they are rather narrow and only practical by day. It is best to go in near LW when the rocks on the S side can be seen.

**Facilities:** Two harbour tugs are stationed here. They are owned and operated by Sean Cunningham, phone 016937-63462.

**Directions**

From seaward, having passed Vidal Rock buoy, No 9, steer towards the houses on Greencastle Point. When the rear Leading Lt. Beacon comes abeam about 0·75 of a cable to starboard look out for a very thin perch – at HWS only 1m of it shows. Keep this perch in line with any part of Greencastle pier, a derelict wooden structure, and as you approach the perch turn to starboard for a moment so as to leave it not less than 10m to port, then head for the inboard end of the pier and when the moorings are reached, it is better not to go SW of them unless the rocks there are visible. Going out this way, keep the Block House just open W of

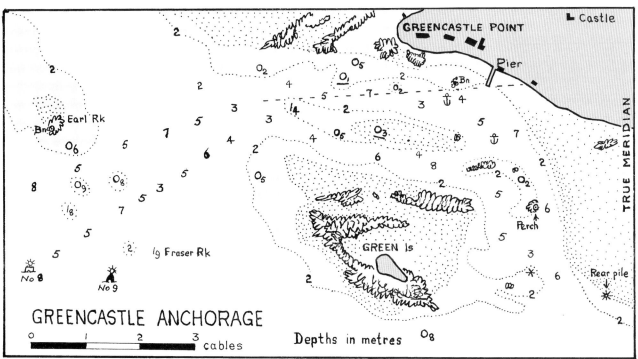

GREENCASTLE ANCHORAGE

*Greencastle Harbour from NW.*

*Greencastle Harbour from SSE.*

the rear light pile till past the perch, which should be immediately kept astern in line with the pier. The rear light pile astern with the pier just open NE of it leads safely NE of Vidal Rock.

**Approaching from Greenore**, Greencastle may be reached by passing between Earl Rock and the rocks S and SE of it which have a least depth of 0·8m. There is no mark for these latter so unless there is ample rise of tide, leave Earl Rock beacon just 0·5 of a cable to port. When this beacon comes on the port quarter, keep the outer end of Greencastle pier in line with the small red bungalow on the shore about 1 cable E of the pier. Just before Greencastle Point comes abeam bear to starboard towards the moored yachts.

### Caution
The large shoal on the S side of the channel SW of the pier very seldom dries and is not marked: take care not to go too close to it. N of Greencastle Point there is a buoy depot with a quay. Yachts should not go near it as the whole approach to it dries out. The small rock which dries 0·5 of a cable W of the pier-head is now marked by a thin perch.

### Anchorage
Much of the area is occupied by yachts on moorings. It might be possible to anchor between them and the rocks which dry S of them, but this should not be

*Greenore from S.*

attempted except at LW. A safer place to anchor is W of the NW moorings, not more than 0·75 of a cable from the perch on the rock W of the pier and not N of the red bungalow and pierhead transit. The tide runs more strongly here than S of the pier. Land on the beach near the pier. There are a few fishermen's and holiday houses in this rather out of the way spot. The Carlingford Lough pilot's house is beside the northern end of the pier.

### GREENORE HARBOUR
Greenore Harbour, just W of Greenore Point, a busy commercial shipping port. It consists of a quay protected by a detached breakwater about 100m NW of it. The quay is not suitable or available for yachts to lie alongside. Anchor about 70m from the W end of the Breakwater in 2·3m, gravel bottom. Further in the bottom shoals rapidly and dries close to the end of the breakwater. A strong tide runs across the entrance of the harbour and weak variable eddies run through it so that a yacht is inclined to sheer about. This harbour should only be used as a refuge anchorage in strong southerly winds and/or when waiting for a favourable tide in the channel.

### Light
Greenore Light Fl. R 7·5s10m5M.

**Facilities:** Landing is at stairs outside the enclosed goods depot and gives easy access to the street. Limited stores at shop. No fuel. The harbour VHF is manned during working hours VHF 16, c/s "Greenore Ferries" Telephone 042-73170. Electrical repairs at Dundalk Telephone 042-73554. Bus to Dundalk. Crane for lifting out could be arranged if required.

### CARLINGFORD HARBOUR
Carlingford Harbour, easily recognised by the town and the old castle, lies nearly 2M beyond Greenore on the SW side of the lough. The harbour dries and is fronted by a large shoal extending to the edge of the buoyed channel. At neaps a yacht drawing 1·4m could anchor 1 cable N of the E pierhead, and one drawing 1·7m 0·5 of a cable further N. This anchorage is seriously exposed only to the N quarter though it is subject to violent gusts in strong SW winds. The harbour offers good protection in all winds alongside either pier. The NW pier has 2·7m at HWN as far as the second steps. The bottom is deep mud and rather unstable so it is somewhat dangerous for keelboats. The E pier has a better bottom but is a lot further from the town.

**Facilities:** Dundalk Sailing Club Telephone 042-73238 is active during the season at weekends, particularly Sunday. VHF, limited meals, showers and bar. fuel, water and most services are available in this quaint village. Hotels, pubs and guesthouses. Good area for walking.

### Entrance Lights
End of the NW pier Fl. G. 3s3M. End of east pier Occ. R. 4s 3M.

### CARLINGFORD MARINA
Telephone 042-9373492 Mariners are recommended to approach the marina from No.18 Port Hand Channel Buoy Fl. R(4) 8s on a course of 192°. This course is on a transit between No. 18 and No. 23

*Carlingford Marina from No. 18 buoy.*

*Carlingford Marina (showing entrance to left), 500 yards off.*

*Carlingford Marina.*

Channel Buoys. The entrance is marked with day marks and lights, Port and Starboard, Lt. Fl. G(16) 60s Lt. Fl. R(16) 60s. There are 20 visitors berths out of a total number of 90 berths. The marina should be called on Channel 16 Working 37 to advise your arrival when a berth will be allocated and assistance given to guide yachts to the designated berth. Depth in marina is 3·5m LWS. Min. Depth in approaches from No.18 Buoy is 2m. Marina Rates 1999 IR£1.20 per metre IR£7.00 per metre per week. Major credit cards accepted.

**Facilities:** Fuel, water, electricity, toilets, showers, public telephone, garbage disposal skip, crane 16·5 tons boat trailer lift unit, slipway, divers, drying out pad, chandlery, winter storage. New bar and restaurant. Carlingford town is 10 minutes walk away and has hotels, restaurants, pubs (folk music evenings), Post Office, well stocked supermarket, newsagent, angling centre, bicycle hire, adventure centre, horse riding, medieval sites to visit, heritage centre showing history of the area. Golf course – Greenore.

## UPPER PART OF CARLINGFORD LOUGH
The SW side is fairly shallow for 0·5M N of Carlingford, but from there a berth of 2 cables clears any dangers as far as Greer's Quay, where the depth 1·5 cables NE of the quay is just 2m. This means it is a suitable anchorage for most yachts in winds between S and W. The quay dries completely and there are no facilities ashore. Beyond Greer's Quay the head of the lough shoals gradually. At MLWN most yachts can proceed NW, minimum depth 0·6m, passing between No. 22 buoy and Black Rock beacon and anchoring in about 1m 1 cable N of the beacon and about 3 cables offshore from Omeath. The boatslip here has approx. 0·5m at MLWS.

**Facilities:** Hotel, groceries and petrol pump are all conveniently close.

## NORTH EAST SIDE OF CARLINGFORD LOUGH
Carlingford Lough Yacht Club, just N of Killowen Point, has a landing slip but at LWS it should be approached with caution. Anchor off the moored yachts. There is 2m 1·5 cables offshore.

**Facilities:** When the Club is open, visitors are welcomed and may use the showers and the bar. Close by on the main road there is a public telephone. 1 cable N of Yacht Club there is a 190m long jetty with slip on either side. A perch marks the seaward end. It does however dry out.

Opposite **Rostrevor Quay**, 1M further NW, the 2m line is 0·5M offshore. Apart from the distance it is a

convenient place to land, except near LW when both the slip and the quay are surrounded by impassable mud. However you can then land on the stony beach about 1·5 cables to the SE where steps lead up to the road. There is a garage with fuel opposite the quay. It is 0·75M to Rostrevor town, EC Wed.

### Anchorage
Anywhere between these two places is very pleasant for anchoring but there is nowhere else you can get ashore. Suitable depth is further offshore the further NW you anchor, holding is good and there is virtually no tidal stream.

## WARRENPOINT
GW +0025 Dover. Rise: 5·4-3·9/1·4-0·2 m. This is a fairly new commercial port. It is approached along a straight buoyed channel 80m wide and dredged to 5·4m. The breakwater light shows Fl.G 3s and the light on corner of dock Fl.G 5s5m3M. The area just NW of the breakwater now dries out completely. The commercial quays have vertical timber fenders and the area around them is dredged to 5·4m. Consult the HM, VHF 16 & 12, c/s "Warrenpoint Harbour", about staying there, as you may have to move. HM telephone 016937-52878 during office hours.

### Berthing
In summer months a floating pontoon is placed behind the breakwater where yachts may berth. There are mooring facilities between the breakwater, the old Customs House, and the old Warrenpoint/Omeath ferry landing point. Lying along the pontoon is safe, with 7ft. depth at low water. The first 25ft. or so is used by the Warrenpoint/ Omeath ferry (Red Star Motor Boats) which finish at 5·00 p.m. After that time the whole pontoon is free, i.e. two 30ft. boats alongside, with the rest rafting up! There is total protection – passing ships cause a bounce!

**Facilities:** Warrenpoint is the best shopping place in the lough. Hotels and pubs. Buses to Newry. Taxis. Warrenpoint Boat Club have toilet and shower facilities in the old Customs House. Excellent restaurants and night life for the young crews.

### Coast
There are no other isolated dangers between Hellyhunter Rock and Roaring Rock near the S end of Dundrum Bay. After steering NE for 1M from Hellyhunter buoy the coast should be given a berth of not less than 0·5M. N of Annalong there are many lobster pots.

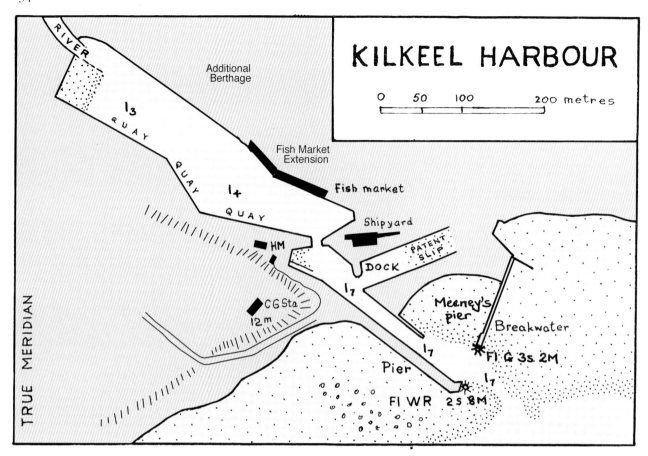

## KILKEEL HARBOUR

HW −0005 Dover. Rise: 5·3-4·4/1·9-0·7m. This busy fishing port is 3·5M NNE of Hellyhunter buoy and is included on chart 2800. It can be a useful place to stop and the inner basin is completely sheltered. It is not the safest harbour for yachts because it becomes very crowded in the evening, but visitors are permitted to berth there. The depth is 1·2m at LAT throughout the harbour. In a SW gale sand builds up near the entrance and makes a drying shoal just outside. The river, which now flows through the harbour, then gradually forms a shallow channel through the shoal. The permanent drying bank extends up to 2·5 cables off the shore E of the harbour and has some stones on it. A shallow shoal extends 0·5M SE of the harbour.

### Directions

From about 1M away approach with the harbour bearing between 341° and 350°. If it cannot be identified, steer first for the CG station (red brick with a white flagstaff) which is easier to see. The recommended approach is with the pierhead bearing 341°. When 100m away from it turn to starboard and steer 010° to 015° till the inner side of the pier is visible, then turn to port and enter. To avoid the edge of the bank on the NE side, the E end of the shipyard building should not come in line with the end of the breakwater. Go straight up the Channel to the inner basin, tie alongside and ask the HM where to stay.

**Facilities:** Water on the quay. Fuel and gas available. Shipwrights operate N of the dock where there are 2 patent slips. All stores in Kilkeel town 0·75M distant. All repairs, except sails. HM on VHF 16/12/14 or Telephone 016937-62287. Hotels, restaurants and pubs, launderette. Area is close to Mourne Mountains for walking. EC Thur. Showers, restaurants and cafe at Nautilus Centre.

### Lights

Pierhead light on small metal post Fl.WR 2s8m8M R 296° to 313°, W 313° to 017°. New light on Meeney's pier, Fl. G 3s6m2M.

*Kilkeel Harbour from SW.*

## ANNALONG HARBOUR

Annalong Harbour is 4·5M NE of Kilkeel and used by local fishing boats. There is excellent shelter in its small tidal basin except in strong onshore wind when it may be subject to swell. If necessary, it can then be closed by a surge gate so obviously yachtsmen should not consider entering in such conditions. It is a very pleasant place in settled weather. It has recently been dredged and now only dries around LWS so it should be about 2m deep 3 hours before HW and at least 2·5m deep 2 hours after HW. The breakwater runs out E with the entrance, difficult to detect until close in, on its N side. There is a small launching slip built about 1 cable N of the harbour, the seaward end of which is marked by a perch.

### Directions

Having made sure that the tide is really high enough, head straight in for the entrance, but not any faster than necessary for control. To avoid the rocky fore-shore keep close to the N side of the breakwater and the harbour wall beyond it. It is all right to move away a little before making the sharp turn to port through the 9m wide entrance to the basin. Seek advice as to where the yacht should be left alongside.

**Facilities:** PO, small shops, good pub.

### Lights

Light on the breakwater head Oc.WRG 5s. 8m9M G 204° to 249°, W 249° to 309°, R 309° to 024°. To enter at night would of course be more difficult for a stranger and cannot be recommended.

56

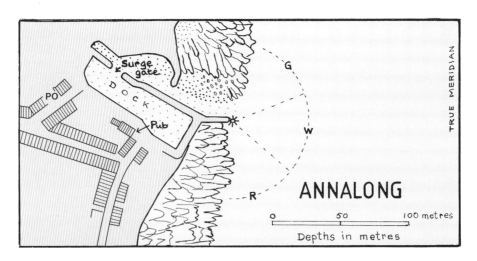

ANNALONG

0          50        100 metres

Depths in metres

*Annalong from W.*

## DUNDRUM BAY

Dundrum Bay, about 9M wide and 4M deep, lies between the Mourne Mountains and St John's Point, described later. Its 2 harbours, accessible only in settled weather and near HW, do not often attract yachts. In westerly winds it is noted for squalls and in strong onshore winds a heavy sea runs into the bay.

**Dangers.** 1·75M N of Mullartown Point, the SW limit of the bay, the unmarked Roaring Rock, which dries at LWS, lies 3 cables offshore. At Newcastle and E of it the shores of the bay are shoal. Cow and Calf Rocks, 3·75M W of St John's Point and 1M offshore, stand at the S end of a submerged reef. They just cover at HWS. They are in the red sector of St John's Point auxiliary light. Between these rocks and St John's Point there are other rocks closer inshore. There are 3 oval yellow buoys in the centre of the bay marking a firingpractice area. A red flag flying from No 8 flagstaff (*see Dundrum plan*) means firing is taking place, or will shortly commence, on the army ranges about 2M E of Dundrum, and yachts should keep away from the area. Red flags on other flagstaffs do not concern the mariner unless there is one on No 8 also.

## NEWCASTLE HARBOUR

HW +0015 Dover. Rise: 5·1-4·1/1·5-0·5m. This is a small artificial harbour at the S end of the town with Fl.R WG Red 232° to 240° White 228° to 232° Green 180° to 228° on end of pier. A strong wind between SE and NE makes the entrance difficult and causes scend in the harbour. However, in summer a fleet of dinghies and motorboats lie on moorings there and take the ground at LW. It dries completely, even at neaps. The approach is shallow, but otherwise free of danger. The entrance faces N. The best berth is at the N pier, anywhere between the end and the steps, clean sand bottom, 2·7m HWN.

### Caution

Watch out for rock amouring which extends 15m S from S pier and covers at HW. A sewage outfall extends 240m due E from the sewage works to S of S pier, and is barely covered at LW. In settled weather a yacht could put in here at HW and perhaps risk drying out, subject to local advice.

**Facilities:** The Newcastle Sailing Club, with showers when open, has premises beside the RNLI house and there is a slip for launching dinghies at HW. The town stretches for 1M along the shore. HM: Telephone 013967-22106.

## DUNDRUM HARBOUR

HW +0010 Dover; it has been found that HW Liverpool gives the closest prediction for HW Dundrum. Rise: HW reckoned to be 0·3m less than at Newcastle and LW 0·3m more; the rise is notably increased by S winds and reduced by N winds. This is a pretty estuary surrounded by sandhills at the head

of Dundrum Bay. Dundrum Bay cannot really be recommended for keelyachts because the narrow bar, which is completely exposed to the S, has only 0·3m, and there is nowhere very suitable for lying afloat. It would be interesting to visit in a twinkeel yacht or a motor cruiser. The channel is liable to change so be prepared to deal with going aground when entering or leaving.

### Directions

Entry should only be attempted in reasonable sea conditions, good visibility and with a rising tide. An old castle on a small rounded hill behind the town bearing about 330° leads to the entrance. Steer for a small round buoy which marks the outer end of the narrow entrance channel and leave this buoy about 11m to port. Next steer for the fairway buoy, a small buoy on the E side inside the entrance, and leave it close to starboard. (Both buoys are black, and may remain so). There are 2 posts to be left to starboard, passing halfway between the second of them and the poles along the shore to port. From here carry on towards the last post (porthand diamond topmark) and when about 45m from it alter course to starboard for the quay.

### Anchorage

The only anchorage with over 2m is in the reach between the last 2 posts but the tide there runs very strongly. On the W side of the fairway and just S of the quay is a better place but the depth there is only 0·3m. However, this might be enough to enable a small yacht to lie afloat at LWN. Drying out at the quay is not recommended, chiefly because of the strong tidal streams.

**Facilities:** Garages, shops, PO, a small hotel. EC Thur.

### Lights

St John's Point, the E tip of Dundrum Bay, is easily recognisable by the prominent lighthouse, 40m high, black with 2 yellow bands, which stands near the end of the long low point. Main light: Q(2) W 7·5s37m25M; auxiliary light Fl.WR 3s14m W15 R11M, W 064° to 078°, R 078° to shore. Horn (2) 60s, Fog Det. Lt. VQ W.

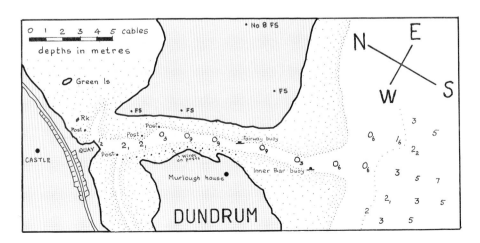

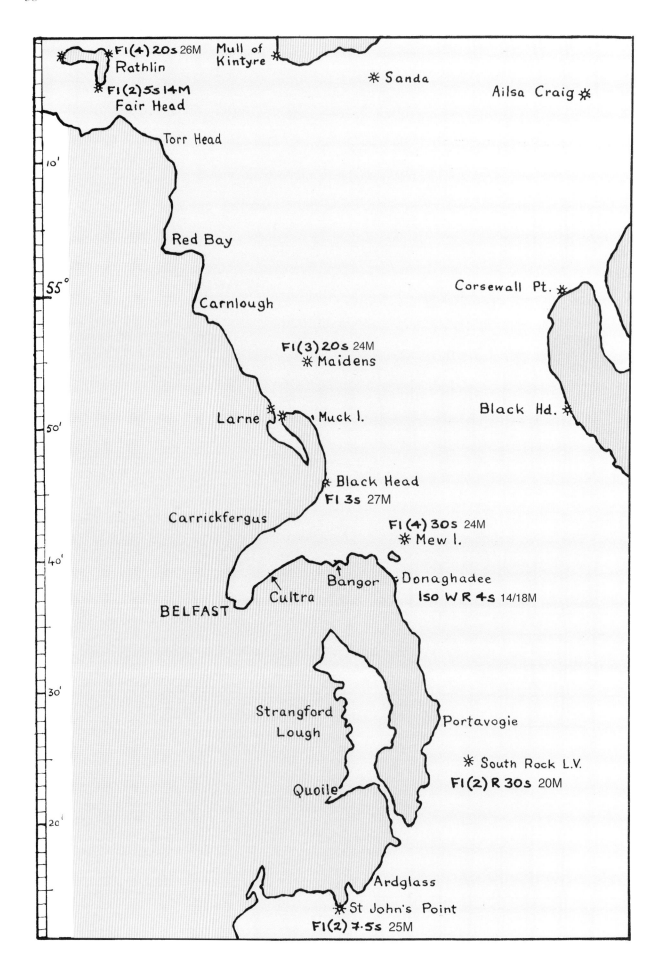

# Chapter 3

## ST JOHN'S POINT
## TO FAIR HEAD

### Charts

The S part of this coast is included on chart 44 (which covers Chapter II). It is possible to manage with three other charts, 2156 Strangford Lough and the coast E of it, and 2198 and 2199 covering the N Channel. Charts 2156 and 2198 just join, at different scales, so 2093, S Approach to N Channel, might be desirable also chart 1753 is useful if going to Belfast, but not essential. 3709 is only needed for investigating the Copeland Island shores. It is possible to anchor in Larne Lough without 1237. The entrance to Strangford Lough is now on chart 2159. (*see Appen-dix 1*).

### ARDGLASS HARBOUR

This is a safe and a handy terminus for a day's sail to or from Dublin. The new Phennick Cove Marina, on the Western side of Ardglass Harbour, is fully operational and offers a very good service to visiting yachts (see below for details). Strangford, just N of it, is undoubtedly one of the best loughs for yachting in Ireland. At present the only sheltered port in

onshore winds on the rockstrewn shore between Strangford and the neighbourhood of Belfast Lough is Portavogie. Belfast Lough is a very popular yachting area with anchorages in offshore winds but rather exposed to the E. There are now two very well equipped marinas in Belfast Lough at Bangor and Carrickfergus. Larne Lough has no closely sheltered spot but it has plenty of space for anchoring in suitable depths and safe conditions. From Larne to Fair Head the handsome coast with bold heads offers limited security in onshore wind. Advice about crossing from there to Scotland is given in Chapter V.

### Tides

The flood tide runs SE and S, following the trend of this coast, while the tide is rising at Dover. The ebb flows out to the N during the falling tide at Dover. In the entrance to the North Channel both the flood and the ebb can reach 4·5 kn at springs. The tides run strongly in the Channel till it widens S of Belfast Lough, and become weak near St John's Point, SE of

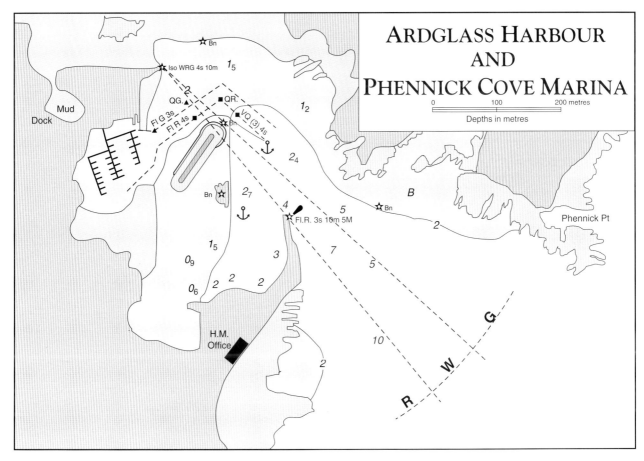

which the flood streams from N and S meet and divide. The time of HW along this coast is not much different from HW Dover. The tidal range decreases from S to N. More detailed descriptions of local tidal streams are given where necessary.

## KILLOUGH HARBOUR

1·75M NE of St John's Point. Killough Pier has been rebuilt but has no depth of water alongside.

### Anchorages

Anchorage in the bay outside the harbour and W of Ringfad Point is not particularly attractive as most of the bottom is rock, it is therefore not recommended. If wishing to go in, the plan on chart 633 gives full details.

### Rocks

The only danger just outside the bay is Water Rocks, which dry 3m and are marked by a red mast. There are more rocks inside.

**Facilities:** None.

## ARDGLASS

HW +0015 Dover. Rise (HW), probably: 4·7-4·0m. VHF Call 16, Work 14, 12. This busy fishing harbour is 3M NE of St John's Point. It consists of a rocky inlet partly sheltered by a substantial breakwater with quays on its inner side. Further in there is a marina and a completely sheltered old tidal dock. Approaching from seaward, the white roof of the fish shed above the pier is a useful landmark. Coming from the S one sees a tower on the conical hill S of Ardglass and a water tower nearer Ringfad Point outside the hill.

### Lights

The principal lighthouse is on the end of the inner pier and shows Iso WRG 4s 10m W8M R7M G5M G shore to 308°, W308° to 314°, R314° to shore. On the end of the breakwater or Outer Pier, there is Fl.R 3s10m5M. On the Starboard side and NE of the Outer Pier there is Ardtole Bn.

### Directions

Keep well away from the rocks on both sides of the shore outside the harbour entrance and go in between the breakwater and an iron tripod marking the rocks on the NE side. At night approach the harbour in the white sector of the inner light.

### Anchorages

The best place to anchor is between the outer quay and the red iron beacon on the rock NW of it, in 2 to 2·5m. This is a safe anchorage but uncomfortable in fresh winds between E and S. It can also be disturbed by heavy fishing traffic. In quiet weather or offshore winds it is suitable to anchor between the entrance and the inner entrance, NE of the two beacons.

*Ardglass from SW.*

## Berths

Yachts may go alongside the quays during the day while the fishing fleet is at sea, but should consult the HM about staying there. The foundation of the N facing quay protrudes 0·6m in places. When the shed on this quay is closed it is not possible to go ashore past it. Small yachts might dry out alongside the inner W facing quay, firm bottom. Beyond the inner lighthouse pier the harbour dries and is mostly rocky. The dock there is normally only worth using in an E to S gale. It is about 3m deep at HW over a bottom of deep mud. To reach it, keep close to N of the Wall W of the lighthouse till it bends towards the entrance. Good fenders are necessary as the quays are built of stones and yachts are apt to move when settling down in the mud.

**Facilities:** Report arrival to the HM whose office is in the Northern Ireland Fishing Harbour Office on the pier Telephone 01396-841291. Excellent Supermarket on Quay. Shops often stay open in the evening. One hotel. Public phone in fishmarket on the quay. Fresh water from tap in fish market. Fuel conveniently available, bulk diesel by arrangement. Buses to Downpatrick and Belfast. Minor harbour dues.

## ARDGLASS (PHENNICK COVE) MARINA

The entrance to Phennick Cove Marina is by way of a lighted, buoyed channel which commences about 120m N of the Port Hand Pier Head light (Fl. R. 3s.) and runs in a NW direction before turning sharply to Port around the NW end of the central rock-armoured breakwater, from where it leads in a SW direction to the Marina (see chartlet). Marina capacity: 55 berths of which 36 are reserved for visitors. Minimum depths in approach channel 3.26m. Depths in Marina 3·16m to 1·66m. VHF Call: Channel 16, Working Channel 37.

## Facilities

Fuel, water, gas, toilets, showers, electric power, limited chandlery and repairs. Telephone, groceries, bars, restaurants, hotel, limited banking facilities, angling club, close to historic castles and very good Golf Club. Charts, marine publications, car hire and laundrette.

## Overnight Stay Charges

| | | | |
|---|---|---|---|
| Under 30 ft. | £10.00 | Over 35 ft. | £14.00 |
| 30–35 ft. | £12.00 | Over 40 ft. | £16.00 |

## Rocks – Ardglass to Strangford Narrows

Between Ardglass and Guns Island 2·75M further NE there are a few outlying rocks within 1 cable of the shore. Guns Island is 30m high and has a white obelisk on its SE side. Ballyhornan Bay (charts 2156 and 2159), N of Guns Island, is foul but Benderg Bay is a pleasant and useful anchorage in suitable conditions. **Beware Craiglewey Rocks** S of Killard. If rounding

Killard Point layoff to pass E of them. If heading for Benderg Bay give their S end a very wide berth, turning in when Benderg Beach is well open to N.

## STRANGFORD LOUGH (*Chart 2156, Strangford Narrows 2159*).

Strangford Lough is the longest inlet on the East Coast. It is convenient to deal with it in two parts, the Approaches and 5M entrance known as the Narrows, and the main body of the Lough which lies beyond to the north.

## The Approaches to Strangford Lough and the Narrows

The Approaches and the Narrows are well marked and lighted (*see Chartlet*). Entry is straightforward by day or night, passing to the E of Angus Rock Lt. Ho., using the east channel. The west channel should not be attempted without local knowledge and a chart. Timing is critical as both the flood and the ebb can reach almost 8 knots in places. It is always safe to enter, but to leave on the ebb, into fresh onshore winds, can be dangerous (see caution below). The Marina berthing at Portaferry and the visitors' buoys there and at Strangford, together with the various safe anchorages, make the Narrows an excellent overnight stop.

## Strangford Lough beyond the Narrows

The Lough widens out and there is plenty of unobstructed water for racing. There are visitors' moorings off the towns and the many yacht clubs. There are some pontoons at the clubs but, as yet, no fully equipped marinas. For a passing stranger with a day or two to spare, the Lough, with its pastoral surroundings, is well worth a visit. The only drawback is the number of shoals and drying patches, known as pladdies, which are usually marked by beacons or poles when near a recognised fairway. Chart 2156 is essential. The tidal flow, though very strong, does not run true and one can be carried off track very quickly if one allows one's attention to wander.

## Lights in Strangford Narrows and Approaches

These are as shown on the three associated chartlets (Strangford Narrows, Strangford Creek and Portaferry).

## Tides and Tidal Streams

HW Killard Point as Dover. (**N.B.** HW Dover relates closely to HW Belfast.) HW Strangford Narrows and all of Strangford Lough as for Strangford Quay +0140 Dover. Rise at Strangford Quay 3·6-3·1/0·9-0·4m. Outside the entrance the stream runs NE from +0200 to +0500 Dover, and then SW for nearly 8 hours. The stream in the Narrows floods in from −0330HW Belfast and out from +0230HW Belfast, about six hours each way and at speeds of up to 7·8 kn in places in the main stream, at Spring tides.

*Strangford Narrows from SE.*

## Caution

Beware the overfalls at the bar and in the SE approaches out to a distance of 1·5M, which only occur when there is ebb in the Narrows. These overfalls are bumpy at the best of times and become severe in strong onshore (E to SSW) winds. It is always safe to attempt entry (though few will wish to do so against a strong ebb), as the attempt can readily be abandoned and safer water regained. However, it is not always safe to depart and the danger lies in this not becoming apparent until it is too late for a yacht to regain safe water. A departing yacht approaching the white water at the bar may wish to make back for shelter but be unable to do so against the ebb, and so be drawn out into the overfalls against its will. These are the only circumstances in which Strangford Lough is actually dangerous. There is never any damaging sea at or N of Angus Rock.

*Sailing down The Narrows—Strangford Village background.*

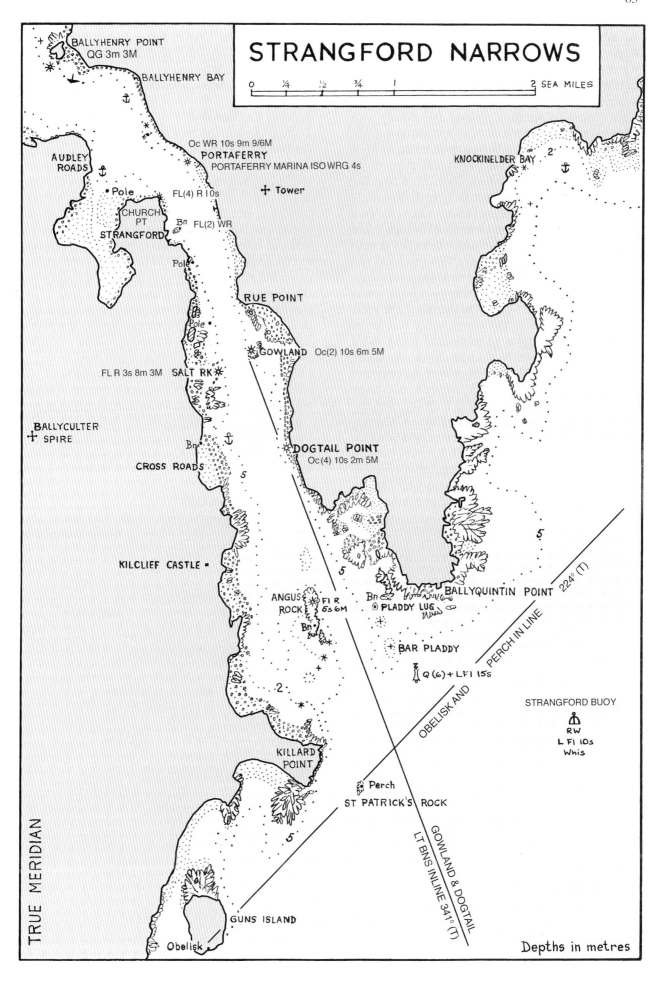

# STRANGFORD NARROWS

0   ¼   ½   ¾   1                    2 SEA MILES

Oc WR 10s 9m 9/6M
**PORTAFERRY**
PORTAFERRY MARINA ISO WRG 4s

+ Tower

KNOCKINELDER BAY

AUDLEY
ROADS

• Pole
CHURCH
PT
**STRANGFORD**

FL(4) R 10s

Bn FL(2) WR

Pole

RUE POINT

Pole

GOWLAND   Oc(2) 10s 6m 5M

FL R 3s 8m 3M  **SALT RK**

BALLYCULTER
+ SPIRE

Bn

**CROSS ROADS**

5

**DOGTAIL POINT**
Oc(4) 10s 2m 5M

5

**KILCLIEF CASTLE** ■

5

ANGUS
ROCK  Fl R
5s 6M

Bn

Bn

BALLYQUINTIN POINT  224°(T)

PLADDY LUG

BAR PLADDY

Q(6)+LFl 15s

2

KILLARD
POINT

Perch

ST PATRICK'S ROCK

5

OBELISK AND

GOWLAND & DOGTAIL
LT BNS INLINE 341°(T)

PERCH IN LINE

STRANGFORD BUOY

RW
L Fl 10s
Whis

TRUE MERIDIAN

GUNS ISLAND

Obelisk

**BALLYHENRY POINT**
QG 3m 3M
BALLYHENRY BAY

Depths in metres

66

*Strangford Creek from SE leading across to Portaferry.*

a 1·4m rock three-quarters of a cable on your right. The tide does not run true, so keep the engine running and take great care to steer so as to stay tight on your transit. Remember that LW at Killard Pt. occurs about 1½ hours before the ebb in the Narrows stops. The advantages of using the West Channel are that when the ebb is running it is weaker in the West than in the East Channel, which helps if you are entering. And when leaving on the ebb, you avoid most of the overfalls by using this route.

**Caution**
In **Strangford Lough** mariners should take particular care as some of the poles and perches are subject to storm damage consequently they may be unreliable. Chart 2156 is therefore essential for safe navigation above the Narrows.

**Anchorage near the entrance**
**Cross Roads**, on the W side, is the nearest anchorage to the entrance and is a suitable place for anyone who does not wish to go ashore. The anchorage is marked by a stone beacon on the bank at the top of the foreshore. There is a second beacon in a hedge about 0·5M inland, but it is now obscured from most bearings due to the tall growth of trees and bushes in the area. This anchorage is seldom used nowadays.

**STRANGFORD CREEK (Strangford Village)**
This small area is sheltered by Swan Island and out of the main stream, there is a counter tide which runs N except from −0100 to +0100 HW. It is fairly crowded. Large car ferries operate from the ferry slip using the fairway to the S of Swan Island. One of them, when not operating, lies alongside the end of the quay, or may be moored fore and aft between the 2 large buoys N of Swan Island. If the quay is unoccupied a yacht might berth there temporarily, but should remain ready to leave at once if requested. If the height of the tide allows, it is possible to berth elsewhere on the quay.

*Audley Roads from SE.*

### Directions

The white stone beacon Fl.(2) WR 6s near the NE end of the reef around Swan Island should be given a berth of 40m. Pass either S of the beacon Fl.(3)10s situated 40m SSW of the island, or N of the beacon Q 100m NNW of it.

**Facilities:** Shops, restaurants, and water at quay. Electrical or other repairs. Bus to Downpatrick. Ferry to Portaferry. Some visitors' moorings – apply Ferry Superintendent/HM Ch 16 or Telephone 01396-881637. Anchor so as not to obstruct fairway NW of Swan island. 2 Slips.

### Caution

Church Point, on the W side about 1·5 cables N of Strangford Creek, has a white stone beacon with a light, Fl. (4) R 10s; the beacon, and the shore S of it which is foul, should be given a berth of at least 0·75 of a cable.

### Anchorages – North End of Narrows

**Audley Roads**, NW of Church Point, is an excellent anchorage. It is within walking distance of Castleward House (National Trust), but there are no shore facilities. Anchor in 4·5m between the small stone pier under the ruins of Audley Castle and a pole which marks the end of a long spit stretching across from the SE side of the bay. The inlet is all shoal further in. There are many yacht moorings and some racing marks belonging to Strangford Sailing Club on the W

*Spinnaker off Audley's Castle.*

*Spinnaker off Castle Ward.*

68

*Quoile from E.*

*Pontoon—Quoile Y.C.*

*Quoile Y.C.*

shore. The scenery and shelter make it very popular with local yachts so at weekends it may be necessary to anchor outside them in up to 10m. There is quite a lot of weed which can cause C.Q.R. anchors to ball up and drag. *(See also Ballyhenry Bay anchorage, p. 74.)*

**Facilities:** None.

## STRANGFORD LOUGH BEYOND THE NARROWS
*(See earlier remarks on page 61)*

**Caution**
It is unwise to sail further into the lough without chart 2156. Careful pilotage is necessary as so many of the islands and rocks are of a similar appearance. Compass courses cannot be relied upon owing to the set of the tides. Many rocks and pladdies are marked by poles or perches but these are unreliable. Yellow buoys are laid in approaches to some anchorages in the Lough, with notices to reduce speed. These should not be used as mooring buoys.

**Lights** – Beyond the Narrows. Killyleagh Town Rock Q.4M. (reported unreliable, 1999). Limestone Rk. Beacon QR 3M.

## EAST DOWN YACHT CLUB
East Down Yacht Club, Telephone 01396-828375, is situated inside **Island Taggart** and is marked on chart 2156. There are yacht moorings somewhat exposed from S to NE 4 cables offshore from Club. Approach with care. There is a pontoon in Inner Pool which has 2m depth alongside, approachable only in latter part of flood. Local knowledge is advisable for this manoeuvre.

**Facilities:** Showers available in the clubhouse which is active on race nights and at weekends when the bar is open. Facility to haul out 32ft. yachts.

## QUOILE
This is another well sheltered spot and is the limit of navigation of this river, which enters the lough at its SW corner.

**Directions**
The approach is between Barrel and Skate rocks, both marked by perches. The transit to pass clear N of Skate Rock is to keep Portaferry pier open of Chapel Island. Keep on this transit till you see between Green and Salt Islands so as to avoid the shoal 3 cables W of Skate Rock and NE of Green Island. This shoal, normally unmarked, is dangerous near LW. When entering the estuary favour the port shore and leave the perch on the Toadstone and the iron beacon beyond it to starboard.

**Anchorage**
Anchor off the moored yachts. The depth is suitable anywhere between Castle and Gibbs islands. Close W of Gibbs Island is well sheltered but probably occupied. Approaching the quay leave the perch just off the end of the jetty to starboard.

**Facilities:** Quoile YC, on Castle Island close to the dam, offers its facilities to visitors from recognised YCs. There is a slip, pontoon and quay suitable for drying alongside and scrubbing. Water hose at end of quay. Clubhouse Telephone 01396-612266. Shops are 3M away in Downpatrick.

*Spinnakers coming down Quoile. Mountains of Mourne background.*

## KILLYLEAGH

HW +0145 Dover. Rise (HW): 3·8-3·3m. This town, on the W coast at the entrance to the Quoile, is approached by the same transit. Development work in quay area may restrict access for yachts. (1999)

### Anchorage

There is ample space to anchor in 2 to 4m SSW of Town Rock beacon, a red brick cylinder QW. It is handy to land at the YC pontoon jetty, W of the beacon, from which the shops and a garage are easily accessible. Showers and bar in YC. The town quay, NW of the beacon, is no longer in commercial use. A yacht drawing 2m could go alongside at −0200 HW and should approach with the spire a little open W of the quay. It is safe to dry out there but not recommended because of the smell.

**Facilities:** Showers and bar in YC. Dufferin Arms Hotel Telephone 01296-828229 is in the vicinity. Good shopping, chandlery, pubs and restaurants. Taxis and buses. Plans for a marina. YC jetty is only to be used for loading and unloading. Long term berthing is not permitted.

## RINGHADDY SOUND

Ringhaddy Sound, the headquarters of the Ringhaddy Cruising Club, is splendidly sheltered and most attractive. Unfortunately it is mostly rather deep and moorings extend the full length of Islandmore. The flood tide runs N at 2 kn.

### Directions

After rounding Ballyhenry beacon (Note: there is a rock awash at LWS and unmarked in position 2 cables NNW of this beacon), steer 337° for the conspicuous Scrabo Tower 14M away. This leads to the Limestone Rock which is marked by a beacon, QR, on its E end,

plus two perches on the N and W ends, and covers at 4 hours flood. Leave this beacon to port and steer 318° for a distinctive circular residence (formerly a windmill) just on the skyline 4M away. There are 2 white leading marks near the shore under the windmill. Astern on the E shore will be a rebuilt cottage in Marlfield Bay which should be kept just open N of the beacon. Hold this line right in. It passes between Verde Rocks sometimes called Rathgorman Pladdies on the NE side, marked by a perch, and Brownrock Pladdy and Brown Rock on the SW side which are not marked. They cover at half tide but their seaweed often shows. Black Rock, a grasstopped islet, is 1 cable SW of Brownrock Pladdy. When Pawle Island and Islandmore come abeam to starboard keep about midchannel. When Ringhaddy Sound opens up, swing round to starboard. Keep near line of yacht moorings to avoid 2 rocks awash at LWS about 0·5 of a cable offshore, slightly S of a jetty below a green wooden bungalow on the SW end of Islandmore. Entering the sound keep towards the SE side as the spit on the opposite shore extends halfway across. Proceeding up the sound avoid the bays, which are shoal, and keep midchannel to clear moorings.

### Berths

On the W shore 1 cable S of Ringhaddy quay there is a floating pier and concrete slip which belong to the Ringhaddy CC. Temporary use of a mooring can usually be arranged. The floating pier should be approached with caution as there is less than 1·8m at LWS. The bottom is soft mud. Yachts may only lie alongside for a short time. Ringhaddy Quay is a stone pier which dries. The bottom there is firm and yachts normally berth on its N side.

**Facilities:** Water tap on the pier. Between the float-

*Killyleagh from S.*

*Ringhaddy Cruising Club.*

*Ringhaddy Sound from SW.*

ing pier and the quay there are private facilities for hauling out. No stores are available as Ringhaddy is remote from any village.

## WHITEROCK
The headquarters of the Strangford Lough Yacht Club.

### Directions
The direct approach is up the middle of the lough, course as shown on the chart, leaving the perch on Dead Mans Rock to port before turning NW leaving Trasnagh to port. The approach from Ringhaddy is between Darragh and Parton. A spit extends 2 cables W of Parton. It dries 1 cable from Parton, where it is marked by a pole, and deepens to 1·2m a further cable

W. Always keep closer to Darragh than to the pole. At LW keep 60m off Darragh shore round to its NW point, then head straight for the E end of Sketrick Island 345°. Keep to E of Braddock Rock which is marked in the sailing season by 3 vertical floats with cardinal markings.

### Anchorage
Anchor outside the moored yachts.

**Facilities:** The club boatman can advise whether a mooring is free and also about obtaining stores, which are available 2M away. There is a pontoon jetty at the Clubhouse Telephone 01238-541202, with 2m 3 hours either side of HW. Water hose available. The bar in the clubhouse opens on Wednesday, Friday and

*Whiterock and Sketrick Island from SW.*

Saturday after racing. Daft Eddie's pub, restaurant, chandlery and sail loft is near the castle on Sketrick Island, and there is a landing pontoon (least depth 1·7m) on the N shore close to the pub. Boatyard in Conly Bay (S of Whiterock) with a slipway for yachts up to 25 tons and some repair facilities. The proprietor, Mr W Smith, lives 0·5M from Whiterock.

### DOWN CRUISING CLUB (BALLYDORN)

Down Cruising club, Telephone 01238-541202, has its headquarters in a converted lightship moored afloat in the narrow channel W of Rainey Island and connected to the shore by a gangway. In summer there are usually members on board and visitors are welcomed. The entrance between Rainey and Sketrick Islands is only 1·5m deep at LWS but inside there is 3 or 4m. There is 2 to 3 kn tide through the channel and numerous moored craft so there is really no room to anchor. Beware of half-submerged mooring buoys when tide is running. A visiting yacht may berth at the extended pontoons alongside the club ship.

*Note: Tides reported in excess of 3 kts, consequently visitors should carefully time their departure from pontoon to coincide with slack water.*

**Facilities:** bar, waterhose and diesel fuel. There is also a derrick for mast lifting. Various shops and services in Newtownards, including laundry facilities.

### NEWTOWNARDS SAILING CLUB

Newtownards Sailing Club lies on the E shore of Strangford Lough about 1M N of the village of Greyabbey. The club is mainly involved in dinghy racing and has no deep water moorings.

N.B.: Anchoring, well offshore, is only practical during top half of tide.

**Facilities:** Showers and bar facilities are available when the clubhouse is in operation. The jetty has water laid on but dries out at LWS.

### KIRCUBBIN

Kircubbin lies on the E side of the Lough and is completely exposed to the west. The approach is strewn with pladdies. From the E end of Long Sheelah steer 035° for 1·5m leaving Gransha Pt to starboard 3 cables then 005° into the bay. Watch for Sand Rock pladdy. There are 2 passages from the W, S of Skart Rock and S of Bird Island respectively, but neither is recom-

*Ballydorn and Down Cruising Club from N.*

mended to strangers. The harbour dries and is of no value.

### Anchorage
Anchor off in 2·7m. Sheltered from N through E to S.

**Facilities:** There is a slip at the sailing club on the N shore of the bay. Limited stores in village.

### BALLYHENRY BAY
Ballyhenry Bay is 0·75M NNW of Portaferry, provides good anchorage – easy access. At the S end of the bay give a good berth to Walter Rocks which dry 3·4m and are marked by a perch. The tide runs strongly across them.

### Anchorage
Anchor off the cottage among the trees. A number of yachts moor here permanently.

### Caution
Beware the remains of a wrecked ship at the NW end of the Bay, 2·5 cables SW Ballyhenry Point beacon, which is partly covered near HW.

### PORTAFERRY MARINA
Portaferry is diagonally across the Narrows from Strangford Creek and is the Eastern terminal for the local ferry service. This substantial town, which is already the centre of a popular tourist area, has recently been provided with a secure 30 berth marina, dredged to a depth of 2.5m below CD.

### Directions
The concrete marina breakwater extends out from the shore in a protective arm and forms an entrance with the land on its southern side *(See Chartlet p. 75)*. This entrance is 230m S of the ferry terminal pier and is marked on its N, or Breakwater side, by a sectored R.W.G. light (Isophase 4 Sec.) and on its S side by outer and inner green, conical, unlit buoys. There are also 3 visitors' mooring buoys provided by the Portaferry Hotel. These are large black buoys, marked "Hotel", two of which are N of the Ferry Pier and the other one S of it. The ferry pier light is OcWR 10s 9/6M.

### Facilities
Portaferry Sailing Club is adjacent to the Marina, on

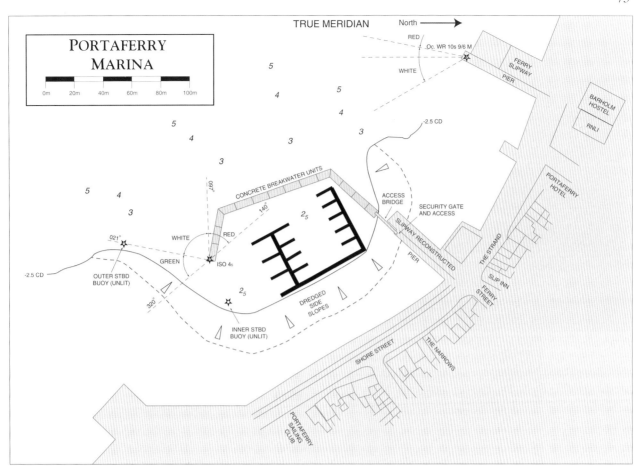

PORTAFERRY MARINA

0m 20m 40m 60m 80m 100m

TRUE MERIDIAN

North

RED
Oc. WR 10s 9/6 M
WHITE

5

5
4

5
4

4
3

3

3
3

5
4

-2.5 CD

FERRY SLIPWAY
PIER

BARHOLM HOSTEL

RNLI

CONCRETE BREAKWATER UNITS

160

140

2₅

ACCESS BRIDGE

SECURITY GATE AND ACCESS

SLIPWAY RECONSTRUCTED

PORTAFERRY HOTEL

5
4
3

WHITE    RED
GREEN
ISO 4s

021°

-2.5 CD

OUTER STBD BUOY (UNLIT)

320°

2₅

INNER STBD BUOY (UNLIT)

DREDGED SIDE SLOPES

PIER

THE STRAND

SLIP INN

FERRY STREET

SHORE STREET

THE NARROWS

PORTAFERRY SAILING CLUB

*Portaferry.*

78

*Ballywalter from S.*

## BURIAL ISLAND
Burial Island, the E point of Ireland, lies 2 cables E of Burr Point. It is 8m high and appears small at HWS. It is surrounded by a reef which seldom covers and extends 3 cables N and 2 cables E and S of the island. The reef is steep-to on its N and E sides. There is a clear channel inside the island and using chart 2156 it would be possible to go straight through in not less than 2m. However, yachts are recommended to pass outside, keeping at least 3 cables E of the top of the island.

## BALLYHALBERT BAY
Ballyhalbert Bay is clean with a good temporary anchorage in W or SW wind 1 cable N of the pierhead in 5m. The pier is just inside Burr Point and has a yellow diamond top on the new breakwater to W of pier. This small sheltered harbour dries out.

**Facilities:** Water 100m from pier. Good shop, fuel (open Sundays) 0·5M NW of pier. Telephone further away in High St (2nd turn left). Pub 1M NW of pier.

## SKULLMARTIN ROCK
Skullmartin Rock is 3M N of Burial Island and 1M offshore. It dries 1·2m and the passage inside it is very foul. It is marked by a red mast with cage and flag topmark 11m high. Light Buoy. Skullmartin Safe Water spherical buoy, LFl.10s, whistle, is moored 1·5M ESE of the red mast.

### Tidal streams
Near the buoy the flood runs SSE starting at +0540 Dover and the ebb starts NNW at −0035 Dover, maximum rate 1·2 kn at neaps, 2·3 kn at springs.

## BALLYWALTER
Ballywalter, 1M WNW of Skullmartin Rock, has a quay facing NW which dries. There is temporary anchorage off it with shelter in winds from S to NW.

### Directions
It is advisable to have chart 2156 as there are rocks near the pier and around the part of the bay NE of it. However, it is quite clear to go straight in with the church spire in line with the pierhead bearing 272°. Anchor 1·5 cables E of the E corner of the pier in 4 or 5m, sand.

### Lights
On the NW end of the breakwater from a metal column 3m high, Fl WRG 1·5s5m9M G 240° to 267°, W 267° to 277° shows the safe approach, R 277° to 314°.

**Facilities:** There is a water tap on pier and a coin-operated electricity supply half way along pier. CG shed with equipment. Shops, hotel, pub and telephone 0·25M in from pier. Fuel 0·25M S of road junction.

### Rocks
Between Ballywalter and Donaghadee there are rocks drying up to 0·75M offshore for 1M N of Ballywalter and up to 0·5M offshore further NW. Give it a good berth by day and at night keep in the white sector of Donaghadee light. (*see below*).

## DONAGHADEE HARBOUR
HW as Dover. Rise: 4·0-3·4/1·1-0·5m. This is a small harbour formed by 2 massive piers. Heavy scend frequently sets into it. It is very congested and has been gradually silting.

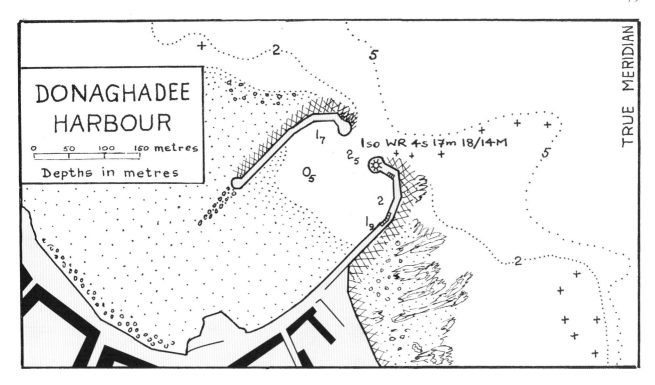

*Donaghadee Harbour from SW.*

## Anchorage

There is very little space for a visiting yacht to anchor. It can only be recommended for a temporary visit in the absence of scend when a visiting yacht should be able to berth alongside the end of the S Pier, or more likely outside other vessels there. Turn to Port immediately upon entering between the 2 piers. There is always sufficient water depth alongside at this point. Report to the HM, who can also advise about taking a yacht into Copelands Marina.

## Lights

The white tower on the S pierhead shows Iso WR 4s17m W18M R14M, R between 326° and the dangerous coast already described, W elsewhere. Siren 12s, only if a vessel is expected.

## Directions and Dangers

A sunken ledge with less than 2m in places extends 1·5 cables ENE from the S pierhead. Coming from

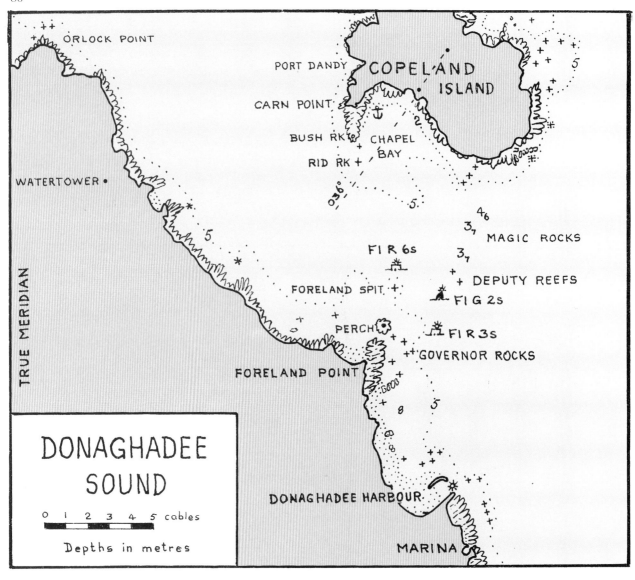

DONAGHADEE
SOUND

0 1 2 3 4 5 cables

Depths in metres

the S, do not approach within 2 cables until the landward end of the N pier is well open of the S pierhead, in fact nearer the N pierhead. There are similar rocks 1 cable N of the harbour. They are inside the normal approach from the sound with the entrance open and bearing more than 180°. By night keep the pierhead light bearing well between 180° and 240°. When approaching the entrance, which is only 45m wide, allow particularly for the S going tide. Fortunately, it runs N for 9 hours from −0300 Dover till +0600 Dover. It is preferable to motor in, but if you have to sail in beware of the blanketing effect of the piers. HM can be called on VHF 16 working 6 or 8. Telephone 01247-882377.

**Facilities:** It is a very convenient place to go ashore for shopping as all provisions are available in the town close to the harbour. There are local engineers and electricians. Water on pier and fuel at harbour yard. Electricity available on S pier. Normal supplies in town – short walk. Hotels, restaurants and pubs. Places of interest include the Moat and Commons.

Bus to Belfast. Taxis. One visitors' mooring – yellow buoy inside harbour mouth during summer season. Lifeboat (*see Appendix 7*).

**COPELANDS MARINA**
This is completely sheltered in a small inshore harbour 3 cables S of Donaghadee Harbour. It is fairly fully occupied by local yachts and boats and is very well equipped. The approach is extremely narrow between drying rocks and is only deep enough at fairly high tide. Permission must be obtained to leave a yacht in the marina, and a pilot must be used for entering and leaving. It is a tricky entrance, new leading marks have been established bearing about 276°.

**Facilities:** A pay telephone is available in office.

**DONAGHADEE SOUND**
Inside Copeland Island just N of Donaghadee, is the normal passage for yachts sailing along the coast. It is very satisfactory with a fair tide but quite possible to get through against the tide with a fair wind or a good engine.

*Donaghadee Sound from S looking towards Copeland Islands. Copelands Marina bottom right.*

## Dangers

There are many rocks 2 or 3 cables offshore between Donaghadee Harbour and the red perch off Foreland Point. Foreland Spit, with less than 1·8m, is between the perch and Foreland red buoy, Fl.R 6s. Governor Rocks, with 2·7m, are between the perch and Governor red buoy, Fl. R 3s. NE of Deputy green buoy, Fl.G 2s, Deputy Reefs have less than 1·8m and beyond them, over the deeper Magic Rocks, there are heavy tide rips. There are a few rocks off the shore NW of Foreland Point. A drying reef extends 1·5 cables S off Carn Point, the SW point of Copeland Island, with Bush Rock 1m high at the S end and rocks with less than 1·8m almost half a cable W and SE of Bush Rock. Rid Rock, awash and very dangerous, is just 1 cable S by E of Bush Rock.

## Tides

In the sound tides change earlier than at sea, the flood starting SE at +0445 Dover and the ebb NW at −0115 Dover, maximum rate 4·5 kn, probably near the buoys – details on chart 3709. From Ballyferris Point 4M S of Donaghadee an eddy starts running N along the coast from about −0300 Dover till the ebb starts. It widens gradually to 1.5M NE of Donaghadee where it runs out E of the sound and the Copelands.

## Directions

Going NW through the Donaghadee sound leave the 2 red buoys to port and the green buoy to starboard. Do not go SW of a line between the red buoys. Keeping the red buoys in line (which should be 147° to 327°) leads well clear of the rocks off Donaghadee and also of Rid Rock off Copeland Island. NW of the buoys the coast as far as Orlock Point should be given a berth of 2 cables. Going SE against the tide it is best to enter the sound along this coast till it is necessary to turn out E towards Foreland red buoy. Beating through with the tide, which would be safest using chart 3709, there is good space for a tack NE of Foreland buoy, but if going SE with the tide be careful not to let Deputy buoy get in line with Governor buoy. The Coastguard Station is in Bangor Marina Buildings.

## Anchorage

**Chapel Bay** is well sheltered in W to NE winds. Great care must be taken to avoid Rid Rock. Approaching from the S keep Donaghadee lighthouse halfway between the two red buoys. Coming from the N keep these 2 buoys in line and turn in when the long grey cottage on the shore comes in line with the white cottage on the skyline, 036°. Anchor in the W half of the bay about 1 cable E of the outer HW rock on Carn Point in about 3m, gravel and clay, not particularly good holding but out of the tide. If rowing to the steps beside the grey cottage, take care to avoid a rock which dries about 0·5 of a cable SW of these steps. There is a small jetty behind the steps.

## COPELAND ISLANDS (*Chart 3709 or 1753*)

Copeland Islands comprise Mew Island and Lighthouse Island which almost touch each other, and Copeland Island divided from them by Copeland Sound. The sound is navigable but not recommended as there are no marks to lead between the groups of rocks across its E end. The only guide to pass between them is to keep the red buoy outside bearing 101°. Unless passing over 2M outside Mew Island, yachts should go through Donaghadee Sound. Only pass close to Mew Island when the Ram Race and North Race are not in operation, giving it a berth of at least 2 cables. Races extend N and S from up to 0·5M E of Mew Island (*see full description under Tides below*).

### Tides

The first of flood sets strongly S through Donaghadee Sound and between Copeland and Mew Islands and continues in this direction for 3 hours. At half flood the stream S of the Copelands slacks and turns N so that from Ballyferris Point, 3M S of Donaghadee Light, to Foreland Point, 0·75M N of it, the stream runs N for 9 hours and S for only 3 hours. The eddy is narrow off Ballyferris but extends at its northern end 1·5M offshore, that is as far out as the E side of the Copeland Islands. It stirs up and lifts much sand in the relatively shallow water and this can easily be seen in calm weather as an indication of the extent of the eddy.

By HWB −2 (2 hours before High Water Belfast) the N going eddy meets the stream coming through the Sound at Deputy Reef and the two run jointly E round the S side of the Copelands. They then turn N over the reefs between the islands, and E to meet the main tide to form the **Ram Race**. This starts SE of Mew Island and runs fiercely NNE until shortly after HWB at a rate of up to 5 kn.

**In Copeland Sound**, locally known as Back Sound, the tide turns a little earlier, SE at HWB +0420 and NW at HWB +0115. This passage should not be attempted without a large chart and then only in good conditions.

**In the Ram Harry or Ram Race** the stream runs N from a point 1·5M SE to a point 0·5M E of Mew Island. It starts at HWB −2 and continues to about HWB +30 minutes. Between the Ram Race and Mew Islands is a narrow stretch of relatively calm water moving slowly S. However, the shore of the island and the area S of it is so studded with reefs that it would be foolhardy for a stranger to attempt to use this stream when the Ram is running. On the last hour

this race comes right into the rocks and remains so throughout the ebb. Ram Harry itself is a black pyramid rock, about 3 ft. high at high water, at the NE point of Mew Island.

**The Northern Race** begins about 3 hours after the end of the Ram Race at HWB +3 and runs N at up to 3·8 kn until low water ie, HWB +0600. It extends from a point about 0·5M SE of Mew Island for about 2M in a NNE direction, passing about 0·25M E of the island itself. It is not nearly so strong or dangerous as the Ram Harry.

### Tidal Lee

On the N going stream or ebb, there is no tide at all along the N side of Old Lighthouse Island, hence this area is favoured by divers at this stage of the tide to work on a wreck or go for clams.

### Lights

Mew Island Lighthouse on the NE end of the island is a conspicuous 37m high black tower with a white band and shows Fl. (4) 30s37m24M Racon.

### Anchorages

A pleasant day can be spent in fine weather exploring the islands. Chapel Bay has already been described. The following 3 anchorages are only suitable for temporary use in settled conditions and chart 3709 is necessary. Port Dandy on the W side of Copeland Island is a useful though very restricted anchorage in E and SE winds. It is a small bay with a grey sandy beach. A reverse transit leading to it is the water tower S of Orlock Point in line with a white flat-topped cottage on the shore. Anchor just inside the arms of the bay in 4·5m, out of the tide. The N side is nearly steepto. Some rocks extend a bit from the S side. Off the N side of Copeland Island, between Bessy Point and Port Rammon, is a pleasant anchorage in light S winds, out of the tide. This must not be approached from the E. Give Bessy Point a berth of at least 2 cables and then close the shore to 2 or 3m and anchor. There are rocks off the inlet marked Port Rammon on the chart. If you open up its sandy beach you have gone too far SE. There is a well behind Port Rammon beach. Lighthouse Island is steep-to on its NE side at the entrance of the gut between it and Mew Island, off which there are some rocks. Anchor there in 5 or 5·6m not more than 0·5 of a cable off Lighthouse Island with its N side bearing about W. There are 2 boat landings on the N and SW sides of Mew Island. Lighthouse Island has a bird observatory in the original buildings.

## BELFAST LOUGH

Belfast Lough, 6·75M wide at the entrance between Orlock Point on the S and Black Head on the N, is free of dangers in its navigable area which has an average depth of 11m.

# TIDAL STREAMS. REFER TO H.W. BELFAST.

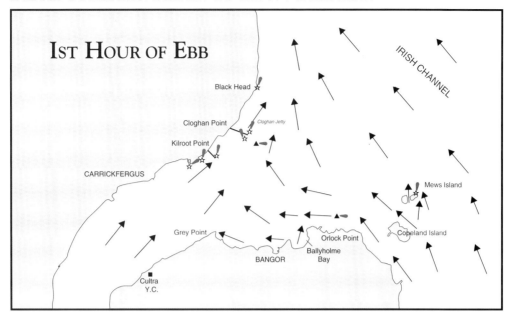

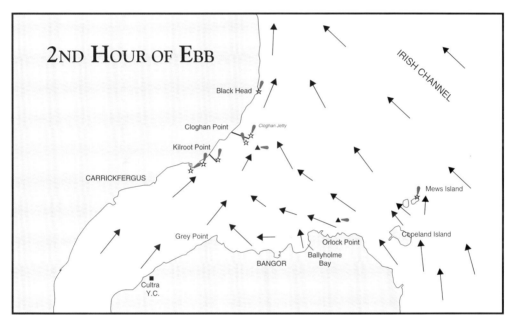

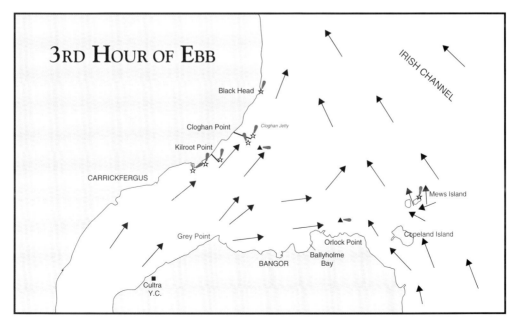

# TIDAL STREAMS. REFER TO H.W. BELFAST.

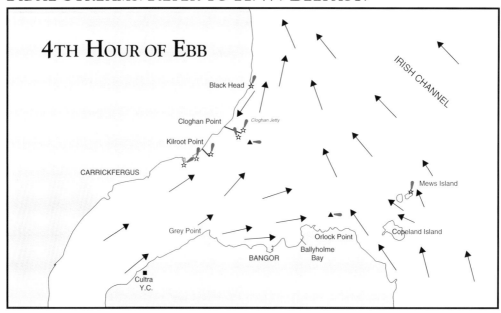

## 4TH HOUR OF EBB

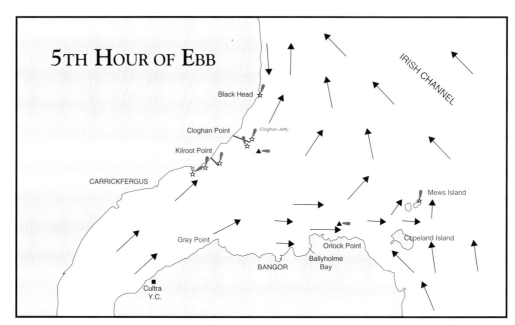

## 5TH HOUR OF EBB

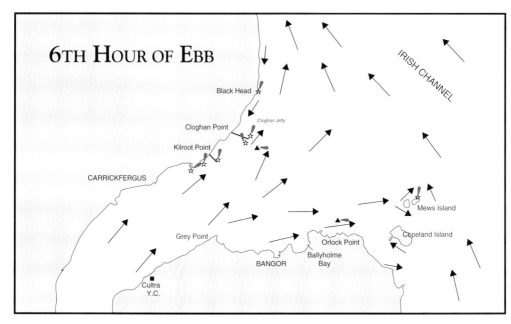

## 6TH HOUR OF EBB

85

# Tidal Streams. Refer to H.W. Belfast.

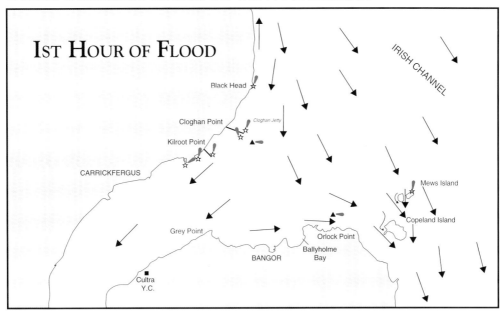

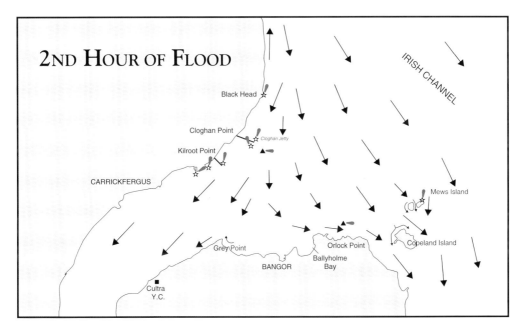

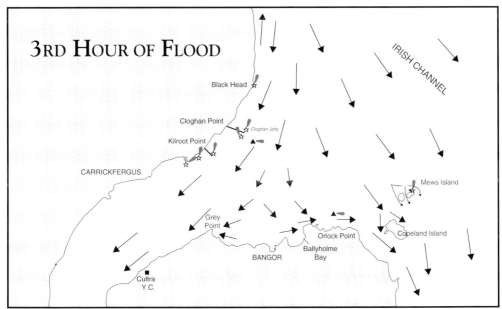

# TIDAL STREAMS. REFER TO H.W. BELFAST.

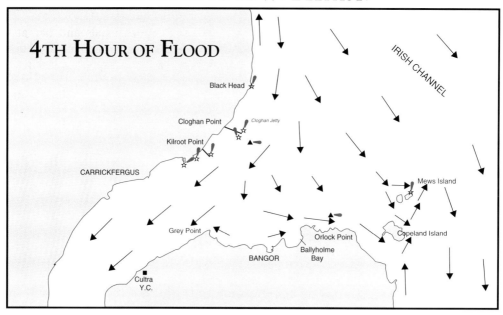

**4TH HOUR OF FLOOD**

IRISH CHANNEL

Black Head ☆

Cloghan Point
*Cloghan Jetty*
Kilroot Point

CARRICKFERGUS

Mews Island

Grey Point

Orlock Point

BANGOR

Copeland Island

Ballyholme
Bay

Cultra
Y.C.

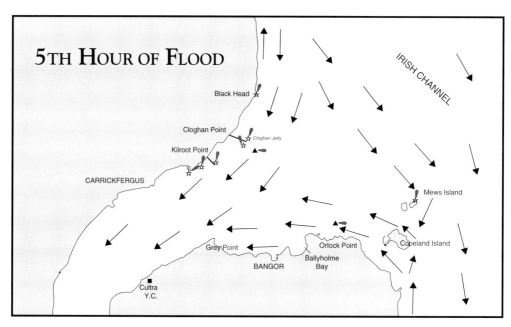

**5TH HOUR OF FLOOD**

IRISH CHANNEL

Black Head ☆

Cloghan Point
*Cloghan Jetty*
Kilroot Point

CARRICKFERGUS

Mews Island

Grey Point

Orlock Point

Copeland Island

BANGOR

Ballyholme
Bay

Cultra
Y.C.

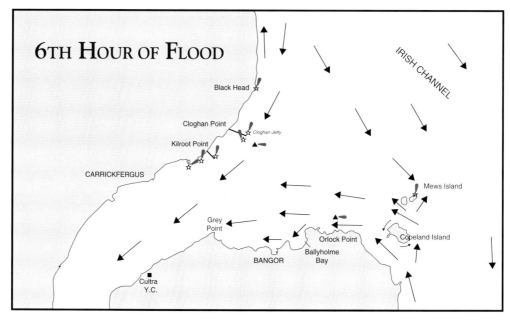

**6TH HOUR OF FLOOD**

IRISH CHANNEL

Black Head ☆

Cloghan Point
*Cloghan Jetty*
Kilroot Point

CARRICKFERGUS

Mews Island

Grey
Point

Orlock Point

Copeland Island

BANGOR

Ballyholme
Bay

Cultra
Y.C.

## Rocks/Buoys

The S shore is rocky and much indented but may be approached to within a few cables except off Orlock Point, about 0·5m NW of which are South Briggs rocks. A red buoy, Fl.(2) R 10s, is moored N of these rocks and yachts should pass outside it. Unlit racing marks are laid, in season, from Ballymacormic Point to Bangor Marina.

## Tides

In the middle of the outer half of the lough the streams are always less than 1 kn and are rotary in a clockwise direction. They run between 160° and 260° during the rising tide and between 330° and 080° during the falling tide. On the N side between Black Head and White Head there is hardly any stream. Along the whole shore SW of White Head, and on the S shore SW of Grey Point, the streams are very weak, the flood running in and the ebb out of the lough. Along the shore E of Grey Point it is also very weak but starts running W at half flood and E at half ebb.

## BANGOR (*plan on chart 1753*)

Bangor is a well known sailing centre and the HQ of the Royal Ulster and Ballyholme Yacht Clubs, Telephone RUYC Bangor 01247-270568; Fax: 01247-273525; E-mail: ruyc@btinternet.com; Web: http://www.btinternet.com/~ruyc, and B.Y.C.

Telephone 01247-271467. Both of these clubs have extensive premises and welcome visiting yachtsmen.

**Facilities:** Showers, meals and bar at the RUYC, which also has a permanent secretary. Catering: 01247-465002. The town has excellent shops with all kinds of stores and essential services. Lifeboat (*see appendix 7*)

## BALLYHOLME BAY

Ballyholme Bay, lying 1·5M W of South Briggs buoy, used to be the principal yacht anchorage at Bangor but it has been superseded by the Bangor Marina (*see below*). The Bay offers a good anchorage in 3·5 to 5·5m in offshore winds but is very exposed to winds from NW to NE. Approaching from the E, Ballymacormick Point is foul and should be given a berth of at least 2 cables. Lukes Point on the W side of the bay is also foul and should be given a berth of 1 cable.

**Facilities:** At HW yachts drawing up to 1·8m can come alongside the club wall to take on water. There are 2 slips at which to land. BYC offer showers, meals at weekend, and bar in the evenings and weekend. RUYC – a large red brick building – is close by and offers similar facilities. VHF channel M. Supplies are all available in Bangor about 0·75M away. A number of Irish Cruising Club members live locally.

*Bangor Bay from E with a backdrop of Belfast Lough.*

*The Royal Ulster Yacht Club on the shores of Belfast Lough at Bangor.*

## BANGOR BAY, MARINA AND HARBOUR

The bay lies 0·5M W of Ballyholme Bay. It has a large marina in the W side of the old harbour. The bay itself is exposed to winds from W through N to E and is not recommended for anchoring. Yachts may lie alongside the N breakwater, but are subject to the interest of the locals and visitors. The marina is sheltered by a new breakwater – Pickie and an extension of the

*Bangor Harbour and Marina.*

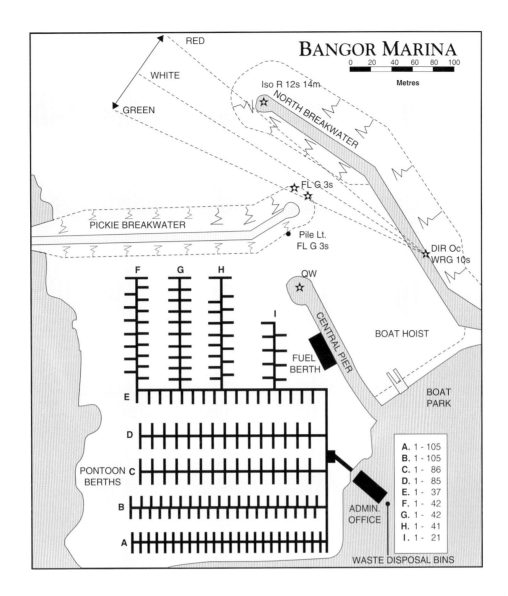

# BANGOR MARINA

RED

WHITE

GREEN

Iso R 12s 14m

NORTH BREAKWATER

FL G 3s

PICKIE BREAKWATER

Pile Lt.
FL G 3s

DIR Oc
WRG 10s

QW

F  G  H

I

CENTRAL PIER

BOAT HOIST

FUEL
BERTH

E

BOAT
PARK

D

PONTOON
BERTHS

C

B

A

ADMIN.
OFFICE

A. 1 - 105
B. 1 - 105
C. 1 - 86
D. 1 - 85
E. 1 - 37
F. 1 - 42
G. 1 - 42
H. 1 - 41
I. 1 - 21

WASTE DISPOSAL BINS

0  20  40  60  80  100
Metres

*Bangor Harbour entrance.*

old Central Pier. Beware of wash in the bay from high speed ferries passing offshore.

### Lights
Light on the N breakwater Iso R 12s9m14M. Dir. Lt. 105°: OcWRG 10s. Pickie Breakwater Hd. 2 FG (vert), Central Pier Hd. Q.W. Marina entrance FL G 3s.

**Facilities:** The marina has all facilities, including a travel hoist with 50 tons lift capacity, all repairs, fuel 24 hours per day. VHF Channel 80 c/s "Bangor Marina" or "Bangor Harbour" on channel 11. Telephone 01247-453297, Fax No. 01247-453450. Marina charge (1995/1996) £1.25p per metre per day including VAT £7.05p per metre per week including VAT. Also based at the marina are HM Coastguard's Marine Rescue Sub Centre and the Bangor Atlantic 21 Lifeboat (*see Appendix 7*). Bangor is a major holiday town with all its attendant features – hotels, pubs, restaurants, dance halls. Good shops. Chandlery in Main Street, Todds Admiralty Chart Agents Telephone 01247-466640. Bus and rail connections to Belfast. Tourist office. Taxis.

Telephone or Fax, in advance, for a handbook with all marina details to be forwarded by post.

Bangor Marina currently holds the Five Gold Anchors Award from the Yacht Harbours' Association.

### Anchorage
**The Long Hole**, a pool immediately E of the harbour, offers complete shelter to small shallow draught boats which take the ground easily. It is only accessible around HW and should not be entered without a pilot who can be engaged at the harbour.

### GREY POINT
Grey Point, 2·5M WNW of Bangor, is a bluff point 23m high. For 1M of Bangor the shore should be given a berth of 1 cable. Nearer Grey Point, and between it and Cultra, a berth of 4 cables is recommended to avoid foul ground. Temporary anchorage may be had

in suitable weather off Helen's Bay immediately E of Grey Point.

### CULTRA
Cultra, 2·5M W of Grey Point, is the headquarters of the Royal North of Ireland YC.

### Anchorage
In offshore wind there is good anchorage in 3·5 to 4m outside the yacht moorings, some 4 cables from the shore which is very shoal. In S winds there is less roll here than in Bangor but it is exposed from WSW through N to E.

**Facilities:** Water and fuel are available, as are showers, bar and meals, throughout the year. It is possible to lie alongside the club jetty at HW in 3·3m in order to take fuel and stores. Nearest good shops – Holywood – are about 1·5M away. Taxis are available. Small shop about 0·5M. Boatyard and patent slip for 15 tons. Fulltime secretary, Telephone 01232-420841. A number of Irish Cruising Club members live locally. Easy access by rail (0·5M) to Belfast Harbour Airport, Belfast City and Bangor. Cultra Folk & Transport Museum nearby.

### HOLYWOOD
There is a drying anchorage off this town about 1M W of Cultra, but one must be prepared to take the ground near existing boats.

**Facilities:** Holywood YC have showers and a bar. The town has good shops, pubs and restaurants. Visitors' moorings are available.

### BELFAST HARBOUR
Chart 1753 has a very much larger plan. HW −0015 Dover. Rise: 3·5-3·0/1·1-0·4m. VHF Call 12, Work 08, 11, 12, 14. This is a very large commercial harbour with vessel traffic surveillance by radar west of a line

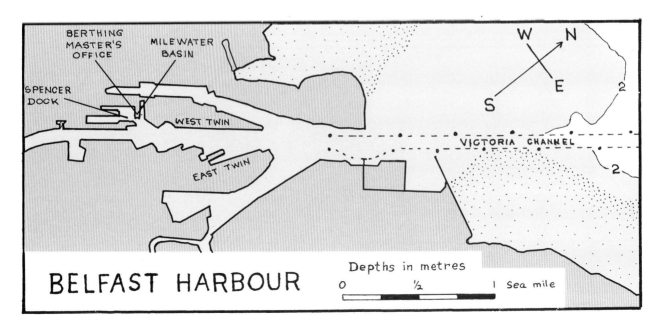

BELFAST HARBOUR

between Kilroot and Grey Point, and yachts may not have any need to enter this harbour since the new marinas at Bangor and Carrickfergus give very adequate shelter from all quarters, and provide all facilities.

## Directions

Yachts do not need to use the seaward part of the dredged channel which starts at a new fairway buoy (R.W. striped Pillar Buoy with R. spherical topmark. Long FL. Ev. 10 sec. Fog Sig. Bl. Ev. 10 sec.) between Carrickfergus and Grey Point but should enter it between the buoy and the beacon N of Cultra. Inside this buoy it is marked by pile beacons with lights, red and even numbers on the SE side, green and odd numbers on the NW side. It is very dangerous to leave the channel inside beacon No 12, the 3rd beacon on the port hand when entering.

Belfast Harbour radio maintains a 24 hour watch on VHF Channel 16 and yachts with VHF should ask for permission to use the harbour before entering the channel at Lt. Buoy No. 1. Those without VHF should phone from a previous port Telephone 01232-553010.

To proceed south of Lagan Weir, call Lagan Weir Control on Ch. No. 71.

**Facilities:** All facilities, including a sailmaker, are available in Belfast.

## North West Shore

The N point of Belfast Lough is Black Head which is steep-to and 62m high with a prominent white lighthouse, Fl.3s 45m27M. Whitehead town, about 1M SSW of Black Head, is the headquarters of the Co

Antrim YC Telephone 019603-72322. The Club has showers, water and bar. The anchorage is not recommended in strong S or SW winds, although the holding ground is good in sand or stones.

## Rocks

**Hailcock Rock**, which dries 0·9m with other shallow rocks NE of it, lies 1·5 cables offshore and 2 cables ENE of the YC slip. A bit S of the slip, between it and White Head, there are more rocks, one with 0·3m being 0·5 of a cable offshore. The anchorage off the slip, in 3m or 4m, should therefore be approached heading W or NW. (see **Rocks** below.)

**Facilities:** Good shops, fuel.

## Buoys

**Cloghan Jetty**, S of White Head, is T shaped and 6·5 cables long with Fl.G 3s2M on the ends of its long head, N end Horn 15s and Fl.G 3s on the S. end. There is a green buoy, QG, 0·5M outside it.

**SW of this is Kilroot jetty**, 350m long with a light Oc G 10s on its outer end. Kilroot harbour is 0·75M W of the jetty and S of a 198m high chimney.

**WSW of Kilroot Jetty** is the unloading berth jetty, the head of which is marked by 2 FG (vert) lights.

**Further WSW of this,** the E entrance to the Intake Basin is marked by an Oc G 4s light.

## Rocks

Between this harbour and Carrickfergus a drying shoal extends up to 0·5M out from the shore. Carrickfergus is described below. For 2M SW of it there are rocks on the sand a long way off the shore which should be given a berth of 3 cables. Beyond this, where the conspicuous obelisk on a hill bears

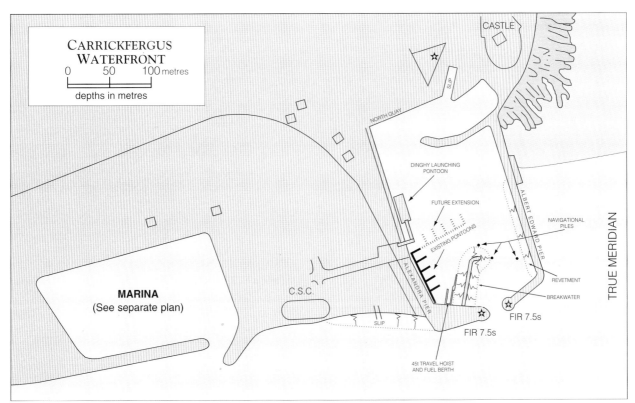

around NNW, it is possible to anchor 2 cables off the shore in 2m, well sheltered of course in NW wind.

**Facilities:** The North Belfast YC, about 1M SW of the little Green Islet, has a slip which is the only place for landing SW of Carrickfergus. The nearest shops are at Whiteabbey 1M away. This is about 2M NNW of the RNIYC moorings at Cultra.

### Anchorage
Further SW there is plenty of anchorage space in between 2 and 3m, but further offshore.

### CARRICKFERGUS HARBOUR MARINA AND WATERFRONT (See Chartlet p. 91)
HW as Dover, Rise 2·9m (9′6″) SP: 1·8m (6′) NP: is situated on the Northern shore of Belfast Lough to the west of Carrickfergus Castle.

The Marine Services facilities are located on the southern end of the west pier as is a purpose built Marina basin accommodating 10 boats behind rubble stone breakwaters. This basin is partly dredged to give depths of up to 2·9 metres (9′6″) at LWS. Carrickfergus Harbour also has an inner harbour area accommodating up to 36 boats and a public slipway that is accessible 3 hours either side of high water.

### Directions
The entrance to the Harbour is open to the South and is dredged to 2·3 metres (7′6″) at LWS. The ends of the East and West piers are marked with red and green beacons showing Fl. G 7·5s 5m 4M and R 7·5s 5m 4M.

Navigational marks are located within the Harbour defining the approach to the harbour basin. Pass between two navigation perches marking the toe of the internal breakwater and revetment. Turn to port to approach pontoons and marine services site leaving the second breakwater perch to port. Note presence of isolated tubular piles in central harbour area. Leave these piles to port on approach to harbour slipway and inner harbour berths.

### Facilities
The Harbour area, now known as Carrickfergus Waterfront, includes the Marina and has been completely refurbished. It includes a Marine Services Area with a 45 tonne Travel Hoist and Boat Parker. 10 new purpose built pontoons have been constructed in the Harbour with more to be added. There is a boatyard capable of most yacht repairs and a slipway which can take boats up to 1·5m draught. Further extensive Waterfront development is in hand (1999). All stores and services, including fuel, available either in the Waterfront complex or in the town. Good road and rail communications with Belfast and Airports. Taxis.

### CARRICKFERGUS MARINA (See Chartlet p. 93)
HW as Dover, Rise 2·9m (9′6″) SP: 1·8m (6′) NP: is situated on the Northern shore of Belfast Lough 330 metres to the west of Carrickfergus Harbour. It is a

purpose built Marina basin to accommodate 280 boats behind rubble stone breakwaters. The basin is dredged to give depths of up to 2·3 metres (7′6″) at LWS.

The entrance to the Marina is situated at the Eastern end of the basin and is open to the South West. The ends of the two breakwaters are marked with red and green beacons showing Qk. Fl. R 7M 3m and G 8m 3M. Red not showing from 245° to 305°.

**Marina Entrance Approach Light**
The entrance approach light is located approximately 30m to port of the red navigation beacon on the West breakwater. The light is a PAL 100 Navigation Sector Light with a total beam width of 24° sectored as follows: 9·5° Red; 5° White; 9·5° Green. The light defines the centre approach line to the entrance.

All visitors to Carrickfergus Harbour and Marina should contact the Carrickfergus Waterfront Office on VHF channels 37; 80; M2; or by land line on 01960-366666 for berth allocation.

The information provided in relation to depths at Carrickfergus Marina and Harbour are guidelines only. As the facilities are situated on the Carrickfergus Sandbank, depths may reduce as a result of siltation. It is the responsibility of skippers to satisfy themselves as to the availability of depths for their vessel at any particular time.

**Facilities:** toilets, showers, sail repairs, pontoon berths for 303 including 30 visitor berths, (water and electricity available at each berth) chandlery, fuel berth, boat and engine repairs, also very good cabin soft furnishing made to order, and marine electrics servicing. An administration office, "Windrose" restaurant and Bar in marina. Fuel is available in the adjacent harbour.

**Carrickfergus** is a good shopping town. Stores of all kinds are available and there are several hotels and restaurants in the area. It is a very old town, with a well preserved Norman Castle – well worth a visit. Many local leisure pursuits.

**Carrickfergus Sailing Club** has its headquarters on the E side of the Marina. The Club has an international reputation for good hospitality and welcomes all visiting yachtsmen. Telephone 01960-351402/359302. VHF Ch. 37, E-mail: csc@btinternet.com; Website: www.bigfoot.com/~CSC.

**Facilities:** CSC has a large club house with showers, bar open evenings and weekends, meals at weekends.

### Coast
The E shore of the peninsula called Magee Island is steep-to for the 5M from Black Head to Isle of Muck, which is also steep-to on its E side. Isle of Muck is 1·25 cables off the shore, to which it is joined by a narrow drying ridge of stones. There is a small temporary

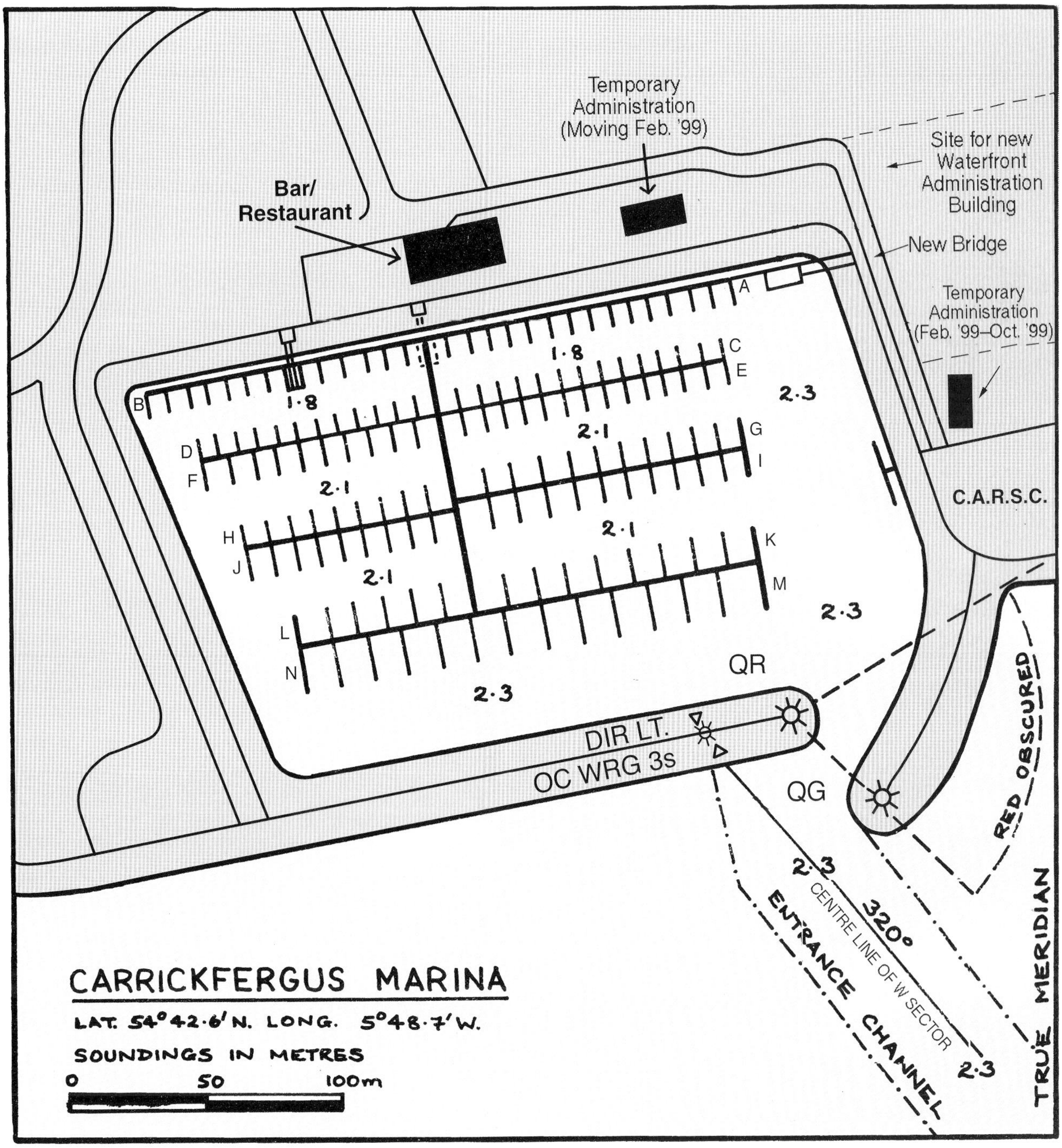
Temporary
Administration
(Moving Feb. '99)
Site for new
Waterfront
Administration
Building
Bar/
Restaurant
New Bridge
Temporary
Administration
(Feb. '99–Oct. '99)
C.A.R.S.C.
A
B
C
D
E
F
G
H
I
J
K
L
M
N
1·8
2·1
2·3
QR
QG
DIR LT.
OC WRG 3s
RED OBSCURED
TRUE MERIDIAN
320°
CENTRE LINE OF W SECTOR
ENTRANCE CHANNEL
CARRICKFERGUS MARINA
LAT. 54°42·6'N. LONG. 5°48·7'W.
SOUNDINGS IN METRES
0 50 100m

anchorage on either side of the ridge, in about 6m on the SE side and 3·5 to 4m on the NW side. At Portmuck (*see chart 1237*), 3 cables SW of the NW end of Muck, there is a small pier which dries. A drying spit extends 0·75 of a cable NE of the pier.

**Rocks**

The coast NW of Muck has rocks close in and needs a berth of at least 0·5 of a cable as far as Skernaghan Point. This point has a reef with a sunken rock outside it so it should be given a berth of at least 1·5 cables when passing N of it.

**Tides**

In the middle of the North Channel the ebb starts flowing out NW at HW Dover and reaches 3·5 kn at springs. The flood starts at +0600 Dover, maximum 4 kn. Off Magee Island the ebb starts 1·25 hours later than in the North Channel. Off Isle of Muck the streams are very strong, possibly up to 6 kn at springs. In the following description, "N going" and "S going" means parallel to the shoreline. At +0115 Dover the main N going ebb starts both off the peninsula and close inshore and continues thus until at +0300 Dover a S going eddy starts close inshore between Larne and Muck. The main stream and the stream inshore S of Muck still run N. This S going eddy probably widens gradually and at −0600 Dover, as countereddy, starts running N inside it along the shore N of Muck. At 0445 Dover the S going flood starts everywhere except along the shore N of Muck, where the new N going eddy continues and runs on till it merges with the start of the ebb at +0115 Dover, but at −0300 Dover a N going eddy starts running from Black Head to Muck. This eddy extends about 1·5M offshore and causes a race off Muck and overfalls 1·5M E of it where it meets the main flood stream. This continues till +0115 Dover when the eddy becomes part of the main N going ebb, as above.

### Rocks/Buoys

**Hunter Rock**, about 2·25M NNW of Isle of Muck, has a depth of 0·8m and is steepto all round. South Hunter buoy is a S Card Q (6) + LFl 15s, Whis. North Hunter buoy is a N Card Q. There is magnetic disturbance in its vicinity.

**The Maidens** are 2 dangerous clusters of rocks mostly above water and separated by a clear channel 1M wide. They are within 4M of Ballygalley Head and their S end is 2·25M 015° from Hunter Rock. The S Cluster is composed of E and W Maiden rocks 7 and 9m high and 0·5M apart. W Maiden is steep-to all round and has an unused stone lighthouse. E Maiden is very foul especially on its S side where a shallow reef with drying and above-water rocks runs out for 7 cables. The E Maiden lighthouse is a 23m high white tower with a black band showing Fl (3) 20s29m24M. 14m below this an auxiliary light Fl R 5s is visible only between 142° and 182° over the N Cluster. The N Cluster forms a triangle up to 1·5M N to NW of the E Maiden lighthouse. Highland Rock, the NE corner, dries 1·5m and is marked by a 10m high red mast with can topmark. Russel Rock, only 0·6m above HW, is 6 cables W of Highland Rock. Allen Rock which dries 1·5m lies 3 cables SE of Russel Rock. There are other rocks less than 2m deep up to 3 cables ESE of Allen Rock.

### Directions

A yacht under power, or with a commanding breeze, may pass safely between the two clusters of the Maidens with a fair tide (*see below*), but this has nothing to recommend it and it is far better to give the Maidens a very good berth, especially in poor visibility. Highland Rock is deceptively far N of the lighthouse. The S danger of the N Cluster is just 1M N of the W Maiden. To pass E of the rocks, E Maiden should not be brought to bear less than 206° while within 2M of it or more than 332° while within 1M of it.

### Tides

Between and around the Maidens the flood starts at +0610 Dover and runs ESE and the ebb starts at −0015 Dover and runs WNW. During the flood an eddy runs NW towards the S Cluster and during the ebb an eddy runs SE towards it.

### LARNE HARBOUR

HW +0100 Dover. Rise 2·8-2·5/0·8-0·4 m. VHF Call 16, Work 14. Call sign "Larne Harbour". This is a very busy commercial port occupying the 0·75M long entrance to Larne Lough. There are very many scheduled movements of ferries during each 24 hours, 7 days a week. It can be safely entered by day or night but yachts must keep clear of the ships entering and leaving. Much of the W side consists of the quays, which are not available for yachts. Beyond them off Curran Point there is a defined area fully occupied by local yachts. On the E side there is a large tanker jetty and further in an L-shaped wharf. N of the tanker jetty there is a small boat harbour.

*Larne Lough entrance from S with the Mull of Kintyre on the horizon.*

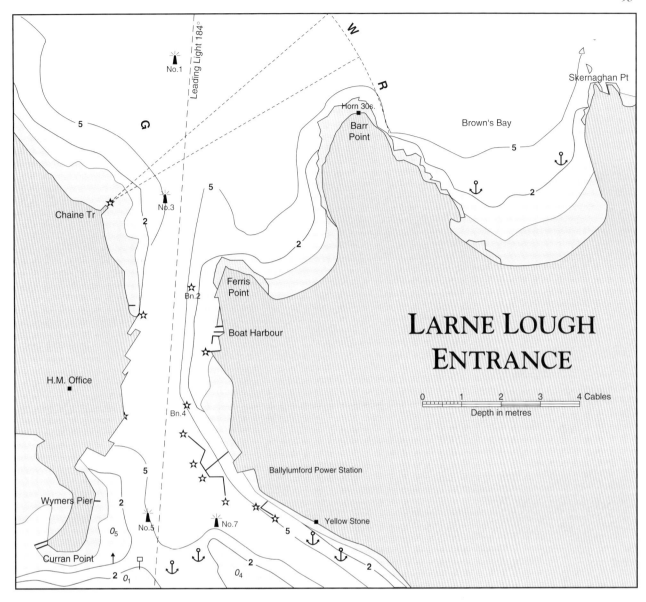

No.1

W

R

G

5

Skernaghan Pt

Horn 30s.

Barr
Point

Brown's Bay

5

5

No.3

2

Chaine Tr

2

2

5

Ferris
Point

Bn.2

Boat Harbour

**LARNE LOUGH
ENTRANCE**

H.M. Office

0        1        2        3        4 Cables

Depth in metres

Bn.4

Ballylumford Power Station

5

Wymers Pier

2

Yellow Stone

5

Curran Point

No.5

No.7

5

2

2

2

## Tidal Streams

Tidal Streams are listed in detail on chart 1237. N of
Barr Point the flood runs SE but W of Barr Point it
runs SSW towards the entrance. In the harbour channel the flood and the ebb start at about LW and HW
Dover, maximum rate 1·5 kn. Off Ballylumford
Lshaped wharf the flood starts about −0545 Dover
but at −0215 Dover a weak eddy starts running N till
HW Dover when the ebb turns NW, maximum rate
1·1 kn. Further in there is little stream.

## Lights

Chaine Tower, 24 m high, shows Iso WR 5s23m16M,
W 230° to 240° leading S of Hunter Rock and N of
Barr Point, R 240° to Magee shore. Barr Point has a
white hut Horn 30s. The leading lights are on structures on the S side of the lough. They show Oc 4s12M
between 179° and 189°, and in line 184° lead towards
and into the harbour. Buoys. No 1 E Card buoy, Q (3)
10s. No 3 Green buoy, Fl (2) G 6s. Nos 5 and 7 Green
buoys, Q G. Two red pile beacons mark the E side of
the channel, No 2, Fl R 3s4M and No. 4, Fl (2) R 6s4M.

The other lights on the piers and jetty on the E side
are 2FR (vert) except at the corner of the
L-wharf which is Oc. R 10s. Both lights on the W side
quays are 2FG (vert).

## Directions

Approaching from the E give Skernaghan Point a
berth of 2 cables and Barr and Ferris Points a berth of
1 cable. Coming from the N leave No 3 green buoy to
starboard and do not go W of a line between it and the
quays. Approaching either way it is best to head next
for No 2 red beacon and leave it and No 4 fairly close
to port. Then if going towards Curran Point head
across, or if going into the lough pass between the jetty
and No 7 green buoy and keep 1 cable off the NE shore
all the way down to Ballydowan anchorage.

**LARNE LOUGH** (*chart 1237 is useful but not
essential*).
The lough is about 1M wide for the first 2M, then it
gets much narrower and mostly dries. A lot of the SW
half of the first 2M also dries. An area immediately S

*Larne Lough from N.*

of the centre of chart 1237 in position 54° 49·37N 05° 46·25W has been made into an island. Though not very snug the lough is a safe place with plenty of room to anchor. Except for the first M of the channel off the NE shore it is mostly fairly shallow. Commercial traffic uses all the channels so in any anchorage a riding light should be shown.

### Anchorages
**Brown's Bay**, E of Barr Point outside the lough, is a good anchorage in winds between SE and SW when it is the best place to stop for the night provided the wind is not likely to veer NW. A depth between 2 and 4m can be found fairly close to either side of the bay or offshore in the middle, the head of the bay being shoal. Landing at SW corner.

**Facilities:** Shop, PO, bus.

**Near the port:** The closest approved area for yachts is NW of a line from Curran Point to No 5 buoy, SW of a line from No 5 buoy to the S end of the ferry quays, and at least 45m away from the buoy. This space is so congested by local boats that a visitor cannot really anchor within its limits. If a vacant mooring is spotted a small yacht might pick it up and check ashore whether it might be used. Another permitted anchorage is S of a line between the SE end of Ballylumford wharf and the beacon about 1·25 cables S of No 5 buoy, where there are anchors on the plan, E and W of which it is shallow. Its only advantage is that it is not too far from the landing place, but the bottom is usually thick with seaweed and the tide is fairly strong. Alternatively, near HW a yacht might berth alongside Wymers pier the end of which just

dries. It is possible to dry out on either side of it if desired.

**Facilities:** Landing at East Antrim Boat Club slip or at Wymers pier. Wymers pier has a fresh water tap and a hose is available. The EABC patent slip can haul vessels up to 15 tonnes. The club, which is used Tuesday, Thursday evenings and Saturday and Sunday, can usually arrange a spare mooring. Telephone 0801574-77204. Their VHF Ch 16 and M is manned during the season on these days. Limited meals and bar. Showers. Harbour office, Customs, PO and bus terminus almost 0·5M distant at entrance to the docks. Fuel and all stores in Larne town, a short bus ride. Larne Harbour VHF Channel 16, Ch 14 working frequency is manned night and day. Larne port information service telephone 0801574-74085. Cranes are available for commercial use only. A passenger ferry crosses between Chaine Quay and Magee shore every half an hour till about 1800. RNLI Lifeboat (*see Appendix 7*).

### BALLYLUMFORD HARBOUR
Ballylumford Harbour, on Magee shore, is a small boat harbour 60 × 40m with least depth 0·6m. It is pretty full in summer, but is very handy for owners of small shallow-draught yachts wishing to visit Larne town.

### Anchorages Inside the Lough
**Yellow Stone**, painted occasionally, is on the edge of the NE shore 1 cable E of the Lshaped wharf. The anchorage SW of the stone or further SE, is the traditional one for cruisers, perfectly suitable for spending a night and the only place inside the lough easily

accessible in the dark. The depth is 3m when the outer side of the wharf is a little open. There is some tidal stream.

**Gas Pipeline.** A submarine pipeline has been laid from Curran Pt. (54°·50′.4 N 5°47′·9 W) to Ballydowan, Islandmagee (54°·50′.3 N 05°46′·5 W). A prohibited anchoring area will be established.

**Ballydowan** is the local name of the anchorage 1M SE of Yellow Stone where there are yachts moored outside a shallow bay off a ruined lime kiln.

### Caution
There is a sunken schooner 0·75 of a cable off the shore of the bay and 1·25 cables SE of the NW tip of the bay. Its masts no longer show at HW. There is good holding and very little tideflow. It is best to anchor NW of the moored boats about 0·5 of a cable offshore in 2 to 3m. Anywhere beyond this anchorage the lough is quite shallow, less than 1m in places, so most yachts should only go further in within 3 hours of HW.

About 2 cables SW of the S point of **Millbay** (which is 0·5M SE of Ballydowan) there is an area 2m deep where boats sometimes anchor. There is a jetty in Millbay, a bay which dries and where the chart indicates stones, so it should only be approached towards HW.

**Magheramorne Bay**, is on the S side of the lough, just NW of the conspicuous cement factory, and is where a lot of local boats and yachts are moored. A channel has been dredged 356° from the cement works harbour marked by a small yellow buoy Q Fl and leading lights. Front OcR 7s9m Rear Oc R 12s12m. Anchor N of the moored boats, choosing a suitable depth which can vary rather suddenly because the mud is dredged out for making cement. It is very well sheltered except in N winds. Land at the wooden jetty with 2 triangular topmarks.

**Facilities:** Concrete slipway. Clubhouse up the road from the shore with showers and phone. Buses to Larne (3M) and Belfast. Hotel ½M.

### Coast
Between Larne and Fair Head much of the coast is very clean. Shallow rocks extend up to a cable in a few places and a berth of 2 cables is safe everywhere. The only offshore danger is The Maidens, already described.

### Tides
The main stream runs past Garron Point and Torr Head at up to 5 kn, the S-going flood starting at +0600 Dover and the N-going ebb at HW Dover. Between Ballygalley Head and Garron Point eddies extend up to 0·5M offshore during the second half of both main flood and ebb, so along this shore the S going stream starts at +0300 Dover and the N going stream at −0300 Dover. Between Garron Point and Cushendun Bay the eddy during the second half of the main ebb runs S from Cushendun to off Cushendall, then across Red Bay and E along the S shore to Garron Point. A weaker eddy runs the other way during the second half of the main flood. There is hardly any stream off the head of Red Bay. As shown on chart 2199, there is a strong local eddy 0·75M NE of Tornamoney Point where the stream runs S for 4 hours maximum 3 kn, starting +0540 Dover, and then runs N for 8·25 hours maximum 4 kn, starting −0240 Dover. Between Torr Head and Fair Head there is an eddy during the second half of the flood. The SE stream runs about 2·5 hours, starting +0600 Dover, and the NW stream runs about 10 hours starting weakly at −0400 Dover but soon increasing and by −0200 extending across the E entrance of Rathlin Sound.

### Anchorages
There is only Carnlough harbour which is best approached towards HW. Most of the other bays are only temporary anchorages in offshore wind and calm sea. Ballygalley Bay is clean with 4m or 5m 1·5 cables offshore and a possible anchorage in W or SW wind, but Brown's Bay 4M SE of it is much preferable (*see above*). Glenarm Bay is 9M from Larne and just W of Path Head which rises steeply to 137m. It is also sheltered in W and SW winds. Anchor in 2 to 4m due N of the harbour, which dries completely. Carnlough Bay is just NW of Glenarm. Close off Straidkilly Point, between the bays, is the small Black Rock which never covers.

### Caution
There are fish farms about 1M offshore in an E direction. Keep a good lookout if approaching from the S. The head of Carnlough Bay is shallow and the place yachts usually anchor, in suitable weather, is 1 cable off the harbour at the N end of the bay.

### CARNLOUGH HARBOUR
HW −0010. Rise (HW) about: 1·8-1·5m. This has always been a popular place for yachts to spend a night as it is the only sheltered harbour between Larne and Ballycastle. The new plan shows Carnlough Harbour, the entrance channel tends to silt up. It is dredged occasionally. There is usually 5·5 ft. when the ledge on the port hand wall is covered. Enter on a bearing of 310° accurately. There are lights on each pier N.Pier Head Fl.G 3s 4m5M, S. Pier Head Fl R 3s6m 5M. The entrance is 18·5m wide. Leading marks have now been fitted consisting of 2 Inverted Yellow Cones. Do not enter with winds onshore above Force 6. Turn to port once inside. There are berths for visiting yachts or tie up to N breakwater but not closer than half way to the slipway from outer end. There is a slip for dinghies in the starboard spur.

*Carnlough from E.*

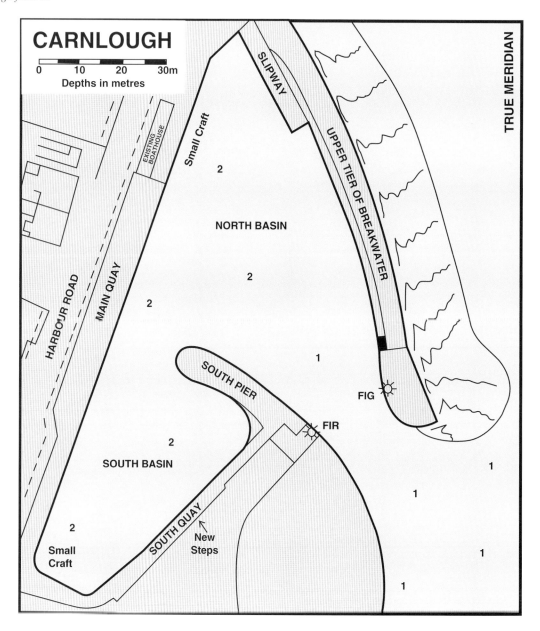

# CARNLOUGH

0 10 20 30m

Depths in metres

TRUE MERIDIAN

SLIPWAY

UPPER TIER OF BREAKWATER

Small Craft

2

NORTH BASIN

2

2

1

HARBOUR ROAD

MAIN QUAY

EXISTING BOATHOUSE

SOUTH PIER

FIG

FIR

2

SOUTH BASIN

1

SOUTH QUAY

New Steps

1

2

Small Craft

1

1

*Carnlough Harbour.*

*Carnlough Harbour from SE.*

**Facilities:** PO, food, hotel, several small cafes, fuel, gas and water all near quay. Small shops. Bus to Larne. Hull repairs – contact Red Bay Boatyard Co. Cushendall. Engineers and electricians – A. McCormack Telephone 0801574-88531 in Carnlough. Tourist representative in PO. Good base from which to explore the Glens of Antrim. Taxis. The

Harbour Authority is Larne Borough Council. HM Telephone 01574-272677. Charges (1996) Up to 5m £2.10 per week; over 5m and under 10m £3.60 per week, over 10m £5.00 per week.

**RED BAY**

HW −0015 Dover. Rise: 1·6-1·5/0·3-0·2m. This fairly

deep bay is quite open to N and E but provides the best anchorages on this part of the coast, out of the tide, and safe in winds between SE and NW. Even in moderate S or SW winds there can be fierce squalls off the hills or down the glen, but the holding is reliable. Approaching from S keep 2 cables off Garron Point and the shore W of it where, as well as a couple of rocks, there are 2 ruined piers. Light established on Glenariff Pier Fl 3s10m5M. In S winds the best anchorage is in the S corner of the bay. The inner ruined pier extends 110m off the shore 0·5M from the head of the bay. E of it there is some tidal stream. Go in past this pier and anchor 2 cables off a white stone arch on the shore, depth 3m or 4m. Yachts have ridden out a SE gale here. In W or NW winds anchor S of the small pier 0·5M NE of Waterfoot village, as close in as draught permits, depth 2m to 5m. There is about 2m alongside the outer part of the pier which is of open timber construction, the inner part being stone. Boats lie here all summer on moorings with stern warps to the pier, though in E wind it gives no protection from swell. Approaching from seaward the pier may be difficult to pick out and is best identified by getting it in line 255° with Lurigethan, a remarkable 350m high spur with flat top and steep sides. Fish Farm in position 1·3M E of Carnlough Pier.

**Facilities:** Some stores at Waterfoot. At Cushendall, 1M N of the pier, there is a YC Telephone 012665-71673 with showers, limited meals and bar during season. It is rather exposed. There is a slip with about 1·7m for 3 hours either side of HW. It is opposite the RNLI boathouse. Boat repairs in village with fuel and water. Occasional VHF watch. Also shops, garage, hotel, hospital, but no shelter or landing facilities except a beach. Lifeboat (*see Appendix 7*)

## CUSHENDUN BAY
Cushendun Bay, 5M NNW of Garron Point, affords temporary anchorage in fine weather off the hotel at the S end of the bay in 9m, or 3·7m fairly close in.

### Caution
Do not anchor more than 1 cable from the S end of the bay as the rest of it has a foul bottom and there is a wreck 2 cables offshore just N of the centre of the bay. Small local boats drawing 0·5m can cross the river bar at HW and dry out on a convenient beach just below the road bridge.

**Facilities:** Hotel and shops.

## TORR HEAD
Torr Head, almost 5M N of Cushendun, has an exCG watch house on its 67m high summit.

### Anchorage
In calm conditions it is possible to anchor just S of the head below the exCG house, landing at a slip protected by a small breakwater. The breakwater is a private dock for a salmon boat. It has a salmon station and a power winch. Permission to enter the dock might be granted to small craft by owners who work the salmon nets in the approach. Capt. McNeill is sometimes resident in the house which has a telephone. It is also possible to anchor on the N side of Torr Head close inshore out of the tide, sheltered from the S. It would be necessary to leave at once if winds changed to the E. The ebb tide has been observed to run at 9 kn. close of the tip of Torr Head and creates a large eddy about 100m NE of the Head.

## MURLOUGH BAY
Murlough Bay is immediately W of Ruebane Point, which is about 1·5M NW of Torr head. At LW a sandy beach shows and at its W end there is a long cottage (occupied occasionally by holidaymakers) with a small boathouse to the right of it and a road leading up NW from the shore. The boathouse slip, which has a winch, gets some protection from the rocks which mark the W end of the bay. In offshore wind there is a possible anchorage SE of the outer rock, in about 2·5m on clean sand and out of the main tide. A small yacht might find some shelter in light N winds S of this rock in 1·8m. Inshore of the rock it almost dries.

### Caution
Beware of salmon nets.

## FAIR HEAD
Fair Head, the NE corner of Ireland 3M NW of Torr Point, is a magnificent headland 190m high and of very distinctive shape. Its top is flat and surrounded by a vertical cliff which drops 90m and from which an even 30° slope of boulders runs down to the sea. Its contour is almost identical as you gradually alter course 45° around it. It is steep-to all round.

102

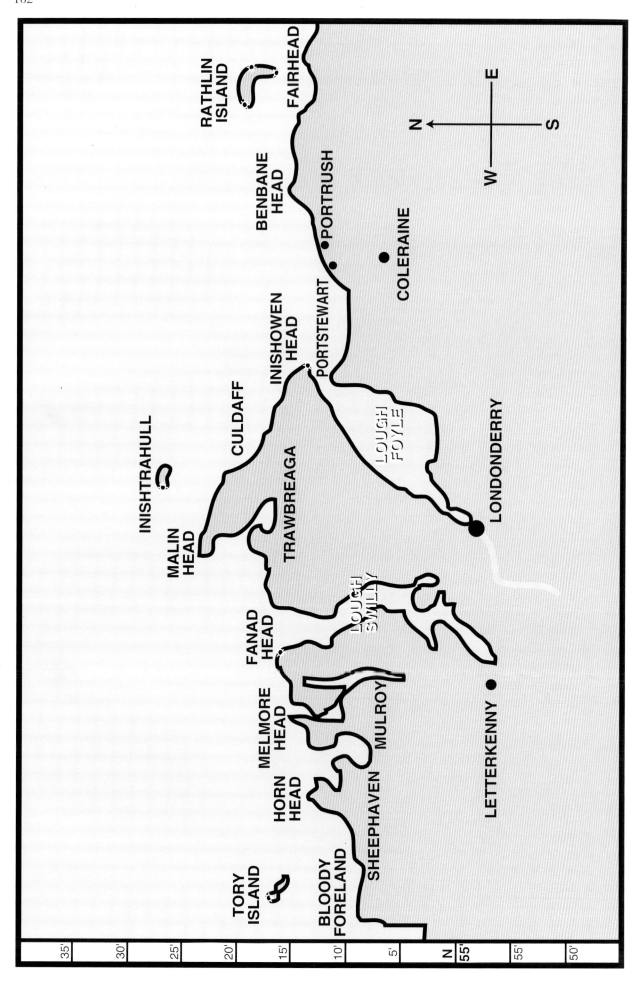

# Chapter 4

## FAIR HEAD TO
## BLOODY FORELAND

Charts 2798 and 2811 (*see Appendix 1*) cover the coast as far as Horn Head. If 2752, which includes Tory, is also carried, the smaller scale 2723 is not needed. Yachts are also advised to have 2699 Sheep Haven and Mulroy, 2697 Lough Swilly, and 2499 Lough Foyle. 49 Portrush is not necessary.

### General

The N coast is about 80M long with a great variety of headlands, cliffs, bays and inlets. It includes half a dozen anchorages secure against all summer winds: Portrush, the River Bann, Culmore (Lough Foyle), Fahan (Lough Swilly), Fanny's Bay (Mulroy) and Downings (Sheep Haven). Many other interesting anchorages are available depending on weather. Yachts sailing out W from the North Channel can have pretty tough beating against the predominant W wind, and in fresh onshore wind some anchorages are not accessible, but SW and S winds are quite frequent and then it is a most delightful coast to cruise along. Swell is much more prevalent W of Malin than E of it where the influence of the tide can kill it quickly. But between Rathlin and Inishowen Head a heavy swell at times accompanies the turning of the tide to the E. This subsides or disappears when the tide turns W. Fog is rare, on average less than 1 day per month, except in Rathlin Sound where it is not uncommon in summer. For crossing to Scotland *see Chapter V*.

### Tides

The time of HW varies by only 1·5 hours along the coast, the W parts being the earliest. HW at inland places such as Londonderry and Milford is of course later than on the coast. MHWS varies from a mere 1m at Ballycastle to 3·9m at Mulroy Bar. The tidal streams are strong near Fair Head but get progressively weaker further W. Maximum spring rate in Rathlin Sound is 6 kn, in Inishtrahull Sound 4 kn and in Tory Sound only 2 kn. Of the three sounds, Inishtrahull is the worst and can produce a steep and dangerous sea very quickly indeed when the tide turns against the wind. Rathlin can be pretty bad too, but even in W or NW wind up to Force 5 a wellfound yacht should have no difficulty in going through either with a fair tide. The period and direction of tidal streams is shown clearly in Admiralty Tidal Atlas No. 218. The table on Chapter 4 page 106 gives the approximate directions of the streams as shown on the Atlas. When the tide changes W of Malin Head at −0430 and +0200 Dover it is in fact the beginning of an eddy which at first runs only within 1M of the coast but extends gradually seaward ending as part of the main tidal stream. There are tidal chartlets for Rathlin Sound overleaf and from Foyle to Swilly on pages 125 and 126. It can be seen that a yacht coming in from the W with a fair wind and passing Bloody Foreland at +0230 Dover would probably have 10 hours of continuous fair tide. Likewise a yacht reaching to the W and leaving Rathlin at HW Dover should get to Malin Head before the tide turns and then have only 2 or 3 hours of foul or slack tide before picking up a further 6 hours of W going tide. The ideal time to pass W through Rathlin Sound is +0330 Dover, when the most turbulent 2 hours of tide there are over. This is just when a yacht might get there when making a fair-tide passage from Carnlough to Portrush. Voyaging from Portrush to Belfast you should leave at +0500 Dover, that is −0300 local HW. Quite good progress can be made by keeping inshore against the last half of the W going stream, and you should be able to get to Rathlin at LW Dover when there will be 6 hours of strong fair tide to take you through the sound and on down the North Channel. If you did not leave Portrush till local HW when the main tide had turned in your favour you would only have 5 hours of fair tide because S of Fair Head the tide turns an hour earlier than off the North Coast. This would scarcely give you time to get through the part of the North Channel where the tide runs strongest and you might, if unlucky, get swept back into Rathlin Sound.

If working a foul tide along the E part of the coast it is worth remembering that the tides are much weaker between Ramore Head (Portrush) and Inishowen Head than elsewhere, and that there is a useful eddy on both ebb and flood between Ramore Head and Barmouth, the River Bann entrance.

### RATHLIN SOUND

Rathlin Sound, between Rathlin Island and the mainland, is 2M to 3M wide and the normal approach to the N coast. Fair Head is quite clean to within a few metres of the boulders but between the head and Ballycastle the shore should not be approached closer than 2 cables as it is much subject to groundswell and there are rocks close in.

### Rocks

**Carrickmannanon** is the only off-lying sunken rock in the sound. It is nearly always breaking and dries 0·3m. It lies 3 cables NE of Kinbane Head and is eas-

104

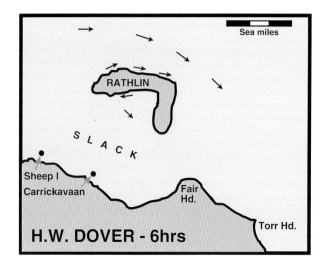

H.W. DOVER - 6hrs

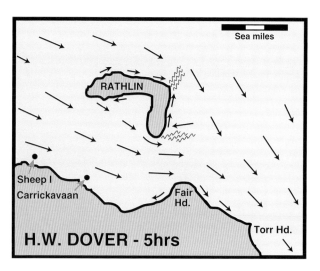

H.W. DOVER - 5hrs

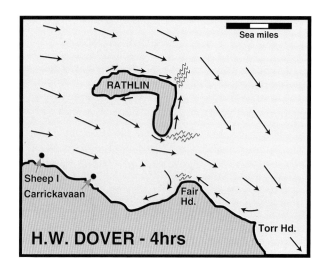

H.W. DOVER - 4hrs

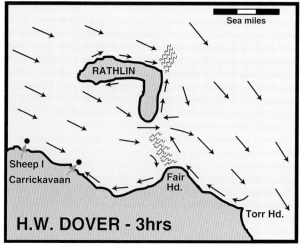

H.W. DOVER - 3hrs

N.W. - going eddy extends from cliffs out as far as Carrickavaan.

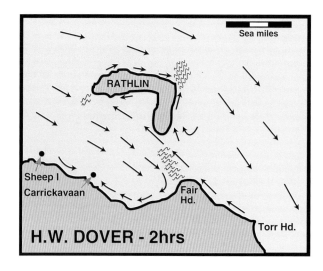

H.W. DOVER - 2hrs

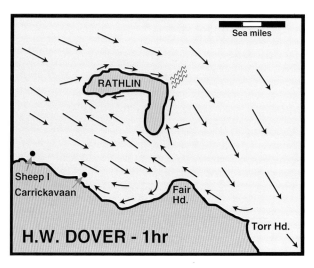

H.W. DOVER - 1hr

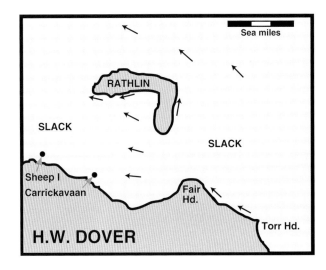

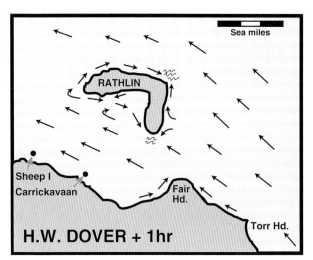

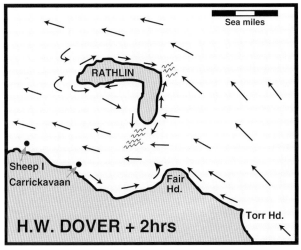

Slough-na-more is a dangerous from Dover + 01.30 to Dover + 02.30

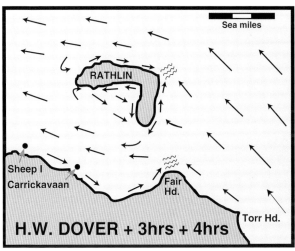

Streams and eddies run strongest at Dover + 3

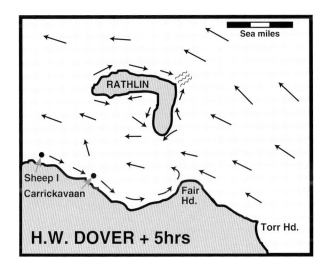

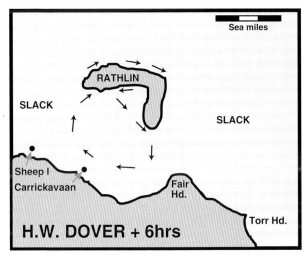

ily avoided by keeping Bengore Head open between Ballintoy Point and Sheep Island, which leads 0·5M outside it. The tidal streams set with full force on this rock, creating powerful eddies in its lee, so it should be given a wide berth, particularly by sailing craft in light weather. Coasters regularly pass inside it and a line for this is to keep the N point of Carrickarade touching the S side of Sheep Island. Sheep Island Sound at the W end of Rathlin Sound is very shoal so yachts should always pass outside the island. On the shore inside the sound there is a white tower almost as high as the cliff behind it.

## Tidal streams

The tides in Rathlin Sound are strong with several eddies. The excellent description in the *Irish Coast Pilot* should be studied by anyone making a stop in the area. The chartlets on pages 104 and 105 also illustrate the tides. For a passage through it is sufficient to know that the main stream in the centre of the sound runs W for 5 hours, starting at HW Dover, and runs E from −0530 to −0030 Dover. If going W it is best to pass through on the second half of the W going tide and if going E on the first half of the E going tide. Sloughnamore, the overfall SW of Rue Point, is dangerous from +0100 to +0300 Dover, otherwise the sound should not cause a wellfound yacht any difficulty up to Force 4 or 5. It is essential to have a fair tide as the maximum rate is 6 kn springs and 4 kn neaps. The roughest water is usually between Fair Head and Torr Head. Close in off Torr Head the Ebb runs up to 9 knots during Spring tides.

## Facilities

Power and water are available at the visitors' berths in the marina and showers, toilets and washing facilities are provided in the adjacent marina office building. The town of Ballycastle is very close to the harbour and has excellent shops, hotels, B & B's, pubs, engineering repairs and most services required by visiting yachts. EC Wed.

## Lights

End of N. Breakwater: Flash (3) G. 6s 6m.
End of Boyd's Breakwater: Fl (2) R. 4s 1m.

## RATHLIN ISLAND – CHURCH BAY

The time and rise of the tide here are as at Ballycastle, but both are somewhat irregular. The island is L shaped and its W leg is surrounded by cliffs 60m to 120m high. Population about 100. There is a very large seabird nesting site below Rathlin West (The Bull) Lighthouse. Major harbour works have recently been completed in Church Bay. These consist of two substantial breakwaters, built to the W of the original harbour, and the dredging, to 3.5m, of the entrance channel, and to 3m as far as the entrance to the Inner Basin, which has a depth of approx. 2m at MLWS.

The additional shelter thus provided has up-graded Church Bay to the status of an all-weather harbour.

## Lights

The island's three main lights are Rue Point: fl.(2) 5s 16m 14M from a white tower with two black bands. Rathlin West (The Bull); fl.R.5s.62m 22M from a

| Tidal Stream Directions | Hours before HW Dover | | | | | | Hours after HW Dover | | | | | |
|---|---|---|---|---|---|---|---|---|---|---|---|---|
| | 5½ | 4½ | 3½ | 2½ | 1½ | ½ | 1 | 2 | 3 | 4 | 5 | 6 |
| Rathlin to Malin Hd | Slack | ——— ESE ——— | | | | | ——— WNW ——— | | | | | |
| Malin Head to Bloody Foreland—Inshore | ENE | | Slack | ——— WSW ——— | | | | ——— ENE ——— | | | | |
| Malin Head to Horn Head—Offshore | ENE | E | SE | Slack | SW | | W | ——— Slack ——— | | | | |
| North of Tory Island | E | | SE | ——— SW ——— | | | W | WNW | N | NE | ENE | |

## BALLYCASTLE HARBOUR AND MARINA

HWS −0445 Dover, HWN −0200 Dover. Rise: 1·2-1·1/0·7-0·2m. The harbour of this popular holiday town has been totally re-developed and deepened in recent years. It is anticipated that all relevant work will be completed by early June 1999. It now offers a well sheltered marina in its inner harbour with excellent facilities. The outer harbour provides berthage for the Rathlin Island and Campbeltown ferries, on the Eastern side of the North Breakwater. *(See Chartlet p. 107)*

## Anchorage

Anchor 50m to 100m off the pier, 5m, sand, sheltered from W through S to ENE but liable to sudden swell.

lantern beside the base of a white tower 18m high, situated halfway down the cliff vis 015° to 225°. Fog Det. Lt. (This is sometimes referred to as the Upside-Down Lighthouse!). Rathlin East (Altacarry Head); fl(4) 20s 74m 26M from a white tower with black band 27m high. Racon.

The harbour at Church Bay now has 3 lights, all of which are essential for night time navigation in the area. End of the N. Breakwater (The Bow); fl R 2s 3m. End of S. Breakwater: fl(2) G 6s 3m. Directional light, close SW of Manor House; Oc RWG 4s 5M. This directional light is for the guidance of vessels entering or leaving the port and is sectored as follows: G 020°–023° W 023°–026°, R 026–029. *(See Chartlet p. 107)*

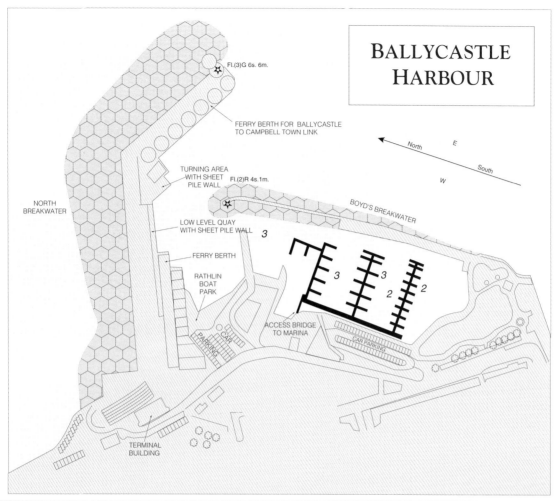

**BALLYCASTLE HARBOUR**

Fl.(3)G 6s. 6m.

FERRY BERTH FOR BALLYCASTLE TO CAMPBELL TOWN LINK

TURNING AREA WITH SHEET PILE WALL

Fl.(2)R 4s.1m.

BOYD'S BREAKWATER

North E South W

NORTH BREAKWATER

LOW LEVEL QUAY WITH SHEET PILE WALL

3

FERRY BERTH

RATHLIN BOAT PARK

3          3     2

2

ACCESS BRIDGE TO MARINA

CAR PARKING

CAR PARKING

TERMINAL BUILDING

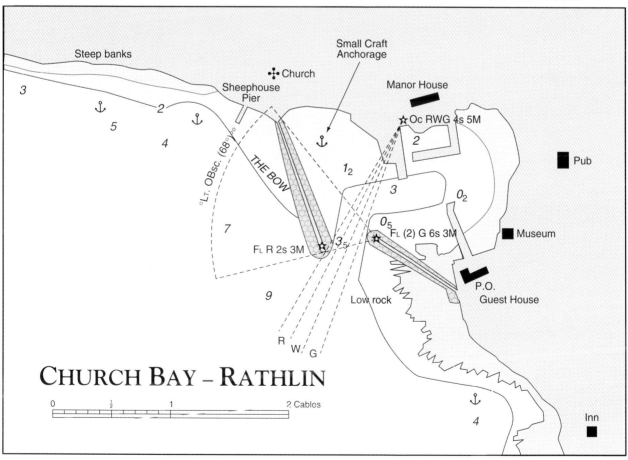

Steep banks

Small Craft Anchorage

Church

Sheephouse Pier

Manor House

3

2

5

Oc RWG 4s 5M

4

THE BOW

2

°LT. OBsc. (68°)

1 2

3

Pub

0 2

7

0 5

FL (2) G 6s 3M

Museum

FL R 2s 3M

3 5

P.O.

9

Low rock

Guest House

R    W    G

4

Inn

# CHURCH BAY – RATHLIN

0    ½    1              2 Cables

*Seals at Rathlin.*                                                      *Chris Hill Photography.*

**Facilities**

PO, telephone, some small general shops, pub (pub grub), guest houses, diving centre and cafe – in season. The Manor House (National Trust) is now a B & B and community centre. Water is available on the quay.

Two ferry sailings a day to and from Ballycastle could facilitate few changes or the leaving of a yacht unattended for a limited period. The inner basin here measures approximately 30m wide by 100m long and has a depth of 2m, MLWS.

**Anchorages**

Church Bay, outside the Breakwaters, provides shelter in winds between NW and SSE through E.

The best anchorage in this area is 1 cable W of Sheephouse Pier, or alternatively 70m west of it, in about 5m, good holding ground.

**Caution**

There is a large wreck in the middle of the bay 1M out from the harbour. There is 0·8m over it so yachts should keep well clear. A S Card Pillar Light Buoy Q (6) + LFl.15s Drake lies 1·5 cables SE of it. Approaching from the S either leave the buoy to port or, if wishing to pass S and W of the wreck, keep Rue Point open till Altacarry light disappears behind the high ground W of it, then steer in keeping it hidden.

**COORAGHY BAY**

Cooraghy Bay, on the S shore near the W end of the island, provides shelter in moderate N winds. Anchor in 4m SE of the boat quay. Convenient for landing to visit The Bull.

**USHET PORT**

This is a rocky gut S of a ruined stone storehouse 0·5M up the E shore from Rue Point. It provides emergency shelter for a small shallow draught boat in winds between SW and NE through N. Drop the anchor about 20m within the E point and take warps to the boulders on either side. Leave immediately if the wind turns S. Craft drawing up to 5′ can usually enter.

**ARKILL BAY**

Arkill Bay, a little further N, is the best anchorage on the E shore and is suitable in offshore winds between SW and NW. Anchor in about 5m. Boulders on the shore make landing difficult. Boats drawing 5′ can, with care, get just within entrance.

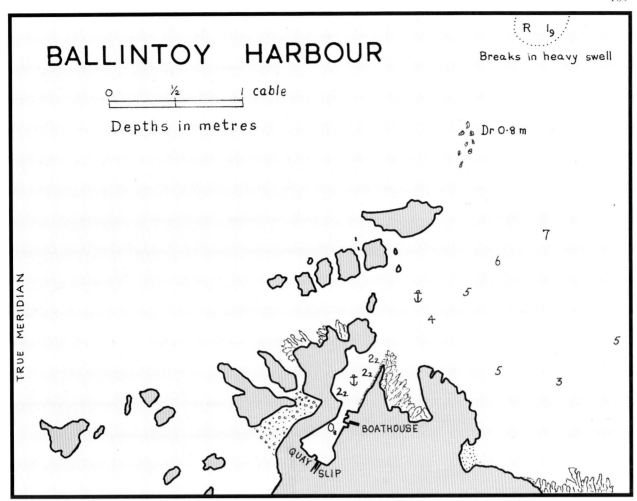

# BALLINTOY HARBOUR

This harbour is on the mainland at the W end of Sheep Island Sound (*see* **Rathlin Sound** *above*). It is very small and used only by local open boats. The depth alongside the quay W of the boathouse is 0·8m, therefore about 2m at HWS. The rockbound gut outside the harbour is about 70m long and 40 m wide and makes an attractive temporary stopping place in settled weather. The gut has been dredged to about 2·2m deep. It is simpler to anchor just outside, as shown on the plan, where the rocks provide some shelter.

## Directions

Head in to pass W of Sheep Island and having left its NW point about 1 cable to port turn to starboard towards the entrance.

**Facilities:** No supplies, but good tea room close to harbour.

## PORTBRADDEN

Portbradden, at the W end of beautiful Whitepark Bay, provides boat landing but no shelter except in moderate offshore wind. A mile further W Dunseverick, also known as Millport, has a boat slip and a small pier with 0·5m alongside. A post with white triangular topmark stands on the outer end of the sea wall. Entering, leave the rocky islet which lies close N of the port to starboard. It should be approached with caution and only in settled swell-free weather.

## BENGORE HEAD

Bengore Head has quite a formidable tide race which can only be avoided by keeping 2M offshore. Two cables E of the head Braddan Rock, with 1·6m over it, lies 1·5 cables offshore. Giants Causeway 1M W of Bengore Head looks quite insignificant from sea and provides no good landing but the multi-layered cliffs E of Bengore Head are of great geological interest.

## PORTBALLINTRAE

Portballintrae can be identified by a conspicuous row of houses above the small horseshoe bay which provides fair shelter in offshore winds. In N wind the swell breaks right across the mouth of the bay so do not chance getting caught there in such conditions. When approaching keep clear of Blind Rock on the E side. The best anchorage is NE of the W pier in 3m or 4m with the gateposts of Seaport Lodge in line with the inner end of the pier. Best landing is at the sheltered slip at the SE pier.

**Facilities:** Some supplies, hotels, PO and yacht club.

*The tiny harbour of Ballintoy – note that even with a substantial swell running outside, there is good shelter for small craft within.*

*Portballintrae from SE.*

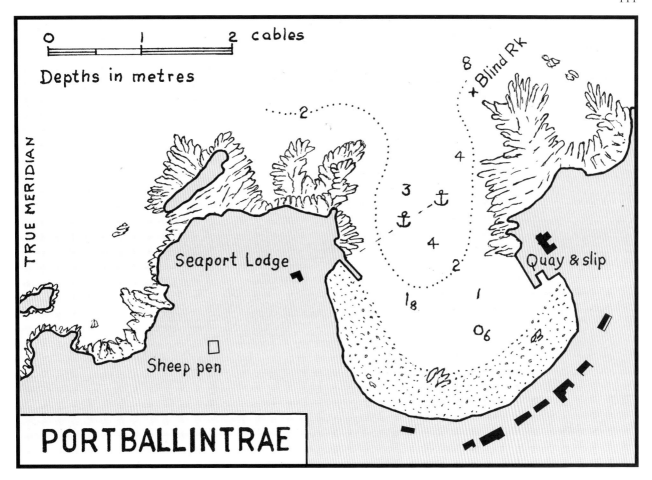

o       1       2 cables

Depths in metres

TRUE MERIDIAN

Blind Rk

8

×

4

2

3

⚓

⚓

4

Seaport Lodge

2

1

8

1

Quay & slip

Sheep pen

0·6

# PORTBALLINTRAE

## Coast

### STORK ROCKS

Stork Rocks, 0·5M offshore at the E entrance to Skerries Sound, are dry at half tide and clearly marked by an 11m high red pillar with can topmark. They are steepto on the N and elsewhere a berth of 1 cable clears the dangers. Skerries Roads provide shelter in moderate N winds. The best place to anchor is abreast the nick in Large Skerrie about 1·5 cables from its E end. This is also the best place to land on the island. In a strong N breeze the swell would make this anchorage uncomfortable for yachts and in a N gale it would probably become dangerous. Skerries Sound is a safe and convenient passage for yachts in moderate conditions. In strong onshore winds or high swell it is advisable to keep outside. There are two dangerous sunken rocks on the N side of the sound SW of the 5m high Carr Rock. Give these a wide berth and remember that the E going tide sets strongly onto them. Going through either way against the tide it is best to keep reasonably close to Reviggerly, a reef part of which always shows, and to Ramore Head. During the E going tide there is a useful eddy off Curran strand and up to Reviggerly. Port-na-Dhu is a small boat harbour obstructed by a drying rock and of no interest to yachts. However, a set of leading marks have been established by HM Coastguard. Upper beacon – Black cone apex down, 31m to seaward. Lower beacon – Black cone apex up 230° T. These are to facilitate the launching of the local coastguard boat.

## Caution

Salmon nets are fixed in summer on both sides of Ramore Head and also off the curve of Curran strand S of the Large Skerrie.

### PORTRUSH

HW −0440 Dover. Rise: 2·1-1·4/1·1-0·4m. This fair-sized artificial harbour lies on the W side of Ramore Head. Once inside it a yacht is secure from all summer winds, though in heavy onshore winds the swell makes it uncomfortable. Unfortunately it is very congested and a yacht cannot be left there unattended unless the HM can allocate a vacant mooring. A berth will always be found for an overnight stay, either on the pontoon or on the N quay.

### Entrance

The ground swell runs right across the entrance and a stranger should not approach in onshore winds of above Force 5. Once the entrance is known there should be no difficulty in entering unless it has been blowing hard from W or NW for some hours. In these circumstances Skerries Roads, or preferably the Foyle, offer shelter. A sunken breakwater runs out about 20m SW from the N pier which should be given a good berth with the harbour mouth well opened up before turning NE to enter. The winds in the entrance are very fluky.

*Portrush Harbour and Skerries Sound from SSW.*

## Lights

N Pier: Fl R 3s 220°-160°; S Pier: Fl G 3s 220°-100°. Leading lights FR on red triangles 028°. These are difficult to pick out with the town lights and are normally only switched on for lifeboat use.

## Anchorage

The S side of the harbour is filled with local yachts and other craft while commercial vessels occasionally use the N quay and require the unoccupied part of the harbour for manoeuvring. The NW part of the harbour has depths of 3 to 5 m. On arrival a yacht should berth alongside the N quay and directions should then be sought from the Harbour Office on this quay. Alternatively call on VHF 16 working 14 or phone 01265-822307 from your previous port of call. The HM may be able to allocate a vacant mooring.

**Facilities:** There is a pontoon at the E end of the N quay where stores, water and fuel by hose can be embarked. Yachts may stay on this pontoon overnight but must be clear by 0900. Charge £3.50 per day. All stores including Calor and camping gas in the town. EC Wed. Rail and bus connections to Belfast and Londonderry. Hotels, good restaurants, wine bars and cafes. This holiday town has many attractions for young people. Lifeboat station. Portrush YC adjacent to the Harbour Office has showers and its members are very helpful. Contact Chris Tinkler 01265-824324. HM Coastguard Sector Office (01265-823356) has a remote aerial connected to Bangor CG VHF 16 and

67. Chandlery at Coleraine (01265-832086). For engine or electrical repairs consult HM. Coleraine is about 3M inland and can be approached by sea up the River Bann. Lifeboat (*see Appendix 8*). Laundry facilities are available ½M from harbour.

New pontoons with a total length of approx. 90m have been recently provided.

## PORTSTEWART POINT

Portstewart Point is 2·5M SW of Portrush. Black Rock 9m high lies close offshore 0·5M NE of Portstewart Point and opposite a distinctive square rock on the shore. Lausons Rock, which dries 1m, extends 0·75 of a cable out from Black Rock which therefore must be given a berth of at least 1 cable. At night keep Portstewart light visible.

## PORTSTEWART

This is a very small harbour 2 cables S of the point. The inner basin is 0·8m to 1·7m deep. In onshore winds the narrow entrance is difficult and the heavy run inside is liable to damage a yacht's topsides. In quiet weather it is very convenient for a temporary visit as it is right beside the town.

**Facilities:** Good shops and hotels, EC Thur. Berth alongside the S side of the inner basin. Water from a tap in the harbour. Gas but no fuel. Tourist Board Office in Town Hall. The patent slip takes out boats up to 12m long and 1·8m draught. River Bann pilots work from the port.

113

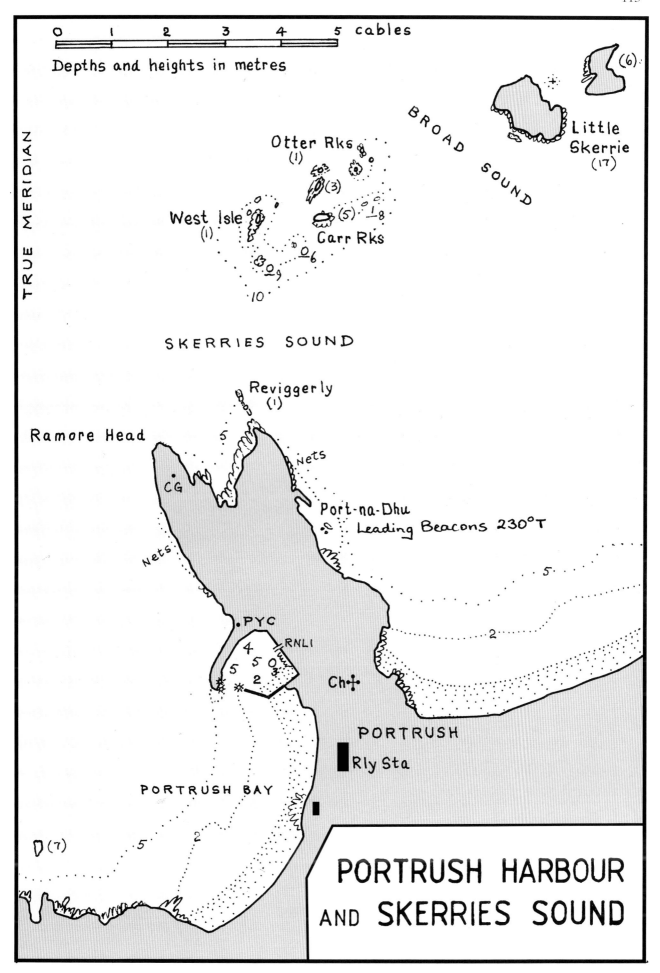

PORTRUSH HARBOUR
AND SKERRIES SOUND

*Portstewart Harbour from SSE.*

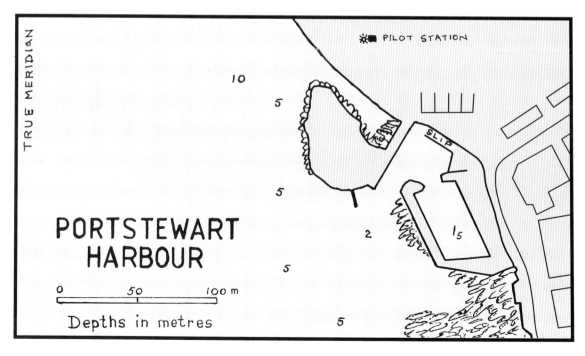

## Lights

Oc R 10s21m5M from 040° through E to 220°. It is shown from the red pilot station on the point at a height of 21m.

## Tidal eddy

From Portstewart to River Bann the coast is rocky for the first mile, then a level sandy beach backed by sandhills. A berth of 1 cable clears any dangers. A tidal eddy runs along the shore during the second half of both ebb and flood between Ramore Head and the River Bann.

## RIVER BANN *Chart No. 2499*

HW Coleraine −0430 Dover. Rise: 2·1-1·6/0·7-0·3m. The river mouth known as Barmouth is between stone training walls projecting 2 cables N from the beaches. The river entrance is maintained at a least depth of 4m and the channel to Coleraine is maintained at a least depth of 3·4m but is subject to silting. It should not be attempted in strong onshore winds or swell. Do not try to enter if the swell is breaking noticeably on the pier ends. If in doubt consult Coleraine Harbour Radio (VHF Call 16, Work 12) or telephone 01265-42012.

## Tidal streams

The outgoing ebb runs at 3 kn and causes uneven seas and eddies up to 2M offshore. The ingoing flood is not strong. The coastal flood stream runs W fairly strongly across the entrance. It is best to enter at slack water or with the first of the flood (+0225 Dover). The river is very well marked with Buoys and Beacons consequently yachtsmen with the latest edition of chart 2499 will have no difficulty making the passage to Seaton's Marina (3M upriver) or Coleraine Marina (4M upriver).

## Lights

E Molehead: Fl R 5s6m 2M from white concrete tower. W Molehead: Fl.G 5s3m2M from black metal mast. Leading lights: in line 165° from piles on SW bank 4 cables inside Oc 5s6m2M and Oc 5s14m2M. River Bann lights: Fl R 5s on the NE side and Fl G 5s on the SW side.

## Entrance

The best time to enter the River Bann is 15 minutes after LW Portrush. Enter with the white leading light beacons in line. The channel is 45m wide and is kept dredged to 3·4m. It is well marked with beacons, red on the NE side and green on the SW side. The first red beacon (tripod) Ballyaghran Point Lt. Fl R 3s appears very far over to the W and unless prepared for this a stranger might take it the wrong way.

## Caution

In summer there may be salmon nets fixed across the full width of the river during the flood tide. On sighting one, stop and shout for the men watching it, who are then bound to lower it for you. But vessels may be held responsible for damage to nets.

## SEATON'S MARINA

Seaton's Marina is on NE Bank 3M from the entrance and 1·2M downstream from Coleraine. No. of berths – 70. Call Ch.37 during office hours to check berth availability. Telephone 01265-832086.

**Facilities:** Landing Slip, Scrubbing Berth. Marina charges (1999) are – 24ft. or more £11 (STG) per day.

## COLERAINE MARINA

VHF Ch 16 and 37. It is on the NE bank 4M from the entrance and 0·5M downstream of the town. It has berths for 63 boats with depths of 3m at the outer

*Coleraine Marina is the longest-established marina on the seacoast of Ireland.*

pontoons and 1·4m near the bank. There is usually a berth available for a visitor but to make sure the supervisor may be phoned between 9 am and 5 pm, 01265-44768.

**Facilities:** Water and electricity on the pontoons. Fuel. Showers and heads, laundry, chandlery, workshop, 13 ton travelift crane. Masts up to 15m long can be stepped and unstepped. Shops are 0·5M away so it is probably necessary to phone for a taxi from the adjacent YC which welcomes visitors and has showers and a bar (limited hours). Marina charges 1999 are STG £7.00 per day up to 25 ft and STG £9.00 over this length.

### Anchorage

The best place is on the NE side just upstream of a high scrubby sandhill which is 0·5M upstream of the old CG Station. Anchor close in or moor to avoid swinging out into the channel, and carry a riding light. This anchorage is known as Dougans Bay or Strawberry Hill. It is reputed to be calmer than the marina in certain cross winds.

### Yachts making passage from Coleraine to Lough Neagh

| | |
|---|---|
| Maximum length overall | 30·0m |
| Maximum Beam | 6·0m |
| Maximum Draft | 1·3m |
| Maximum Air Draft | 3·3m at LW Neaps |

Official minimum depth in navigation is 1·8m but in places it is as little as 1·3m. For passage information yachts should contact Department of Agriculture at the Cutts. Telephone 01265-42357.

### COLERAINE

Yachts do not normally go there now but it has a long commercial quay close to all the shops. Before going there phone the HM for permission and then phone the railway bridge (between the marina and the quay) to arrange to have it opened. Telephone HM 0126542012; bridge 0126542403.)

### Coast

From the Bann to Lough Foyle is all an open sandy beach except between Castlerock and Downhill where there is 1M of cliff on the edge of which there is a prominent classical temple. The shore is shoal and should be given a berth of at least 2 cables.

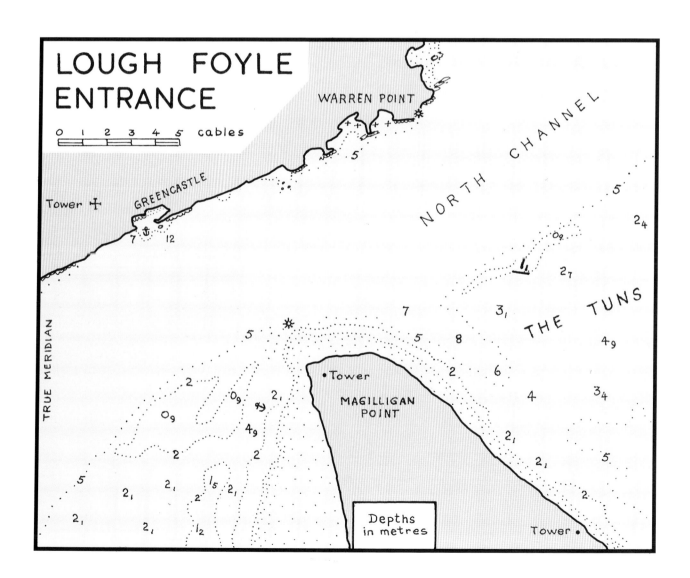

*Lough Foyle entrance from NE.*

## TUNS BANK

Tuns Bank, very shallow in places along its NW edge, extends 3M NE from the E side of Lough Foyle entrance. It has been reported that a large area of the SSW central part of the bank dries about 1m. either side of LWS, consequently mariners wishing to pass between the bank and the shore should do so with care, as the charted depths may be unreliable.

## Caution

Approaching inshore from the E there is nothing to indicate the start of the bank. Once W of Binevenagh Mountain you should either keep about 3 cables off the shore or head out for the Tuns buoy off the NE end of the bank.

## LOUGH FOYLE

HW at Moville 0350 Dover. Rise: 2·3-1·8/0·8-0·3m. A good stopping place for yachts bound W but otherwise there is not much to attract the average cruiser. The SE side is Northern Ireland and the NW side is the Republic. The lough is sheltered from the sea by the lowlying sweep of Magilligan Point which leaves an entrance about 1M wide. The E and S shores are lowlying and very shoal far out. The NW shore rises steeply. There is a good deal of commercial traffic. The border between Northern Ireland and the Republic of Ireland lies at the top end of Lough Foyle on the starboard side just before the entrance to the river. *See Customs Requirements Appendix 14.*

## Approach

The ship channel, about 0·75M wide, lies NW of the Tuns Bank. A berth of 2 cables clears all dangers along the NW shore from Inishowen Head.

## Caution

In June and July the channel is often obstructed at night by salmon nets. Coming from the E it is often more convenient to approach along the Magilligan shore, locally known as the back strand, particularly if trying to enter against the ebb in offshore winds. In these conditions you could anchor anywhere off Magilligan strand to await the flood. The channel between Tuns Bank and the shore has a least depth of 3·4m. Approach it about 3 cables offshore and when 0·5M from Magilligan Point move in to 2 cables offshore, taking care to keep just this distance off till the point is abeam. If the tide is ebbing it sets strongly across the channel towards the bank.

## Tidal Streams

Tidal streams run through the entrance at 3·5 kn at springs. The ebb commences −0320 Dover in mid channel and 1 hour earlier around Magilligan Point. On the NW side of the entrance from Warren Point to Moville there is a useful eddy extending from 45m to 90m offshore on both ebb and flood. Between the entrance and Culmore the maximum speed is 2·5 kn. Detailed information in *Irish Coast Pilot.*

118

*Greencastle in Donegal.*

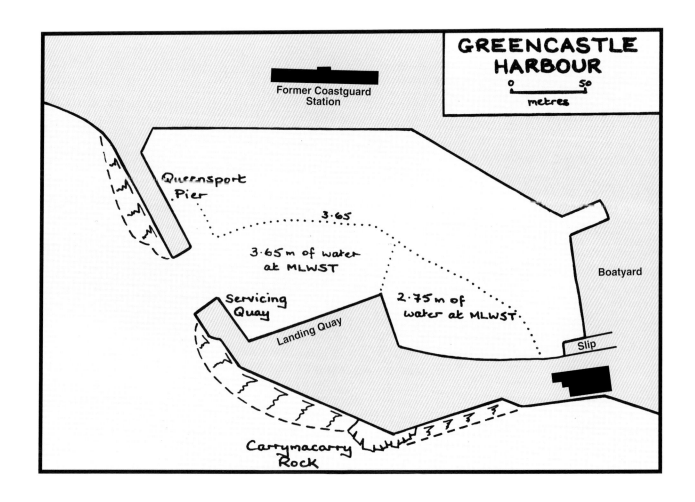

## Lights

Inishowen (locally called Stroove) is a substantial white lighthouse with 2 black bands 23 m high on Dunagree Point (0·5M S of Inishowen Head). Fl .(2) WRG 10s28m W18M R14M G from 197° to 211°, W211° to 249° covering the ship approach, R249° to 360°. Horn (2) 30s. Fog Det Lt. A disused lighthouse, white with 1 black band, 15m high, stands 0·75 of a cable E of the main lighthouse. Lough Foyle Buoy, a Safe Water pillar buoy, L Fl 10s, whistle, lies about 2M NE of Inishowen Head. Tuns Buoy, red, Fl R 3 , is about 1M E of Inishowen Head. Warren Point, Fl 1·5s9m10M from a white tower, from 232° to 061°, obscured close inshore. Magilligan Point, QR, 7m4M from a pile structure off the point. The channel up to Londonderry is very well lit and beaconed as shown on chart 2499.

## Anchorages

### GREENCASTLE

Greencastle, on the NW shore just within the entrance, is a busy fishing harbour. It is not very suitable for yachts as they would have to berth alongside fishing boats which are frequently on the move, particularly at night. The pier has recently been greatly enlarged and rebuilt. It is now unwise to anchor in the middle of the harbour. In winds between NNE and WSW there is a convenient anchorage just outside the harbour. If anchoring outside the harbour in the bay it is advisable to be clear of the fishing boat route. If the wind comes onshore it is best to move without delay to a suitable place up the lough. If this is not possible tie alongside a fishing boat and ask for advice. Buoy the anchor as the bottom is foul with old moorings. Land either at Queen's Port pier, which has 2·7m alongside, or in the harbour.

**Facilities:** There is a water tap on the pier in the harbour and this pier is closer to the shops, garage and hotel in the village.

### MAGILLIGAN POINT

There is a comfortable though remote anchorage in the lee of Magilligan Point in E and NE winds. Approach with Magilligan light structure close to port and then keep it in line astern with Warren Point white tower. As soon as the low round tower on Magilligan Point comes abeam, bear to port and keep Magilligan light structure bearing 021°. This leads down the centre of the gut, which is not less than 2m deep, increasing to 4·9m when the tower ashore bears 055°. Do not go further in than this.

### MOVILLE PIER

Moville Pier is about 3 cables NW of Moville Bank light structure, a white house on black piles. The pier collapsed in 1995. Not recommended for yachts to approach this pier. There are 8 visitors' mooring buoys located about ·3M SW of Moville Pier Head.

## CARRICKARORY PIER

Carrickarory Pier, 0·5M SW of Moville is now in disrepair but the bay offers good shelter in winds from NNW to SW. The outer 25m of the quay has a depth of 2m. It is best to anchor NE of the quay and ask at the pilot office on the pier whether it would be possible to haul in closer to it, which is desirable in winds from SW to NNE. In SE winds there is no suitable anchorage until the lough narrows into the river at Culmore. There is complete shelter in Culmore Bay on the NW side. Anchor about 1·5 cables W of Culmore Point in 2m to 3·5m outside the moorings. Buoy the anchor.

**Facilities:** Stores at Londonderry, 4M.

## LONDONDERRY

Londonderry is 18M from the sea.

**Tidal streams**

Tidal streams are fairly strong in parts of the river. Full details of the streams should be studied in the *Irish Coast Pilot*. There is a bridge with 32m clearance just above Boom Hall and before Rosses Point. Otherwise there are no difficulties for a yacht and the river is very well marked. However, it would be desirable to have chart 2499. Berth at the extensive new quay on the W side below Craigavon bridge.

**Facilities:** The city has all facilities including marine engineering but there is no yacht chandlery or boatyard. VHF Ch 16 and 14 c/s "Harbour Radio", HM 01504-263680. Londonderry Harbour office is now located at Lisahally just south of Culmore Point.

**Coast**

Inishowen Head to Culdaff Bay consists mostly of cliffs rising 100 to 200m. A berth of 1·5 cables clears all dangers. Kinnagoe and Tremone bays provide boat landings on the beach in offshore winds but no facilities.

**Passage timing**

For a yacht making 4 to 5 kn: Foyle to Swilly: leave Foyle entrance at HW Dover. This gives a fair tide round the head and should catch the last of the flood into Swilly. A yacht bound W along the coast can do well by arriving at Malin Head at 0500 Dover at the end of the fair tide, by keeping inshore W of Lough Swilly slack water followed by another fair tide will be picked up after 2 hours. East bound – for a coastal passage leave Melmore Head at −0600 Dover (−0100 Mulroy Bar) or leave Lough Swilly entrance at −0500 Dover. Going to Foyle leave Lough Swilly entrance at +0400 Dover or be at Malin Head at −0600 Dover. This should just enable you to catch the last of the flood into the Foyle.

extends to the centre of Inishtrahull Sound at +0200 Dover, and starts to subside after +0300 Dover. It is particularly severe at springs and with NW wind, in these conditions a race extends 0·75M E of the head. At +0400 Dover the tide is slack inshore at the head. At −0500 Dover it runs strongly SE within 2 cables of the head, but the direction changes to E as you go further out.

## MALIN HARBOUR OR SLIEVEBANE BAY

Malin Harbour, 3M E of Malin Head, offers temporary shelter in offshore winds but is much more subject to swell than Culdaff and not so easy to approach. The entrance is between Lackgolana and Rossnabartan. The small pier extends SSE and has about 1·2m at its head. It is best to lay an anchor out to the S and tie a stern warp to the outer bollard.

**Facilities:** Fuel, hotels, some supplies.

## INISHTRAHULL

HW - 0500 Dover. Rise: 3·3-2·5/5·1-6·0.4m. This island lies 4M off the coast and 5M NE of Ireland's North Point. It is about 1M long and consists of 2 rounded

hills about 40m high forming the E and W ends and joined by a stretch of low ground. The Island is a Bird Sanctuary and recently a herd of Red Deer has been established on the Island. Except for the lighthouse keepers (who were withdrawn in 1987) no one has lived there for the last 55 years. All the shores are rocky. Torr Sound, between the W end of the island and Torr Rocks N of it, is 0·5M wide in the fairway which has quite a tide rip. It is foul on the S side where sunken rocks run out 3 cables N from Inishtrahull. On both sides of the E half of the island a berth of 1 cable leads clear of all dangers.

### Lights

From a 23m high slim white tower on the SW point of the island, Fl.(3) 15s59m25M, obscured 256° to 261° within 3M Racon.

### PORTMORE

Portmore is on the N side of the island. Coming from the W it is best to approach by going S of the island and round the clean E point. On the N side of this point there is a circular eddy with a whirlpool during

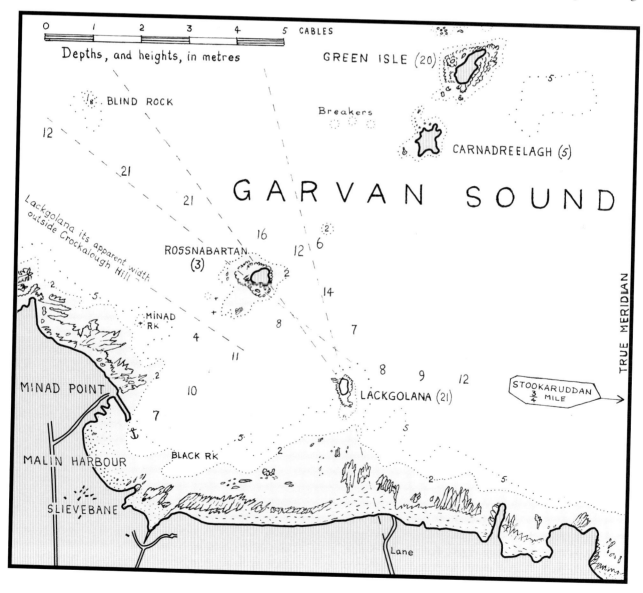

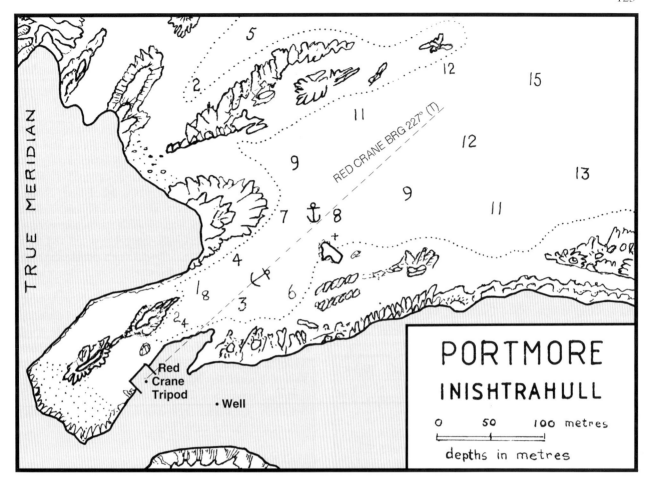

TRUE MERIDIAN

RED CRANE BRG 227° (T)

5

2

12

15

11

9

12

13

9

7 8

11

4

+

1 8

3 6

2 4

Red
Crane
Tripod

• Well

# PORTMORE
## INISHTRAHULL

0   50   100 metres

depths in metres

*Portmore at Inishtrahull.*

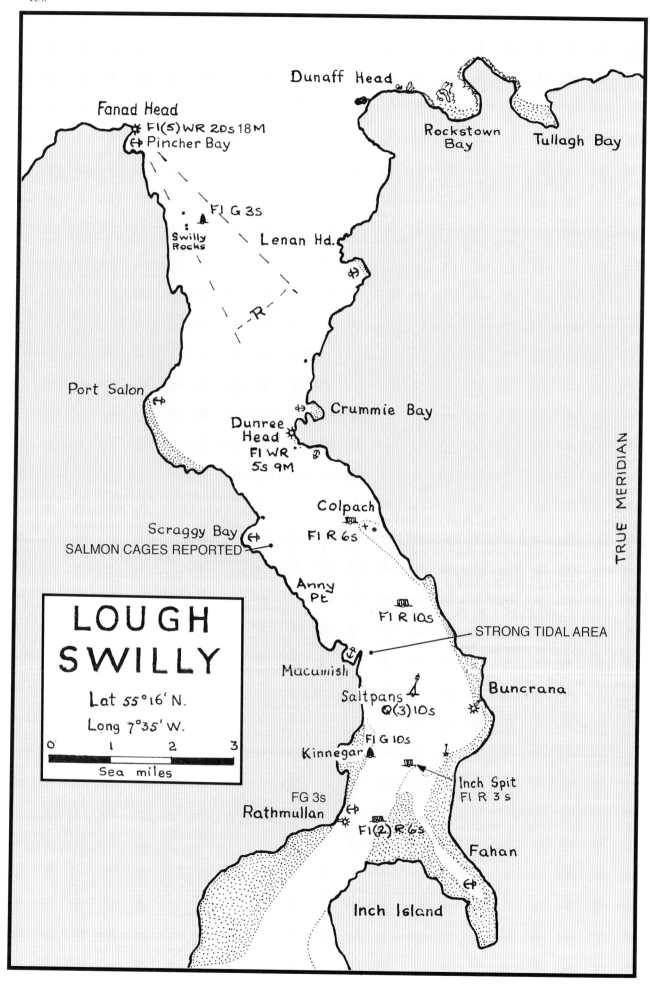

Dunaff Head

Fanad Head
✳ Fl(5) WR 20s 18M
⊕ Pincher Bay

Rockstown Bay

Tullagh Bay

Fl G 3s

Swilly Rocks

Lenan Hd.

⚓

- - R - -

Port Salon ⊕

Crummie Bay
⊕

Dunree Head
Fl WR 5s 9M
✳

⚓

Colpach
Fl R 6s

Scraggy Bay ⊕
SALMON CAGES REPORTED

Anny Pt.

Fl R 10s

STRONG TIDAL AREA

⚓

Macamish

Saltpans
Q(3) 10s

Buncrana
✳

Kinnegar
Fl G 10s

Inch Spit
Fl R 3s

FG 3s
Rathmullan
✳ ⊕

Fl(2) R 6s

Fahan

⊕

Inch Island

## LOUGH SWILLY

Lat 55°16′ N.
Long 7°35′ W.

0      1      2      3

Sea miles

TRUE MERIDIAN

*Dunaff Head marks the eastern side of the entrance to Lough Swilly.*

fore ideal to round Malin Head at +0130 Dover, when the inshore tide has been running W there for about 3 hours. You then have 6 hours of flood into and up the lough. Dunaff Hill at the E of the entrance is 219m high with steep sides. Fanad Head at the W side is very low. About 2M in from Fanad Head a G con Fl.G 3s marks Swilly Rocks and should be left to starboard. Coming from the W round Fanad Head, steer SE till the buoy is seen. When passing Dunree Head in heavy weather do not go E of midchannel as the sea then breaks on Dunree Bar.

### Dangers and Buoys

Dangers in the lough are relatively few but there are a number of unmarked rocks within 1 cable of the shore, so keep further off than this until you have examined the chart. Four of the buoys mark other dangers which yachts should avoid. Colpagh red buoy Fl.R 6s marks a shoal and rocks drying 3m and 4m. The shore from here to Buncrana should be given a berth of 3 cables. Kinnegar drying strand stretches out to within 1 cable of the green buoy Fl.G 10s and Kinnegar shoal with 0·4m extends 4 cables N from the buoy. Two red buoys mark the W side of Inch Spit Fl. R 3s and Flat Fl.(2) R 6s which must be avoided except at HW. A Fish Farm has been established in position 55° 08′·50N 7° 30′·65W.

### Anchorages West shore

Pincher Bay, just inside Fanad Head, is a possible temporary anchorage in 4 or 5m, sand, for those not wishing to sail up the lough. It is less subject to swell than one might expect.

### PORTSALON BAY

Portsalon Bay, 4·5M from Fanad Head, is an excellent anchorage in W winds and quite suitable for an overnight stay in any reasonably settled weather. Anchor off the end of the pier or SW of it in 3m to 5m. There is about 0·5m alongside the pier. At night, the pier and village lighting is very distinctive from seaward. There are 8 visitors' mooring buoys located about 100m S of the Pier Head.

**Facilities:** Rita's Bar, general store and restaurant are adjacent to the pier. Visitors may dine at the local golf club, which is nearby.

### SCRAGGY BAY

Scraggy Bay, 2·5M further in, provides shelter similar to and perhaps slightly better than Portsalon. The house is a Youth Hostel. Coming in from seaward give the shore a berth of 2 cables to avoid Yellow Rock which dries 0·8 m.

### Anchorage

Anchor at the S end of the bay beyond the beach in about 3m.

*Portsalon from SE.*

*Scraggy Bay in Lough Swilly from N.*

**Facilities:** None

**MACAMISH**

Macamish is easily identified by the Martello tower on the point. It is a pretty place and well sheltered in winds between WNW and SE. Tide runs strongly past entrance, but no stream inside.

**Anchorages**

There are 2 small places for anchoring as shown on the plan. The nicest is beside the Martello tower. Keep about 80m off the point when entering to avoid the 1·7m shoal NW of it. Anchor just past the tower in about 5m, sand. The other anchorage is close inside Lamb's Head in 3m, sand. There is a shallow ridge about 0·5m deep about 125m away from the shore. Land on the beach.

**Facilities:** Shop on the main road 0·5M away. Home of Ottway Golf Club.

*Macamish Anchorage from N.*

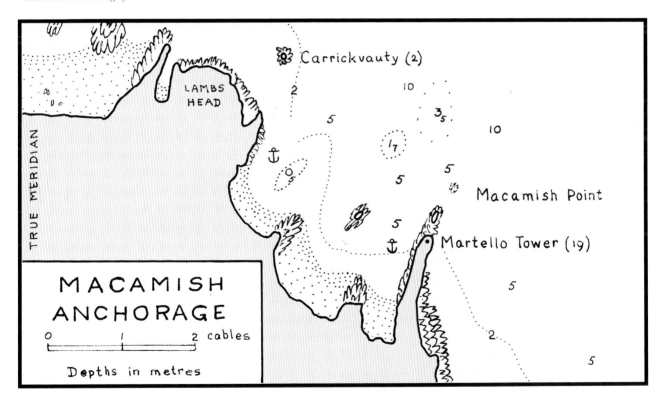

**RATHMULLAN**

Local craft remain on moorings all summer off the beach N of the pier. Visiting yachts should anchor outside or N of them. Well sheltered in prevailing SW to NNW winds. Land at the steps on the solid part of the pier or at LW on the beach nearby. The deepwater berths on both sides of the head of the pier being against open piles and in strong tide are not recommended except for large motor vessels. Yachts can berth alongside the Pontoon on the Southside of the Pier in deep water. Yachts may tie up on either side but the shore side is used mostly by small motor boats.

*Unlike most Lough Swilly anchorages, Macamish is not tiderode.*

*Rathmullan from SW.*

*Ramelton from SW.*

There are berths alongside for about 12 boats, but numbers can be increased by doubling-up, or rafting. It is hoped to develop this facility into a marina in the near future. The pontoon is accessed by a walkway from the pier. A council workman is stationed in a hut on the pier and a charge of £10 is made for an overnight stay. Phone Jim Deeney at the Pier Hotel, 074-58178, for further information.

**Facilities:** There is a water hydrant at the pierhead and a water tap at the toilet at the shore end of the pier. Shops and PO in town, also fuel and telephone. Two good hotels near the shore about 0·5M N of the town are most easily reached by outboard dinghy. Bus to Letterkenny and taxis. There are good pubs adjacent to the pier.

**RAMELTON**

Ramelton, about 3M up the Lennan river, can be reached on a rising tide by judicious sounding. Yachts drawing 1·5m can enter at Whale Head at halftide and go up to the town. It is a very pretty spot and well worth a visit for those who like a turn at "ditch-crawling". If staying it is best to dry out alongside the quay which fronts the town and has 3m HWS. The port is very occasionally visited by coasters.

**Facilities:** Hotel, shops, water on quay. EC Wed. Turners yard builds and lays up yachts and takes care of yachts left alongside the town quay.

**Anchorages, East shore**

Leenan Bay, 2·5M in from Dunaff Head, is a wide sandy bay facing SW.

**Caution**
Beware of rocks off the N point of the bay and fishing nets on its N side. Anchor outside local boats.

**Facilities:** None.

## CRUMMIE BAY
Crummie Bay is just N of Dunree Head. Anchor between the points of the bay – the inner part is all shoal.

**Facilities:** None.

## DUNREE BAY
This bay is just S of Dunree Head. **Note** that there is a drying rock almost 1 cable SW of the head. No part of the shore of the bay is clear, so anchor not closer than 1 cable, depth about 4m. On the W side of the head, 4 cables from the anchorage, there is a small pier, much exposed to swell, with 0·4m alongside. Permission to land required from CO of fort, Telephone Linsfort 404.

## BUNCRANA
It is necessary to anchor a long way out to remain afloat so it is only suitable in calm weather. Alongside the SE side of the pier there is about 2·5m at half tide. However, the pier is made of open piles so a yacht is not safe there without someone on board.

**Facilities:** There is a water hose from the toilet on the quay and petrol at a store nearby. There are good shops in the town 0·5M away. EC Sat. Fuel at garage 0·25M up road to SE.

## FAHAN CREEK
Fahan Creek, inside Inch Island, offers sheltered anchorage for small craft and yachts, and is accessible to vessels of up to 2m draft, at all states of the tide except Low Water Springs. The only time it becomes uncomfortable is when a NW wind blows against the strong ebb. The entrance has been silting and the rise of tide is irregular so it is suggested that a visiting yacht should enter between 1·5 and 1 hour before HW and turn out if she goes aground. Yachts drawing over 2m should not attempt to enter.

**Directions**
The entrance to Fahan Creek lies between Lisfannan Bank and Inch Flats. Approaching from seaward, steer 150° from Inch Spit buoy till the conspicuous chimney (45m) near the shore at Buncrana comes into transit with Barnan More (the easterly and larger of the 2 prominent paps 6M to the NE), bearing 030°. Keep these in line steering 210° until Rathmullan Pier bears 252°, then steer 156° for the first low summit on the ridge west of Grianan Fort. (The fort appears like a long shed on top of Grianan Mountain, 5M to

*Fahan Creek from NW.*

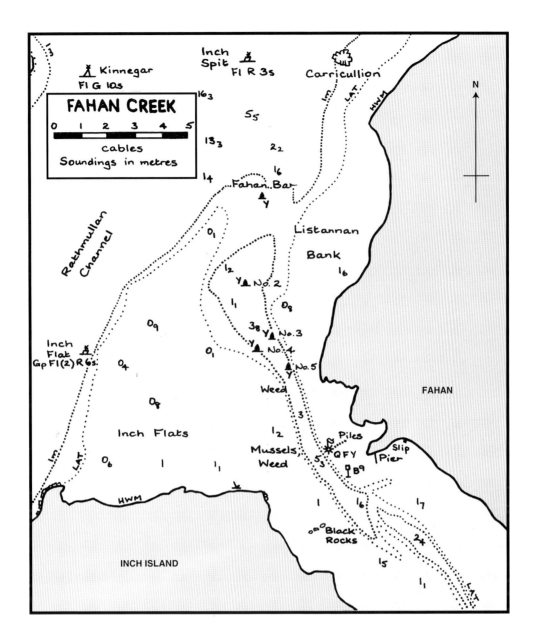

**FAHAN CREEK**

```
0   1   2   3   4   5
          cables
   Soundings in metres
```

Kinnegar Fl G 10s

Inch Spit Fl R 3s

Carricullion

Rathmullan Channel

Fahan Bar

Listannan Bank

Y No.2

Y No.3

Y No.4

No.5 Y

Inch Flat Gp Fl(2) R 6s

Weed

FAHAN

Inch Flats

Mussels Weed

Piles

Q F Y

B9

Slip Pier

Black Rocks

HWM

INCH ISLAND

the SSE.) Keep this heading till abeam of the pole marking the end of the derelict Low Water Pier (55°05′15″N, 7 28′53″W). Give this pole a berth of 25m, then steer between the lines of moorings into the upper creek. A sandbar with a maximum depth of 0·9m LAT crosses the creek S of Rinnaraw Point, and the deeper water lies on the Fahan side. Use of an echo sounder is recommended.

**Anchorages**
Anchor S or SE of moored yachts in 2m to 5·5m, good holding, sand and mud.

**Facilities:** The Lough Swilly Yacht Club slip is just E of the pier. There is a pub and a PO beside the club but no shop. Bus service to Buncrana and Londonderry. Ferry to Rathmullan. Reliable boatman in whose charge a yacht could be left.

Work has commenced on the construction of a marina but completion is not anticipated before Autumn 1999.

**THE LETTERKENNY CHANNEL**
This channel is pretty and interesting as far as Castle Grove. Above this, the narrow channel winds through an expanse of very soft mudflats to a small quay at the roadside outside Letterkenny, 3m HWS, which is often occupied by a coaster.

**LOUGH SWILLY TO MULROY BAY**
This coast is very foul. For clearing lines see below in Mulroy Bay.

**Directions**
Off-lying Danger. Limeburner Rock with a depth of 2m lies 3M N of Melmore Head and has a N Card QW (whis.) buoy. The red sector of Fanad Head light shows over the rock and the buoy.

**MULROY BAY**
HW at bar −0500 Dover. Rise (HW): 3·9-2·9m. Fanny's Bay, 4M in from the open sea, is the best anchorage on the N coast. Mulroy Lough extends

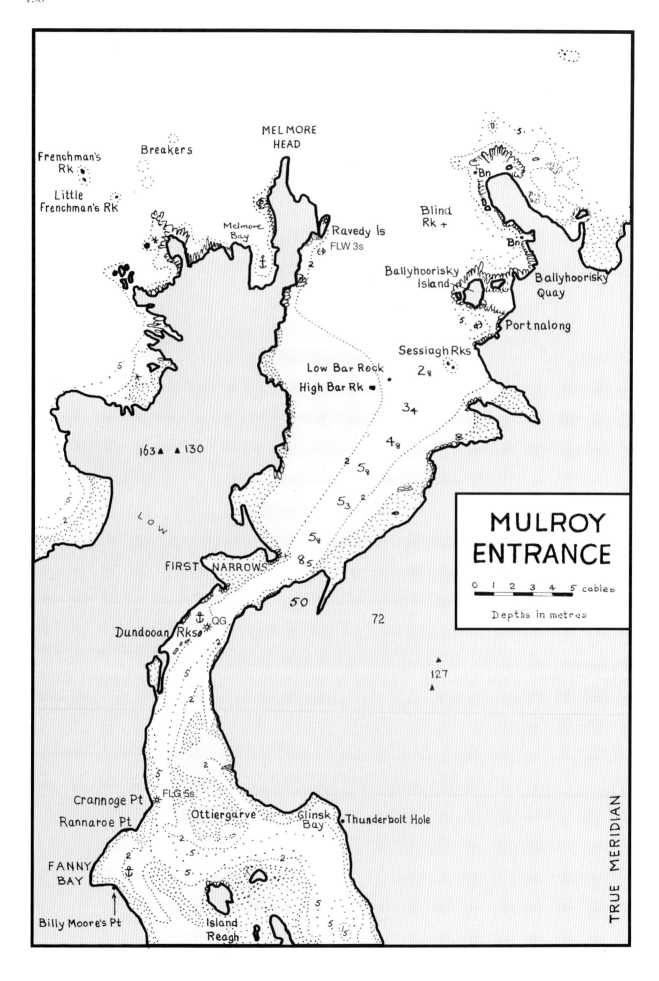

Frenchman's Rk

Little Frenchman's Rk

Breakers

MELMORE HEAD

Melmore Bay

Ravedy Is
FLW 3s

Blind Rk +

Bn

Bn

Ballyhoorisky Island

Ballyhoorisky Quay

Portnalong

Sessiagh Rks

Low Bar Rock
High Bar Rk

163 ▲  ▲ 130

LOW

FIRST NARROWS

Dundooan Rks   QG

Crannoge Pt   FLG 5s

Rannaroe Pt

Ottiergarve

Glinsk Bay

Thunderbolt Hole

FANNY BAY

Billy Moore's Pt

Island Reagh

## MULROY ENTRANCE

0 1 2 3 4 5 cables

Depths in metres

127

72

50

TRUE MERIDIAN

*The entrance to Mulroy Bay and the First Narrows from SW.*

some 10M inland and provides sailing on sheltered water in most attractive surroundings and with fairly intricate pilotage.

## Caution
There are now mussel rafts and salmon fish farms in the bay. A good look out is necessary. Chart 2699 is essential to really enjoy one of the most beautiful cruising areas of Ireland.

## Directions
The coast between Lough Swilly and Mulroy Bay is very foul and should be given a wide berth using the clearing marks shown on chart 2699. Highest part of Dunaff Head open of Magheraguna Point (beside Fanad Head) is the clearest. Keep on this bearing until almost abreast of Melmore Head, the tower on which is in ruins but distinguishable. Then approach the entrance bearing S and keeping a bit nearer the W side. Blind Rock has 1·5m over it. If approaching the bay from further offshore Limeburner Rock must be avoided. If approaching from the W see **Mulroy to Sheephaven** on p 142.

## Lights
Ravedy Island, Fl.3s9m3M vis 177° to 357°. Dundooan Rocks, QG.4m1M. Crannoge Point, Fl.G 5s5m2M. These are for the guidance of local boats. No stranger should attempt to enter in the dark.

## Temporary anchorages
If passing along the coast or waiting to enter the lough, Ravedy Roads is most convenient if wind is between NW and S. Anchor 0·75 of a cable S of Ravedy Island in about 2·5m, clean sandy bottom. It is surprisingly well sheltered from swell. Portnalong, the bay S of Ballyhooriskey Island, is better in winds between NE and S but is much more exposed to swell than Ravedy Roads. Anchor in 3m or 4m with the S point of the island in line with its summit. Ballyhooriskey Quay is used by local lobster boats but is quite unsuitable for yachts. Anyone who nevertheless wishes to take a small boat in should only attempt this near HW and not if there is any swell. Pass close N of the beacon and note that the narrow channel between it and the quay has a rocky bottom which dries about 1m.

Chart 2699 (or old chart 2698) is not necessary to reach Fanny's Bay but is essential for going further into the lough. Though based on a 1856 survey, the chart is accurate inside the lough, but not in the inner part of the bay N of the First Narrows as the Note beneath the title indicates. The channel shown on the plan on page 138 has been amended to show depths over the bar as taken in 1984.

The entrance has been E of Bar Rocks for at least 50 years. The shallowest part of the bar is SE of Bar Rocks where the depth is 2·8m. If the sea is not rough

*The Second Narrows in Mulroy Bay from S.*

one may enter at any time, provided the yacht can progress against the tide which may reach 4 kn in the First Narrows at springs. If there is swell or N wind there may be breakers W of the Bar Rocks. In such conditions the bar should be carefully observed before approaching it and it would be prudent to enter with the flood or leave at HW.

**Timing the passage**

HW at the head of the lough is 2·25 hours later than at the bar and as this is about the time it takes to go in with the flood, then if you enter as recommended at half flood it will still be half tide when you arrive at Milford. This convenience when entering becomes the converse when leaving. It is then best to pass through the Third Narrows at HW or even a bit earlier in order to find a helpful depth of water in the Ottiergarve Bank area and later at the bar. As stated, about half flood is the best time to enter if bound for the Broad Water or beyond. At springs it might be better to start an hour earlier and thus avoid the strongest flow at the Third Narrows and also have a good liftoff in the unlikely event, if you are a

prudent navigator, of running aground or hitting a rock. Beating in or out under sail and with the tide is quite feasible but new visitors are advised to motor against head winds.

**Directions**

Before approaching identify High Bar Rock which at HWS is covered but marked by breakers. At half tide Low Bar Rock is visible. Leave High Bar Rock 2 cables to starboard, i.e. pass midway between it and the Sessiagh Rocks (*named on plan*) and 1 cable E of Low Bar Rock. Then steer towards the First Narrows, about 215°, and pass through it slightly nearer the SE side. Next steer towards the beacon on the N Dundooan Rock but when abeam of Dundooan Point, aim to pass halfway between the beacon and the SE shore. After leaving all Dundooan Rocks 0·5 of a cable to starboard follow a curved course between 0·5 of a cable and 1 cable off the W shore till near Crannoge Point light tower which should be given a berth of 0·5 of a cable. From the light tower if making for Fanny's Bay steer about 192° for the left (SE) end of a row of houses SE of Billy Moore Point.

*The Third Narrows in Mulroy Bay from SE.*

When a small white beacon on this point comes in line 230° with a similar beacon on a rock on the skyline enter Fanny's Bay on this line. If the beacon cannot be seen head for the boatyard shed on the same bearing. (*Anchorage described below*). If continuing up the lough, after passing Crannoge Point steer about 192° (*see above*) and when Rannaroe Point comes abeam steer for the middle of Island Reagh till on a line joining Billy Moore Point (or the left side of the boatyard shed) and Thunderbolt Hole which can be seen just S of where the road runs close to the Glinsk Bay shore and which is immediately S of the word Binderg on the chart. Hold to this line (076°) till about 11 cables from the shore, then head S to leave the high shore of Island Roy 0·5 of a cable to starboard. When this is well abeam start turning gradually to port so as to approach the Second Narrows heading about 085°. Pass through slightly nearer Rawross Point the S side of the narrows and continue E across Millstone Bay till 1 cable off its E shore, then turn SE to pass between the shore and Seedagh Bank. From here to the Third Narrows the E shore is all clear to within 0·5 of a cable (less in parts) and should be followed along accordingly. When within 1·5 cables of the stone beacon on the rocks in the middle of the channel keep 15m off the E shore and as soon as the

rocks extending S of Marks Point (Umrycan Point on chart 2698) come abeam, make good a due S course to the W shore. At this stage the tide may make steering seem peculiar to newcomers, as maximum spring rate is 8 kn with a drop of 0·4m causing rapids, so have the engine running even if there is a good wind. Keep the W shore close aboard (to avoid being swept onto Scalpmore Rock) until well into Pan Bay before turning out to pass the SE point of that bay. Pass 1·5 cables off Deegagh Point (Cranford Point on chart 2698) and beyond Cranford Bay leave Cranford Rock beacon close to starboard. Next steer for a small islet 4 cables close in down the shore (a black dot on the chart inset, Otter I on chart 2698) and when it is nearly abeam turn to port so as to leave Greencastle Islet (a rock capped with grass) and Gowan Black Rocks (marked with a bent perch) 0·5 of a cable to port. When halfway between Gowan Black Rocks and Ranny Point (with a stone beacon) turn to starboard and steer about 205° towards an island 1M away covered with conifers. It is called Inishyweel. This course leads between the unmarked and dangerous Williamson and Ranny Rocks. When the first of the Long Islands comes abeam to port alter course to SW so as to avoid the spit off these islands. When Milford Flour Mill comes in line with the E side of Inishyweel steer to pass close NE of that island. Turn to starboard and pass midway between Inishyweel and McSwyne's Bed. (The centre of the bed seldom covers and is marked with a stone beacon.) Finally, if bound for Milford Port pass midway between Hewitsons Island and the beacon SW of it off Ross Point. There is a rock pinnacle 0·5 of a cable outside this beacon.

### Anchorages

North of Dundooan rocks in 3·5m to 5·5m, sand. A well sheltered but isolated anchorage out of the main tide but with variable eddies which makes a yacht sheer about. Handy if leaving in the morning as it is only 1·5M from the bar.

### MELMORE BAY

Inside Low and High Bar Rock to the W is reported to be well sheltered and to have good holding ground in 3m. This bay is on the starboard side going in and is not the Melmore Bay which faces W.

### FANNY'S BAY (*Fanny Hole on chart 2698*)

Approach described above. An excellent anchorage secure in all winds, uncomfortable only in SE wind and relatively calm in W and NW gales. Head towards the boatyard and anchor in 2m when Crannoge Point touches the E shore of the seaward channel. It is advisable to buoy the anchor.

**Facilities:** The patent slip can be used for landing. No shops nearer than Downings, a 1M walk across the hill.

### ROSNAKILL BAY

Rosnakill bay, just N of Broad Water, is easily entered and well sheltered. Anchor in 3·5m towards the SE side.

### Caution

North Water is inaccessible due to a high voltage cable 6m above HW which crosses the N end of Moross Channel. There is a low telephone wire 0·25M S of this dangerous cable.

### CRANFORD BAY

Cranford Bay in Broad Water is a good anchorage. Towards the NW end in 3·4m is a suitable place. The chart, and local moored boats, indicate other suitable places for anchoring.

**Facilities:** None, except a road along the shore.

### MILFORD PORT

HW −0245 Dover. Rise (HW): 1·4-1·1m. There is 1·8m alongside Milford Bakery quay which may be used with permission from the company office nearby. Plenty of space to anchor SW of the quay in 3m or 4m, soft mud.

**Facilities:** Small shop nearby, water from bakery. At Milford, 1M away, all stores, large garage, good small hotel, bus to Londonderry. EC Monday.

### Coast

Between Mulroy and Sheep Haven there are many

*Fanny's Bay from S.*

*Cranford Bay from SW on the edge of Broadwater.*

rocks and if coming in from seaward the coast should not be approached within 1M. However if going in good conditions from Mulroy to Sheep Haven or vice versa, the passage inside Frenchman's Rock and between Carrickguill and Carnabollion is safe and interesting. Chart 2699 has useful transits.

## TRANAROSSAN BAY
This is a pleasant temporary anchorage in offshore wind. Anchor either in 8m E of Carnabantry or in not less than 5m off Rosses Strand, which is believed to extend somewhat further out than is shown on the chart.

**Facilities:** None. Tormore Rocks provide some shelter in NW wind but in general Ravedy Roads in Mulroy Bay is preferable in W and NW winds. Doagh Bay, used by curraghs, is very exposed and not recommended.

## SHEEP HAVEN
HW −0515 Dover. Rise (HW): 4·0-3·0m. This bay is 4M wide. It is easily accessible in daylight and provides safe anchorage in all summer weather. Rinnafaghla Point on the E side is lowlying, rocky and foul for 3 cables off. The W point is Horn Head, the end of a peninsula with up to 200m high cliffs.

### Tidal streams
Tidal streams in the bay are weak except off Ards Bay.

### Danger
Wherryman Rocks, which dry 1·5m and 2m, lie about 1 cable off the E shore 2·25M in from Rinnafaghla Point. Be sure to avoid them when approaching or leaving Downings. Duncap Head in line with Horn Head is a good clearing transit – the chart shows 2 others.

*Milford Quay from South looking towards Broadwater.*

## Lights

Portnablaghy Leading Lts. Oc 6s7m/12m2M in line
125° 15′. Downings pierhead Fl.R 3s.

## Anchorages

### DOWNINGS (*"Downies" on chart*)

Downings has a pier with about 1·5m alongside its
outer end which provides security against all summer
winds but is subject to scend. Anchor SW of the pierhead. SE of it there is less depth than charted. There
are 8 visitors' mooring buoys located about 0·1M SE
of Downies Pier Head.

**Facilities:** Grocery shop beside the pier. Water from
pump. Fuel 300m away. Hotels. Downings is a
very busy holiday village. Bus to Londonderry.
EC Wed.

## POLLCORMICK INLET

Pollcormick Inlet, 2 cables W of Downings pier, provides excellent anchorage in peaceful surroundings
in 3m, sand. It is a short scramble across the point to
the pier. Local boats remain here all the year.

## ARDS BAY

Ards Bay, 1·5M S of Pollcormick, probably provides
the best shelter in Sheep Haven, but the bar can
be dangerous if there is a big sea running in. The
tide runs strongly over the bar and along the channel
inside, the flood starting in at +0120 and the ebb
at −0500 Dover. As well as the beacon (painted
green) on Bar Rock on chart 2699 there are 3 perches
along the NW shore inside: one on Yellow Rock,
the second on the rock about 1·5 cables SW of

*Downings ("Downies" on chart) from SE.*

Yellow Rock, and the third on a rock just N of Bath Point.

**Directions**

The least depth on the bar in the entrance is 2·4m so in settled conditions most yachts can enter safely at LW. After passing 0·5 of a cable E of Bar Rock beacon, head S till the second perch opens to the left of the Yellow Rock perch (they are in line 220°). Then turn in and pass close SE of these 2 perches, anchoring outside their line about 0·5 of a cable beyond the second one.

**Facilities:** Slip. The estate ashore belongs to a Friary so one should ask for permission to walk through it, and to use the slip. On the S side of Bath Point there is a quay which dries. The anchorage shown on the

chart in the centre of the bay is intended for larger vessels. It should be quite safe for a yacht but is less convenient, not accessible near LW and probably rather difficult to find, particularly as the position of the channel is understood to have altered somewhat.

**MARBLEHILL BAY**

Marblehill Bay is 0·75M wide and very pretty. In off-shore wind and absence of swell it is a good temporary anchorage. Anchor towards the NW end in 3m or 4m. The beach here is not as flat as elsewhere. It is frequented by holidaymakers and is the only place to land.

**Facilities:** None.

*Ards Bay in Sheephaven from NE.*

## PORTNABLAGHY BAY

This bay is foul with rocks all round and is much exposed to swell which could be dangerous. There is temporary anchorage in the middle of the bay in about 4m in suitable weather.

### Leading lights

Oc 6s 7m/12m 2M bearing 125° 15′. The pier dries alongside with rocky bottom.

**Facilities:** Stores, fuel, hotel.

## DUNFANAGHY QUAY

Dunfanaghy Quay is accessible at HW but the bay dries out 7 cables to seaward of it and there is nothing to mark the way in. The bay is fully exposed to dangerous swell. The quay is therefore definitely not recommended, nor is the anchorage in the bay.

### Coast

Ummera Rocks, which dry at LW, lie 2 cables offshore with a reef inside them 0·5M SW of Horn Head. To be sure of avoiding them keep Melmore Head in sight till past Ummera Head. From here a direct course to Inishbofin is clear. There are dangerous rocks N of Tramore Bay, a temporary anchorage in off-shore

wind. If heading there it is possible in calm conditions to pass inside all the rocks by keeping 1 cable off the cliffs S of Templebreaga Head. Otherwise pass 2 cables outside Carricknaherwy, which does not cover, and then steer for the SW end of Tramore strand till Marfagh Point at its NE end comes abeam, when it is safe to turn in.

## BALLYNESS HARBOUR

This harbour is too shallow for most yachts and can only be entered in very settled conditions. The bar is fully exposed and variable in position. The leading marks shown on chart 2752 are Iso W 4s. Ldg. 119°29′. Ebb tide runs at about 3 knots. Anchor off the pier, the wooden end of which is now ruined.

**Facilities:** Nearest stores at Falcarragh 1·5M away.

## INISHBOFIN, INISHDOOEY AND INISHBEG

These are low-lying grassy islands extending from the mainland halfway towards Tory. Only Inishbofin is now inhabited. The passage between it and the mainland dries and should not be attempted. Keelasmore Sound the passage N of Inishbofin, is a good short cut if bound from Horn Head to Bloody Foreland. Reefs and rocks which dry extend from the SW side of

*Marblehill Bay from S.*

Inishdooey, 1 cable off its S point and over 2 cables at the NE end of the sound. In the SE entrance of the sound keep just a little nearer the S end of Inishdooey to avoid Toberglassan Rock which has 1·5m over it and at the NW end keep between 1 and 2 cables off the N end of Inishbofin.

## TOBERGLASSAN BAY
Toberglassan Bay, the SW side of Keelasmore Sound, is most attractive in the absence of swell, to which it is fairly open. It is sheltered in winds from SSE through SW to WNW. Chart 2752 is necessary to avoid Toberglassan Rock when entering. Anchor in about 4m, sand.

**Facilities:** Fresh water spring in the rocks on the SE side of the bay. Small shop on the SE side of the island.

## INISHBOFIN BAY
Inishbofin Bay, S of the island, is exposed to swell and W winds. Magheroarty pier at the S end of the bay is used by the Tory Island mailboat. It is sometimes possible to anchor temporarily 3 cables off the pier in 4m. The roadstead at the N end of the bay has somewhat better shelter. Inishbofin boats lie on moorings off the village pier W of the drying spit. Lt Fl.8s3m3M on pier. HW −0530 Dover. Rise (HW): 3·9-3·0m.

## Coast
Between Magheroarty and Bloody Foreland is steep-to and a berth of 4 cables clears all dangers.

## TORY ISLAND
Tory Island is a slab of rock 2M long tilted towards Bloody Foreland with cliffs on its N side and a low S

148

*Portnablaghy to the South of Dunfanaghy Bay from W.*

shore. The high torrs from which the island gets its name are a fine sight at its NE corner. As the most isolated inhabited island on the Irish coast it is an interesting port of call and, unless there is a high swell, it is usually possible to stop for a few hours or overnight.

**Anchorage**

Local boats remain at anchor for much of the summer in Camusmore Bay and if the islanders are not pulling them up for the night it is usually a sign that it is safe to stay. However the weather is particularly liable to sudden change in this area so one must be prepared to leave quickly. A new pier and break-water is under construction here (1999) which will, on completion, provide greatly improved shelter for boats. *(See page 150.)* Toberglassan Bay, described above, offers good shelter close at hand. The population is about 170.

**Facilities:** Mailboat 3 times a fortnight to Magh-

eroarty. Wintertime services are planned for 3 times a fortnight but this is entirely dependent on weather. PO with telephone. Limited groceries. The island has a licensed Hotel, Ostan Thoraigh, just above the pier, which opens daily at 1600. No fuel.

**Lights**

On the NW point of Tory Island Fl (4) 30s40m27M from 27m high black tower with one white band, obscured from 277° to 302° Racon. Radiobeacon, *(see Appendix 5).*

**Tidal streams**

In Tory Sound tidal streams start running NE at +0230 Dover and turn SW at −0330 Dover, max rate at springs 2 kn. There is a tide rip off the NW corner of the island.

**Caution**

Between Camusmore Bay and the W of the island sunken ledges extend up to 3 cables off-shore and

*Port Doon on the Southern Shore of Tory Island from SSE.*

outside their W end are Rinnamurreeny Rocks which dry. In bad weather there are breakers a long way outside the rocks so this coast should be given a berth of 1M. This danger is of course greatest when coming from the SW at night. Elsewhere round the island a berth of 2 cables clears all dangers.

**Anchorages**
There are three available to be chosen according to weather.

**CAMUSMORE BAY**
Camusmore Bay is the most convenient for exploring the island in fine weather. A new extention to the pier, along with a substantial breakwater, is under construction here *(see Chartlet)*. The entrance channel and outer area of the proposed harbour have been dredged to a depth of 3·0m, but work on the southern L-shaped section of the pier and breakwater has yet to be carried out in 1999–2000.

**PORT DOON**
Port Doon, at the E end, is sheltered from SW through W to NNW. Anchor in the mouth of the bay in about 6m, sand. In the bay there is a quay 24m long with a least depth of 1·5m alongside, almost twice as much in places as the bottom is rock. If the sea is calm, it is convenient for berthing.

**PORTNAGLASS** (*The Green Port*)
Portnaglass is on the N side 0·5M E of the lighthouse. It is sheltered from NW through W to SE. There is a small jetty and steps up the cliffs where the lighthouse stores used to be landed. Anchor off in 10m to 18m.

**PORTACHULLA**
Portnachulla is just NNW of Port Doon and not named on the metric chart. It is not recommended. It looks a possibility on the chart but is in fact a bad place with many boulders and difficult for landing.

150

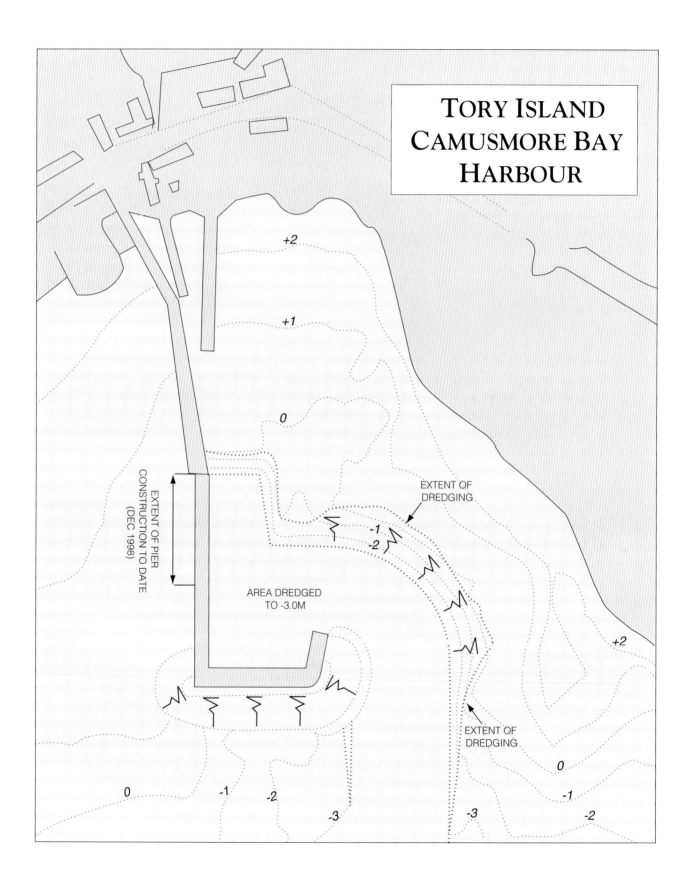

TORY ISLAND
CAMUSMORE BAY
HARBOUR

EXTENT OF PIER
CONSTRUCTION TO DATE
(DEC 1998)

AREA DREDGED
TO -3.0M

EXTENT OF
DREDGING

EXTENT OF
DREDGING

+2

+1

0

-1
-2

+2

0
-1

0

-1

-2

-3

-3

-2

## BLOODY FORELAND

Bloody Foreland, the NW extremity of Ireland, is a very low point from which reefs extend for 1 cable. It slopes up very gradually towards Bloody Foreland Hill which is 1·5M inshore and 315m high. Swell is apt to run high off the point so it should be rounded at a respectful distance.

### Light

A small concrete beacon near the end of the point shows Fl WG 14m 7·5s W6 G4M W to seaward between 062° and 232°, G between these bearings and the land on either side. The green sector should of course be avoided at night but note that it has a luminous range of only 4M which is less than the distance to Inishbeg which is within the sector. However if sailing round this coast at night it is simplest and safest to pass outside Tory Island.

The coast south beyond Bloody Foreland is described in a companion volume, *South and West Coasts of Ireland – Sailing Directions*, published by Irish Cruising Club Publications Ltd. In order to assist visiting yachtsmen, a fifth chapter was added in the previous edition. It is in two parts: (i) Crossing to Scotland and (ii) Refuge Harbour – Dunmore East.

154

bound for Port Ellen from Portrush with a commanding breeze sailing at around 5 kn, a good time to leave is 4 hours before HW Dover. You can then steer the direct course to Port Ellen and the tide will change at about halfway and should even out but you should be prepared to alter course depending on how you find you have been set at the halfway mark, keeping a bit in hand to the E to avoid being set W if arriving late at the S end of Islay. The total set of a tide in the outer part of the North Channel at springs usually works out at about 10M.

Winds tend to change direction a point or two and blow harder in the narrows between Kintyre and Fair Head due to the funnel effect of the land. NW and SE winds are most affected. NW winds in the Irish Sea often back a couple of points as you round Fair Head. The same funnel effect increases the speed of S winds between Jura and Kintyre.

### Very Small Craft
Best departure point is Cushendun, for passage 16M to Southend (average 4 hours). Leave at −0130 Belfast, which is 1 hour before local LW. This gives you time to get clear of the overfalls which occur on the Antrim coast on the first hour of flood and lets you be in the open water during the slack, to get a bit of help from the flood into the Clyde to work E. It is advisable in a small boat to keep at least 3M S of Deas Point, now called Sron Uamha, the S tip of Mull of Kintyre, as there is a tendency to ground swell and broken water round it, particularly near LW. Returning from Southend, 1 hour before local LW is again a good time to start to get clear of Sanda at slack water and have the help of the flood S along the Antrim coast. The rip extending 3M or 4M N of Garron Point on the ebb at +0200 Dover is bad enough to be troublesome to small craft and should be avoided if possible.

### Places to Avoid
If there is any sea running avoid the tide rip off the Mull of Kintyre, the close vicinity of Sanda, and, on the Irish side, the vicinity of Torr Point and Rathlin. If forced to cross the North Channel from Islay in bad weather, which should be avoided if at all possible, the fishermen say it is better to keep down the Kintyre coast as the sea runs a little easier there than farther W. The worst tide rip in the whole area is off the Rhinns of Islay and in a blow this should be avoided at all costs. However, Portnahaven, at the SW tip of Islay inside Orsay Island, is a good bunkhole and a good departure point for a visit to Donegal (29M to Inishtrahull). Directions given below.

### PORTNAHAVEN
HW−0110 Oban (roughly +0540 Dover). Rise: 2·6-2·3-1·3-0·5 m. The tide runs at 8 kn at springs outside Orsay where it can cause dangerous overfalls. It is fairly strong inside the island. Entry should not be considered except in reasonably quiet conditions. Old Chart 3116 did not show great details and metric Chart 2168 is slightly smaller scale. The NW entrance between unmarked rocks is impossible in onshore winds. The entrance N of Orsay Island is used by locals but dangerous for visitors. Only the SE entrance can be recommended. Keep slightly closer to the Islay shore than to Orsay, follow it round N and anchor inshore off a new concrete pier in 3·3 m, sand. There is a completely sheltered pool with 0·8 m just inside the gut leading to Portnahaven village; it is best to pass N of the covered rock outside the gut.

**Facilities:** Small shops, pub, PO.

### LOSSIT BAY
Lossit Bay, 3M N of Portnahaven, is a good anchorage in offshore winds, clean sand.

**Facilities:** None

## Part 2 – Refuge Harbour of Dunmore East to Tuskar Rock

A yacht coming from the S to cruise on the E coast of Ireland will normally pass outside Tuskar Rock and head for Rosslare or Arklow. In the event of strong N to NE winds it may be advisable to leave Tuskar Lt, the Saltee Islands with Coningbeg Lt.F to starboard and head for Dunmore East until the weather moderates. These directions are included to cover such an eventuality.

### Caution
The sea area off the SE corner of Ireland is one to be avoided in bad weather. The tide runs strong right across the entrance to St. George's Channel, 2·5 kn at springs, so it can be very rough even right out to sea. Between the Coningbeg and the Tuskar there are many rocks, shoals and irregular soundings up to 7M offshore. In gale conditions with wind against tide there may be heavy overfalls and par-

ticularly in bad visibility, yachts should stand well off the Saltees until conditions improve or alternatively set course for Dunmore East or Rosslare Harbour.

**Tuskar Rock** is 5m high and lies 6M E by N of Carnsore Point, the SE extremity of Ireland. A tall white lighthouse and a radio mast stand on the island. It is clean on the E side but foul for 1 cable N and W. Gypsy Rock is 2 cables NNW with 2m over it, 2·5 cables SW is a rock awash and 6·5 cables SSW is South Rock with 2·4m over it.

Yachts should give the Tuskar a good berth, especially in light weather for as well as the tide setting onto the rock there is probably an eddy running back towards it on the other side.

### Lights
A light is shown from a lighthouse on the rock, Q

155

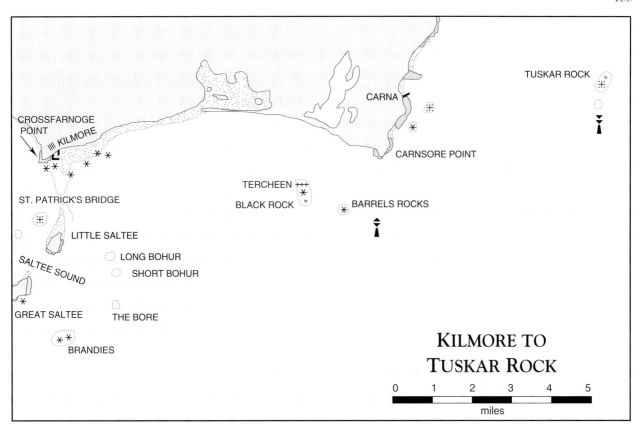

### KILMORE TO TUSKAR ROCK

CROSSFARNOGE POINT

KILMORE

CARNA

CARNSORE POINT

TUSKAR ROCK

ST. PATRICK'S BRIDGE

TERCHEEN

BLACK ROCK

BARRELS ROCKS

LITTLE SALTEE

LONG BOHUR

SHORT BOHUR

SALTEE SOUND

GREAT SALTEE

THE BORE

BRANDIES

0 1 2 3 4 5
miles

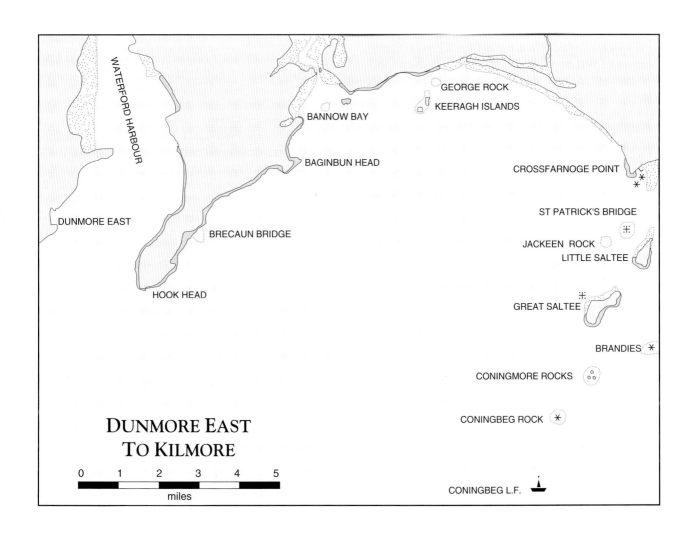

### DUNMORE EAST TO KILMORE

WATERFORD HARBOUR

BANNOW BAY

GEORGE ROCK

KEERAGH ISLANDS

BAGINBUN HEAD

CROSSFARNOGE POINT

DUNMORE EAST

BRECAUN BRIDGE

ST PATRICK'S BRIDGE

JACKEEN ROCK

LITTLE SALTEE

HOOK HEAD

GREAT SALTEE

BRANDIES

CONINGMORE ROCKS

CONINGBEG ROCK

CONINGBEG L.F.

0 1 2 3 4 5
miles

*Kilmore Quay from S.*

lies 3 cables W of the centre of the island. 2·5 cables S of the S point of the island lies Shoal Rock with 0·9m over it, but its position is usually indicated by a tide ripple. Panstown Rock, close to the SW side of the S point of the island, shows above HW and Molly Hoy lies a little over 1 cable to NW of Panstown and shows. There is a group of drying rocks close to the E side of the S tip of the island called the Seven Heads. Makestone Rock shows and is close to the shore on the E side of the island.

### NORTH SALTEE ISLAND

North Saltee Island is 35m high and 1·75M off the shore. The beacon shown on the chart at its SE end is a cairn of loose stones. There are a number of rocks off the island. There is a ledge extending N which almost joins Kilmore Spit, a ledge running S from the shore, which together are called St. Patrick's Bridge, described below. Murroch's Rock, awash at LW, lies over 0·5M NW of the North Saltee and there is a rock with only 0·2m over it 0·5M W of the centre of the island. Jackeen Rock lies 1M to the WNW of the S of the North Saltee and has 1·5m over it. Galgee Rock, awash at LW, lies 0·75 of a cable to the SW of the S point of the island. Goose Rock which dries 2·5m is 0·25M NW of Galgee Rock and 0·75 of a cable off-shore.

### Ornithology

There are reputed to be over 300 different species of birds to be found at various times during the year on the Saltee Islands.

### SALTEE SOUND *(see Chartlet)*

This must be approached with caution owing to the numerous outlying rocks. Making the sound from the E steer for the N tip of S Saltee until you are nearly midway between the two islands and then steer 330° through the sound so as to avoid Sebber Bridge and the shoal soundings running N from S Saltee. Do not carry on too far on this course as it leads up near Jackeen Rock so alter course for the Hook when the cairn of stones on SE corner of N Saltee is in line with the SW point of that island, bearing 104°. Generally keep closer to the N Saltee when going through but not within 2 cables of it. Tidal streams in the sound are strong, reaching 3·5kn at springs, but do not set fairly through.

### ST PATRICK'S BRIDGE

St. Patrick's Bridge is the shortest and simplest route from Carnsore Point to Hook Head and is constantly used by fishing boats with seasonal marks to guide the stranger.. The deepest water is only 2·4m and is about half-way between Kilmore Quay and

N Saltee, a little nearer the latter. It can be recommended to an E or W bound yacht in fair weather, clear visibility, with no heavy swell. When a heavy swell is running Saltee Sound is to be preferred.

### KILMORE QUAY (see Chartlet)
Kilmore Quay is just E of Crossfarnoge (or Forlorn) Point and just W of St. Patrick's Bridge. The harbour consists of a W pier with 2·4m alongside and an E pier with 4·4m alongside. It is in active use by locally owned fishing boats. There is a marina with a capacity for 55 boats with about 2·4m water depth in the NE corner of the Harbour.

### Directions
Coming from the W take care to pass at least 0·5M S of Crossfarnoge Point so as to avoid Forlorn Rock with 1·5m over it which is 0·5M SSW of the point. When the E end of the breakwater bears 010° alter course to port until the leading Lts (Oc4s) are in line bearing 008°G. Coming from the E this line will be picked up almost immediately after crossing St.

Patrick's Bridge. It leads in safely between the rocks called Lings on Chart 2740 (but known as the Blackberries locally) which never dry but have very little water over them. A light, QRG 7m, 5M is shown from the end of the breakwater, visible between 269° through N to 077°. The G sector which leads safely in being from 354° to 003°.

There are leading lights which consist of White pylons with Red stripes to the E of the Harbour, Oc.W 4s 20m Brg 007°.8 in position Rear 52°10.44N 6°35.06W Front 52°10.34N 6°35·07W. These mark a dredged channel which clears the E side of the W breakwater. This channel is dredged to a depth of about 1·9m. Between the 1st April and 12th September each year the passage across St. Patrick's Bridge will be marked by Port and Starboard Channel Buoys.

(a) Green Starboardhand Conical Buoy Fl.G6s 2M in position 52°09.14N 06°34.7W

(b) Red Porthand Can Buoy Fl.R6s 2M in position 52°09.3N 06° 34.7W

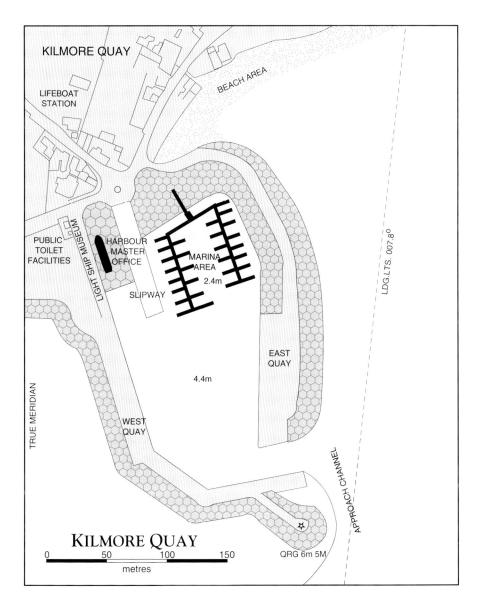

KILMORE QUAY

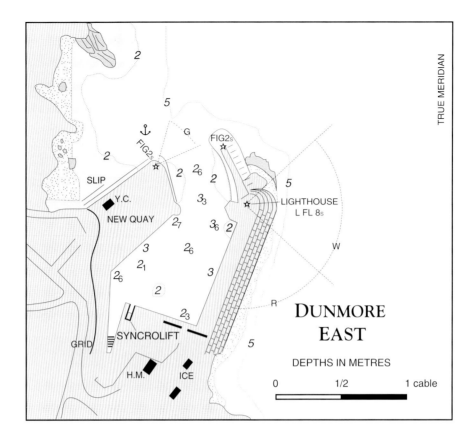

**DUNMORE EAST**

DEPTHS IN METRES

**Facilities**

Water and diesel on quay. Showers and Toilets available at 'Stella Maris', Petrol, PO and groceries in village, also chandlery, Hardware and Marine Supplies, 2 Pubs, plus Hotel Saltees and Silver Fox Restaurant. HM can be called on VHF Ch 16,8,37 (occasional manning only) Marindus Engineering reported offering very good service. A RNLI lifeboat is stationed here. Blue Flag Marina. HM Phone and Fax 053-29955.

**SALTEES TO HOOK**

The rocks W of the islands have already been described. Ballyteige Bay lies W of Crossfarnoge Point, and while its E end is clear, there are rocks and shoals in its NW end. The Keeragh's are 2 islets 6m high and are 1M offshore with a reef extending from them in to the mainland. George Rock over 0·5M NE of the Keeragh's has only 1·2m over it and is 0·5M offshore. Bannow Inlet W of the Keeragh's is very shoal and has a bar with only 0·3m of water over it. Selskar Shoal is in the centre of the entrance and has 0·3m over it while Selskar Rock dries 2m and lies 0·25M off Clammer's Pt. on the E side of Bannow Bay. Entry to Bannon Bay Inlet should not be attempted without local knowledge. There is a shoal rock about halfway between Clammer's Pt. and Ingrid Pt., over which there is only ·3m at LAT. Baginbun Head is conspicuous with its Martello Tower and is SW of Bannow Bay. If beating down for the Hook the tides are slack inshore. Do not go too close in between Baginbun Head and the Hook as

the shore here is foul for a few cables off and Brecaun Bridge 2M from Hook Head extends 3 cables off the shore and has a depth of only 1·4m at its outer extremity. Forth Mountain, the only high point in SE Wexford, open to Baginbun Point 048° clears Brecaun Bridge. On a SW'ly course, keeping Hook Tr. to the E of Slade's Castle will also clear this danger.

**Offshore Anchorage**

Baginbun and Bannow Bays are completely exposed to the SE but give good shelter in fresh W wind, so in these conditions, when the Hook Race is a formidable obstacle to any small yacht, they might provide a welcome overnight stopping place. The recommended anchorage is at the SW end of Bannow Bay just N of Ingard Point off the small drying dock there in 3m sand, good holding. Ingard Point, 1M N of Baginbun Point, is foul for 1·4 cables offshore; the mark to clear this is the largest house in Fethard village open N of the dock. Selskar Shoal, mentioned above, is 0·75M ENE of Ingard Point so if beating in do not go too far in that The dock has been dredged, exposing the rock in places; it has a depth of 1·5m at half tide except towards the head; the best berth is just within the E pier.

**Facilities**

Water at the dock. Fuel, diesel, provisions at Fethard, 1M. Also hotel, restaurants, P.O., pubs and doctor.

Baginbun Bay also offers excellent shelter and holding. Watch out for lobster pots up to 10M off-

*Dunmore East from N.*

shore between the Hook and Kilmore, and salmon nets extending from this point and more pots about 2M SE of it.

## HOOK HEAD

Hook Head is the end of the low peninsula at the E side of the entrance to Waterford Harbour. A rocky ledge extends 2 cables SW of the point. There is a dangerous wreck 1·25 cables W of Doornoge Point, or about 0·5M NW of the Hook.

## Lights

The Hook lighthouse is very distinctive consisting of a massive 12th century tower, 24m high and about 12m wide, white with 2 black bands, upon which stands a shorter modern light-tower. It shows Fl W 3s, 46m, 23M. Horn (2) 45s Racon.

## Tidal Streams

From the Hook to the Saltees the tidal streams set E and W. The E-going stream begins at −0050 Cobh (+0545 Dover) and the W-going stream at +0553

Cobh (−0015 Dover). The rate near the Saltees is about 2kn. Off the Hook itself, especially in strong W winds there is a dangerous tidal race known as Tower Race, which extends about 1M S of the head. In general it is at its strongest from +0420 Cobh to −0455 Cobh (−0130 to +0140 Dover). If the race is expected to be bad a yacht should keep outside the 20m line, when rounding Hook Point. (*See also tidal streams Waterford Harbour entrance*)

## Distances

Carnsore Point to Coningbeg Light Float 14M
Coningbeg Light Float to Pollock Rock Buoy
56·25M
Carnsore Point to Hook (via Saltee Sound) 21·5M

## DUNMORE EAST (see Chartlet)

Dunmore East is a small artificial harbour on the W side of the entrance to Waterford Harbour. The village of Dunmore East is a popular holiday resort. The harbour is the base for the important autumn herring fishery during which it is crowded with fishing boats.

Recent major improvements have given it a depth of 2m to 3·4m and made it safe in all summer weather, though there may be a swell along the NW wall in S winds. It is a popular port of call for yachts which are made welcome, though owners are reminded that it is primarily a fishing port and they should take care not to inconvenience fishing boats.

## Lights

The large grey granite Tower White Lantern on the pier shows Fl WR 8s, 13m, W 17M R 13M, W from 225° to 310°, R 310° to 004°, obscured elsewhere. A pillar on the end of the breakwater which forms an extension of the pier shows Fl R 2s 6m 4M. Vis 000°–310°. On the N point of the W quay a light Fl G 2s 6m 4M shows from 165° to 246°.

## Directions

By day the white pilot look-out on Black Nob just S of the harbour is conspicuous as is the ice plant and the pier itself. Enter under power or much reduced sail and berth at the E pier, then report to the HM for instructions. The Waterford Harbour SC has a club-house on the NW quay. There are Yacht moorings outside the harbour in the bight N of the NW quay which is a good sheltered berth in fine weather and W winds; these moorings are allocated by the HM. There are two baulks of timber with tyre fenders alongside the New Quay to facilitate yachts, 3m at LAT.

Alternatively yachts may lie alongside berthed fishing boats but must be prepared to move at the request of the Harbour Master or fishing skippers. 3m at LAT. Yacht moorings are laid outside the harbour in the Bays N of the North West quay where good shelter is to be obtained in all but strong winds from NE to SE. Advice on vacant moorings can be obtained from WHSC on VHF 16 or 39.

By night approaching from the E, give Hook Head a berth of 0·5 M or more depending on the state of the sea. Alter course for Dunmore East light when in the red sector. From the W hold course for Hook Head until the red sector of Dunmore East light is entered then alter course for it. The white sector of the light shows across the estuary and up it and clears Creadon Head.

## Facilities

Water from a tap at SE corner of quay and from tap at WHSC. Diesel obtained on E quay. Good restaurants, pubs, hotels, shops and P.O. in village. WHSC has its Club House on the W quay. Visiting yachtsmen are made welcome and showers and toilets are available during normal hours. RNLI lifeboat lies afloat. There are good public heads on the S quay at HM office and showers with plenty of hot water near the syncrolift open at 0800.

WHSC 051-383230/383389 VHF 16/33, HM 051-383166 Diesel, V. Cobden 051-383651.

Dunmore East has the Pilot Station for Waterford Harbour, telephone and fax 051-383261. VHF Ch. 16, 14,12.

# INDEX CHART

*Large scale charts of individual places are denoted by a number against the relevant name.*

*633   indicates that a plan is shown on chart  633*

*For details of smaller scale general charts see Catalogue of Admiralty Charts NP 131.*

## NOTE

*The charts shown on this index represent those published at the date given at the foot. They are liable to alteration and amendment.*

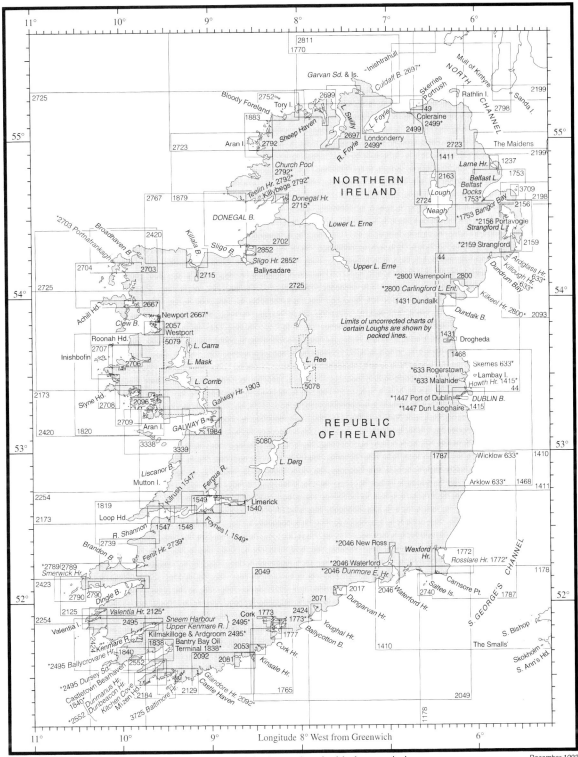

*December 1993*

# Appendix 1

## ADMIRALTY CHARTS AND PUBLICATIONS

| Chart No. | Title of Charts (most plans larger scale) | Scale 1: | Publication Date |
|---|---|---|---|
| 1123 | Western Approaches to St. George's Channel and Bristol Channel | 500,000 | 11-97 |
| 1121 | Irish Sea and St. George's and North Channels | 500,000 | 11-92 |
| 1410 | St. George's Channel | 200,000 | 2-92 |
| 1787 | Carnsore Point to Wicklow Head | 100,000 | 11-91 |
| 1772 | Rosslare and Wexford Harbours with approaches | Various | 3-95 |
| 1468 | Arklow to the Skerries Islands | 100,000 | 24-8-84 |
| 633 | Plans of Arklow, Wicklow, Malahide, Rogerstown, Skerries Killough and Ardglass | Various | 11-11-77 |
| 1411 | Irish Sea – Western Part | 200,000 | 4-92 |
| 1415 | Dublin Bay | 25,000 | 23-9-88 |
| 1447 | Port of Dublin and Dun Laoghaire Harbour | 7,500 | 8-96 |
| 44 | Howth to Ardglass | 100,000 | 20-12-85 |
| 1431 | Drogheda and Dundalk | Various | 28-7-88 |
| 2800 | Carlingford Lough (plans of Entrance, Warrenpoint and Kilkeel) | 20,000 | 12-94 |
| 2093 | Southern approach to North Channel | 100,000 | 14-10-88 |
| 2156 | Strangford Lough | 37,500 | 24-6-88 |
| 2159 | Strangford Narrows | 12,500 | 12-83 |
| 2198 | North Channel – southern part | 75,000 | 25-9-87 |
| 3709 | Copeland Islands and Donaghadee Sound | 12,500 | 7-12-73 |
| 1753 | Belfast Lough (with plans of Belfast Docks and Bangor Bay) | 3,750 | 2-91 |
| 1237 | Larne Lough and approaches | 10,000 | 4-91 |
| 2199 | North Channel – northern part | 75,000 | 13-9-89 |
| 2798 | Lough Foyle to Sanda Island including Rathlin Island | 75,000 | 2-9-88 |
| 49 | Portrush and approaches | 15,000 | 7-2-75 |
| 2499 | Lough Foyle | 40,000 | 4-95 |
| 2811 | Sheep Haven to Lough Foyle, including Inishtrahull | 75,000 | 25-9-87 |
| 2697 | Lough Swilly (including Culdaff Bay, scale 10,000) | 37,500 | 27-2-76 |
| 2699 | Horn Head to Fanad Head with Mulroy Bay | 30,000 | 11-98 |
| 2752 | Bloody Foreland to Horn Head, including Tory Island | 30,000 | 12-12-75 |
| 2723 | Western Approaches to the North Channel | 200,000 | 12-90 |

**Publications:**

Irish Coast Pilot (14th Edition 1998).

Admiralty Tide Tables, volume 1.

Admiralty List of Lights, volume A, 1998.

Tidal Stream Atlases: No. 256 Irish Sea and Bristol Channel 1992.
                No. 218 N. Coast of Ireland and W Coast of Scotland 1995

Chart No. 5011 Symbols and abbreviations used on Admiralty Charts 1998.

*International Admiralty Chart Agent:*

Todd Chart Agency Ltd., 4 Seacliff Road, BANGOR, County Down, N. Ireland BT20 5EY.
Tel: +44 (0) 1247 466640. Fax: +44 (0) 1247 471070. E-mail: admiralty@toddchart.co.uk
*From 01 June 1999:* Tel: +44 (0) 28 91466640. Fax: +44 (0) 28 91471070.

*Admiralty Chart Agent:*

Windmill Leisure & Marine, 3 Windmill Lane, Sir John Rogerson's Quay, DUBLIN 2.
Tel: +353 (0) 1 677 2008. Fax: +353 (0) 1 671 4107.

*Non-Correcting Admiralty Distributors:*

Union Chandlery Ltd., Anderson's Quay, CORK. Tel: +353 (0) 21 271643. Fax: +353 (0) 21 273426. Telex: 75912.
Galway Maritime Services Ltd., Merchants Road, New Docks, GALWAY. Tel: +353 (0) 91 64456
Greencastle Nautical Supplies, Carrowhugh, GREENCASTLE, County Donegal. Tel: +353 (0) 77 81148.

# Appendix 2

## FOR CALCULATING TIMES OF LOCAL HIGH-WATER AND LOW-WATER

Difference of time between secondary ports and the local standard ports.

| Standard Port **DUBLIN** (North Wall) | HW at GMT | | L.W. at GMT | |
|---|---|---|---|---|
| | 0001 & 1200 | 0700 & 1900 | 0500 & 1700 | 0001 & 1200 |
| Secondary Ports | *Time differences* | | | |
| Rosslare Harbour | −0440 | −0710 | −0440 | −0710 |
| Wexford Harbour | −0350 | −0720 | −0325 | −0725 |
| Polduff | −0321 | −0431 | −0340 | −0414 |
| Courtown | −0300 | −0400 | −0315 | −0345 |
| Arklow | −0215 | −0255 | −0225 | −0245 |
| Wicklow | −0035 | −0047 | −0038 | −0044 |
| Greystones | −0008 | −0008 | −0008 | −0008 |
| Dun Laoghaire | −0006 | −0001 | −0003 | −0002 |
| Howth | −0005 | −0015 | +0005 | −0005 |
| Malahide Inlet | −0019 | −0013 | +0006 | +0014 |
| Balbriggan | −0021 | −0015 | +0002 | +0010 |
| River Boyne Bar | −0025 | −0015 | +0001 | +0110 |
| Dundalk (Soldiers Pt) | −0010 | −0010 | +0045 | +0001 |
| Cranfield Point | −0027 | −0011 | −0007 | +0017 |
| Warrenpoint | −0020 | −0010 | +0040 | +0040 |

| Standard port **BELFAST** | H.W. at GMT | | L.W. at GMT | |
|---|---|---|---|---|
| | 0100 & 1300 | 0700 & 1900 | 0001 & 1200 | 0600 & 1800 |
| Secondary ports | *Time differences* | | | |
| Kilkeel | +0010 | +0010 | +0001 | +0001 |
| Newcastle | +0025 | +0035 | +0020 | +0040 |
| Killard Point | +0011 | +0021 | +0005 | +0025 |
| Killyleagh | +0157 | +0207 | +0211 | +0231 |
| Portavogie | +0010 | +0020 | +0010 | +0020 |
| Donaghadee | +0020 | +0020 | +0023 | +0023 |
| Carrickfergus | +0005 | +0005 | +0005 | +0005 |
| Larne | +0005 | +0001 | +0010 | −0005 |
| Red Bay | +0022 | −0010 | +0007 | −0017 |
| Cushendun | +0010 | −0030 | +0001 | −0025 |

| Standard Port **LONDONDERRY** | H.W. at GMT | | L.W. at GMT | |
|---|---|---|---|---|
| | 0200 & 1400 | 0900 & 2100 | 0700 & 1900 | 0300 & 1500 |
| Secondary ports | *Time differences* | | | |
| Ballycastle Bay | +0053 | −0147 | +0056 | −0125 |

| Standard Port **LONDONDERRY** | H.W. at GMT | | L.W. at GMT | |
|---|---|---|---|---|
| | 0200 & 1400 | 0800 & 2000 | 1100 & 2300 | 0500 & 1700 |
| Secondary Ports | *Time differences* | | | |
| Portrush | −0105 | −0105 | −0105 | −0105 |
| Coleraine | −0020 | −0130 | −0020 | −0110 |
| Moville | −0046 | −0058 | −0052 | −0108 |
| Culdaff Bay | −0136 | −0156 | −0146 | −0206 |

| Standard port **GALWAY** Secondary Ports | H.W. at GMT 0200 & 1400 | 0900 & 2100 *Time differences* | L.W. at GMT 0200 & 1400 | 0800 & 2000 |
|---|---|---|---|---|
| Inishtrauhull | +0100 | +0100 | +0115 | +0200 |
| Trawbreaga Bay | +0115 | +0059 | +0109 | +0125 |
| Rathmullan | +0125 | +0050 | +0126 | +0118 |
| Mulroy Bar | +0108 | +0052 | +0102 | +0118 |
| Fanny's Bay | +0145 | +0129 | +0151 | +0207 |
| Mulroy Broad Water | +0329 | +0313 | +0351 | +0407 |
| Downings Bay | +0057 | +0043 | +0053 | +0107 |
| Inishbofin Bay | +0040 | +0026 | +0032 | +0046 |

If a tide table for the standard ports Dublin, Belfast, Derry or Galway is available these time differences, from the Admiralty Tide Tables, enable H.W. at the corresponding secondary ports to be found more accurately than in relation to H.W. Dover as indicated in the text. If the tide table gives L.W. this can also be determined. For example: To find the time of L .W. Rosslare. Supposing L .W. Dublin is 2130 BST, i.e., 2030 GMT, this is halfway between the GMTs 1700 and 0001 at the head of the L.W. columns. Between the two Rosslare L.W. Time differences −0440 and −0710 there is 2 hours 30 minutes (2 = 1 hour 15 minutes which is halfway between both time differences, this is then added to the lowest figure ie 0440 + 1 hour 15 minutes = 0555. So deduct this amount from L.W. Dublin 2030–0555 = 1435GMT + 1 hour to arrive at BST, therefore LW at Rosslare is 1535 hours BST.

# Appendix 3

## SHORTEST DISTANCES BETWEEN PORTS (NAUTICAL MILES)

Longships to Wicklow Head . . . . . . . . . 173
Longships to South Rock L. V. . . . . . . . 260
Dun Laoghaire to Port St. Mary . . . . . .  68
Dun Laoghaire to Holyhead . . . . . . . .  52
Dun Laoghaire to Dunmore East . . . . . 100
Dun Laoghaire to Bangor . . . . . . . . . . 101
Donaghadee to Port Patrick . . . . . . . .  19
Larne to Campbeltown . . . . . . . . . . . .  38
Carnlough to Gigha . . . . . . . . . . . . . . .  42
Portrush to Port Ellen, Islay . . . . . . . .  30
Portrush to Gigha . . . . . . . . . . . . . . . .  43
Howth to Bangor . . . . . . . . . . . . . . . . .  90

# Appendix 4

## WAY POINTS

These positions have been prepared to give approximately 1M clearance of prominent headlands, buoys, etc. or approximately 0·5M off the entrance to harbours, when visual fixing should be possible in clear visibility. They should be carefully checked before entering in a Decca Navigator or GPS Aid to Navigation.

| Place | Way Point Positions | Way Point | |
|---|---|---|---|
| Carnsore Point | 1M SE | 52 09 70 N | 06 20 60 W |
| Tuskar Rock Lt. | 1M N | 52 13 20 N | 06 12 40 W |
| Tuskar Rock Lt. | 2M E | 52 12 20 N | 06 09 00 W |
| Rosslare Pier | 0·5 M | 52 16 00 N | 06 20 20 W |
| E Blackwater Buoy | 1M E | 52 28 00 N | 06 06 40 W |
| Cahore Point | 1M E | 52 33 90 N | 06 09 85 W |
| Arklow Harbour | 0·5M E | 52 47 60 N | 06 07 35 W |
| Arklow Lanby | 1M E | 52 39 50 N | 05 56 40 W |
| N Arklow Buoy | 1M E | 52 53 90 N | 05 53 40 W |
| Wicklow Head | 1M E | 52 57 90 N | 05 58 25 W |
| Wicklow Harbour | 0·5 M NE | 52 59 30 N | 06 01 25 W |
| W Codling Buoy | 1M W | 53 06 95 N | 05 56 20 W |
| Muglins Lt. | 1M E | 53 16 05 N | 06 02 70 W |
| Kish Bank Lt. | 1M N | 53 19 65 N | 05 55 40 W |
| Dun Laoghaire Harbour | 0·5M N | 53 18 60 N | 06 07 50 W |
| Baily Lt. | 1M E | 53 21 70 N | 06 01 40 W |
| Howth Harbour | 0·25M N | 53 23 85 N | 06 03 90 W |
| Lambay Island | 1M W | 53 29 35 N | 06 03 70 W |
| Rockabill Lt. | 1M W | 53 35 80 N | 06 01 80 W |
| Drogheda Entrance | 1M E | 53 43 25 N | 06 11 90 W |
| Clogher Head | 1M E | 53 47 70 N | 06 11 20 W |
| Pile Light Dundalk | 1M SE | 53 57 85 N | 06 16 50 W |
| Hellyhunter Buoy | 1M S | 53 59 25 N | 06 02 05 W |
| St John's Point | 1M S | 54 12 60 N | 05 39 50 W |
| Ardglass | 0·5M SE | 54 15 25 N | 05 35 50 W |
| Strangford Lough Whistle Buoy | 0·5M W | 54 18 65 N | 05 29 50 W |
| South Rock LV | 1M E | 54 24 45 N | 05 20 20 W |
| Mew Island Lt. | 2M E | 54 41 90 N | 05 27 30 W |
| Bangor Bay | 0·5M N | 54 40 50 N | 05 40 18 W |
| Carrickfergus Harbour | 0·5M S | 54 42 15 N | 05 48 30 W |
| Black Head Lt. | 1M E | 54 46 00 N | 05 39 52 W |
| Larne Harbour Buoy | 0·5M N | 54 52 20 N | 05 45 55 W |
| Maiden Light | 1M E | 54 55 70 N | 05 41 90 W |
| Carnlough | 0·5M E | 54 59 57 N | 05 58 30 W |
| Red Bay Lt. | 0·5M E | 55 03 95 N | 06 02 20 W |
| Fair Head | 1M N | 55 14 65 N | 06 08 85 W |
| Altacarry Lt. | 1·5M E | 55 18 12 N | 06 07 60 W |
| Bull Point Lt. | 1M W | 55 18 05 N | 06 18 45 W |
| Portrush Harbour | 0·5M W | 55 12 35 N | 06 40 48 W |
| River Bann Entrance | 0·5M N | 55 10 82 N | 06 46 60 W |
| Lough Foyle Whistle Buoy | 0·5M S | 55 14 80 N | 06 52 50 W |
| Inishtrahull Lt. | 1M S | 55 24 82 N | 07 14 55 W |
| Malin Head | 1M W | 55 22 50 N | 07 25 70 W |
| Fanad Head Lt. | 1M N | 55 17 59 N | 07 37 85 W |
| Melmore Head Lt. | 1M N | 55 16 10 N | 07 46 85 W |
| Horn Head | 1M N | 55 14 70 N | 07 59 00 W |
| Inishbeg Island | 1M N | 55 13 40 N | 08 09 62 W |
| Tory Island | 1M N | 55 14 37 N | 08 14 90 W |
| Bloody Foreland Lt. | 1M N | 55 10 50 N | 08 17 00 W |

# Appendix 5

## WEATHER FORECASTS AND MARINE RADIO SERVICES

**Radio Telefis Eireann (RTE Radio 1)** gives forecasts for all coastal waters at 0602, 1253, 1902, 2355 civil time. These are broadcast on RTE Radio 1 566 kHz. They include shipping forecasts for coastal waters all round Ireland and for the Irish Sea. They are broadcast on 567 kHz and on VHF 90·4 mHz (S half of Chapter I), 89·1 mHz (N half of Chapter I and Chapter II), 97 0 or 91 9 mHz (Chapters III and IV); however on VHF there may not be a forecast at 1823. Gale warnings are broadcast at the first programme junction after receipt.

**Central Analysis and Forecast Office** gives forecasts on request. Tel. (01) 8064255. (These calls are chargeable.)

**Weatherdial (voice):** Sea Area Forecast for all Irish Coastal Waters and the Irish Sea (+ any gale/swell warnings, reports from coastal stations, sea conditions on ferry crossing routes) available on 1550-123-855. Cost per minute 58p.

**BBC Weather Services by Radio:** Shipping forecasts are broadcast on BBC Radio 4 (198kHz, 1515 long wave) at the following clock times: 0048, 0555, 1355 and 1750.

**Inshore Waters:** A forecast for all UK inshore waters, ie up to 12 miles offshore, covering the period up to 1800 clock time, is broadcast on BBC Radio 4 at 0550 and at the end of programmes daily, at approximately 0052.

**UK Met. Office, Weather Services by Telephone:** For 2-day inshore forecasts, phone 0891500 plus the area number. The number for Ballycastle, Bangor Harbour and Malin Head areas is 465.

**UK Met. Office, Met-Call Direct:** Provides a direct line to a Met. Office forecaster, 24 hours a day. For example, when planning a trip or looking for a weather window, one can discuss the weather in detail.

Payment by credit card (on-line) Visa, Master Card, Delta, Switch. Phone 0374-555-888.

**UK Weather Services via the Internet (Met-Web):** A full range of meteorological information is now available. For service details, Met-Web can be found on http://www/met-office.gov.uk.

**UK Weather Services by Fax:** For 2-day inshore forecasts and charts, dial 0336-400 plus area number. The area No. for Northern Ireland reports is 465.

## VHF/MF BROADCAST SERVICES

Traffic lists, Navigational Warnings, Gale Warnings, Decca Warnings and Weather Forecasts are broadcast on the Coast Stations Working Channel/Frequency at scheduled times GMT after a preliminary announcement on Channel 16 VHF and 2182 kHz MF.

**MALIN HEAD CONTROL.** Tel. 077 70103. Fax. 077-70221

| MALIN HEAD RADIO | CLIFDEN RADIO |
|---|---|
| VHFCh23C | VHF 16, 67, 26 |
| MF 1667 kHz A | |
| GLENHEAD RADIO | BELMULLET RADIO |
| VHF Ch 24 C | VHF Ch 83 C |

**VALENTIA CONTROL.** Tel. 066-76109. Fax 066-76289

| VALENTIA RADIO | BANTRY RADIO |
|---|---|
| MF: 2182, 1746, 1752kHz (B) | VHF: 16, 67, 23, 85 (D) |
| VHF: 16, 67, 24, 28 (D) | |
| CORK RADIO | SHANNON RADIO |
| VHF: 16, 67, 26 (D) | VHF: 16, 67, 24, 28 (D) |

**GALWAY RADIO:** VHF (D) is planned for 1999.

*Note:* GMDSS A1, DSC System. IMES will begin installation of a nation-wide GMDSS A1 VHF system early in 1999. Notices will be issued when the system is declared operational.

**DUBLIN CONTROL.** Tel. 01-6620922 Fax 01-6620795

| WICKLOW HEAD (C) | ROSSLARE (C) |
|---|---|
| VHF CH. 16, 67, 87 | VHF CH. 16, 67, 23 |
| DUBLIN RADIO (C) | MINE HEAD (C) |
| VHF CH. 16, 67, 83 | VHF CH. 16, 67, 83 |

For calling and answering use Channel 16 VHF and 2182 kHz MF to call the nearest station to your own position. The control centre will answer on the same channel or frequency. Working channels VHF, frequencies MF and broadcast group schedules are shown under each station.

**NOTE: Ch. 67 is not monitored continuously by Irish Coast Radio Stations.**

| Broadcast Group | Traffic Lists | Navigation Warning | Weather Bulletin | Gale Warning | Decca Warning |
|---|---|---|---|---|---|
| A | 0103 1503<br>0503 1703<br>0903 1903<br>1103 2103<br>1303 2303 | 0033<br>0433<br>0833<br>1233<br>1633<br>2033 | No<br>Service | No<br>Service | (Note 1) |
| C | 0103 1503<br>0503 1703<br>0903 1903<br>1103 2303 | 0033<br>0433<br>0833<br>1233 | 0103 1303<br>0403 1603<br>0703 1903<br>1003 2203 | 0030<br>0630<br>1230<br>1830 | |
| | | 2033 | (Note 5) | (Note 3) | (Note 1) |
| D | 0333 1533<br>0733 1733<br>0933 1933<br>1133 2133 | 0233<br>0633<br>1033<br>1433 | 0103 1303<br>0403 1603<br>0703 1903<br>1003 2203 | 0030<br>0630<br>1230<br>1830 | |
| | 1333 2333 | 223333 | (Note 5) | (Note 5) | (Note 1) |

## NOTES

1. Decca Warnings are broadcast on receipt and repeated at three minutes past the next hour and again one hour later.

2. Gale Warnings are broadcast on (MF) at the end of the first silence period after receipt and repeated at the next one of the following times 0303 0903 1503 2103 or, if the first broadcast is at a scheduled time, the message is repeated at the end of the next silence period.

3. Gale Warnings are broadcast on (VHF) on receipt and repeated again at the next one of the following times 0030 0630 1220 1830 or, if the first broadcast is at a scheduled time, the message is repeated one hour later. **N.B.** Times one hour earlier when DST is in force from last Sunday in March to 4th Saturday in October.

4. Gale Warnings, if in force, general synopsis and area forecasts for SHANNON and FASTNET valid for 24 hours from the time of issue. (Issued by the UK Met. Service Bracknell).

5. Gale Warnings, if in force, general weather synopsis and detailed weather forecasts for Irish coastal waters, within 30 nautical miles of the coastline and for the Irish Sea. (Issued by the Irish Meteorological Service.)

**NOTE: Schedule times are one hour earlier when DST is in force from last Sunday in March to 4th Saturday in October.**

**Other Forecasts:**
RTE 1 television carries weather forecasts after main news bulletins provided by the Irish Meteorological Service.

WEATHERDIAL forecasts for other areas of Ireland:

| | |
|---|---|
| Munster | 1550-123-850 |
| Leinster | 1550-123-851 |
| Connacht | 1550-123-852 |
| Ulster | 1550-123-853 |
| Dublin | 1550-123-854 (includes winds on Dublin Bay and High Water at North Wall). |

## WEATHER DIAL ON FAX FROM MET EIREANN

To obtain any of the following Meteorological Services, dial 1570 131 838 on your fax telephone. Follow instructions given and use product codes from the list below.

| Products | Daily Updates | Code | Product Description | First Update |
|---|---|---|---|---|
| 5-day Text forecast for Munster | 3 | 0001 | Plain language forecast | 0600 |
| 5-day Text forecast for Leinster | 3 | 0002 | for the area with farming | 0600 |
| 5-day Text forecast for Connaught | 3 | 0003 | or national forecast and | 0600 |
| 5-day Text forecast for Ulster | 3 | 0004 | some other information. | 0600 |
| 5-day Text forecast for Dublin | 3 | 0005 | | 0600 |
| Forecast charts explanation | | 0014 | | |
| Latest analysis chart | 4 | 0015 | Fronts, isobars, wind | 0500 |
| Forecast chart 24 hour | 4 | 0016 | arrows W. Europe & | 0500 |
| Forecast chart 36 hour | 4 | 0017 | N. Atlantic | 0500 |
| Forecast chart midday (day 3) | 1 | 0018 | ditto for 48 hours ahead | 0500 |
| Forecast chart midday (day 4) | 1 | 0019 | ditto for following day | 0500 |
| Sea area forecast explanation | | 0020 | | |
| Sea Area Text (+GW +Crossings) | 4 | 0021 | Forecasts for Irish Coastal Waters and Irish Sea | 0100 |
| Beaufort scale of wind | | 0025 | Explanation and conversion to wind speeds | |
| Wave charts explanation | | 0030 | | |
| Wave forecast chart midday day 1 | 1 | 0031 | Forecast of sea and swell | 0700 |
| Wave forecast chart midday day 2 | 1 | 0032 | wave heights and periods | 0700 |
| Wave forecast chart midday day 2 | 1 | 0032 | ditto | 0700 |
| Wave forecast chart midday day 3 | 1 | 0033 | ditto | 0700 |
| Wave forecast chart midday day 4 | 1 | 0034 | ditto | 0700 |

### SEA PLANNERS

*Sea Planners* are computer-generated graphical forecasts, showing the expected winds and waves at specified locations off the Irish coasts, for up to 5 days ahead. They should be used in conjunction with the latest Sea Area forecast.

| Product Sea Planner | Lat/Long | Updates (per day) | 1st Update by (local time) | Code |
|---|---|---|---|---|
| Help Page | | | | 0040 |
| East | 53°N, 5·5°W | 1 | 0430 | 0041 |
| Southeast | 51°N, 6°W | 1 | 0430 | 0042 |
| Southwest | 51°N, 10·5° | 1 | 0430 | 0043 |
| West – 1 | 53°N, 11°W | 1 | 0430 | 0044 |
| West – 2 | 54°N, 11°W | 1 | 0430 | 0045 |
| Northwest | 55°N, 10°W | 1 | 0430 | 0046 |
| North | 56°N, 8°W | 1 | 0430 | 0047 |

Weatherdial Fax Calls cost 100p per minute (VAT incl.)

**Malinhead Radio Station.** A Radiotelephone service, with facilities for connection to subscribers ashore, is now available through Malinhead Radio to yachts with suitable radio equipment. Call 2182 kHz, on which the station answers and will state working frequency either 1841 or 2593 kHz.

## MARINE RADIO BEACONS

| Name | Range | Freq kHz | Signal | Mode |
|---|---|---|---|---|
| Tuskar Rock | 50 M | 286.00 | TR __ .__. | AIA |
| Baily | 50 M | 289.00 | BY __... __.__ __ | AIA |
| South Rock LV | 50 M | 291.50 | SU ... ..__ | AIA |
| Black Hd. (Antrim) on request | 5 M | 294.50 | BA __... .__ | AIA |
| Tory Island | 100 M | 313 | TY __ __ .__ __ | AIA |

During recognition and DF Transmission BFO.ON

## AIRCRAFT RADIO BEACONS

| Name | Signal | Freq. kHz | Lat | Long |
|---|---|---|---|---|
| Killiney | KLY __.__ .__.. __.__ __ | 378 | 53°16'·2 N | 6°06'·3 W |
| Rush | RSH .__. ... .... | 326 | 53°30'·6 N | 6°06'·8 W |

All beacons A2A transmission. During recognition BFO Off. During transmission BFO On. Beacons operate continuously.

# Appendix 6

## PORT VHF RADIO STATIONS

| Port | Channel | Times | Call Signs |
|------|---------|-------|------------|
| Rosslare | 16/14/12/6 | 24 hrs | Rosslare Harbour |
| Wexford Boat Club | 16 | Limited | Wexford Boat Club |
| Courtown | 16/8 | Limited | Courtown Sailing Club |
| Arklow | 16/14 | 24 hrs | Arklow Harbour |
| Wicklow | 16/14 | 24 hrs | Wicklow Harbour |
| Dun Laoghaire | 16/14 | 24 hrs | Harbour Office |
| Royal St. George | 16/37 | Limited | Royal St. George |
| Dublin | 16/12 | 24 hrs | Dublin Harbour |
| Howth Marina | 80 | 24 hrs | Howth Marina |
| Malahide | 37/80 | Limited | Malahide Yacht Club |
| Drogheda | 16/11 | 24 hrs | Drogheda Harbour |
| Dundalk | 16/12/6 | Working days | Dundalk Pilots |
| Greenore | 16 | Working days | Greenore Harbour |
| Warrenpoint | 16/12 | 24 hrs | Warrenpoint Pilot |
| Kilkeel | 16 | 24 hrs | Kilkeel Harbour Master |
| Ardglass | 16/14/12 | 24 hrs | Ardglass Harbour |
| Strangford | 16 | Office hours | Ferry Terminal |
| Portavogie | 16/14 | 24 hrs | Portavogie Harbour |
| Donaghadee | 16/08/06 | Limited | Donaghadee Harbour |
| Bangor Marina | 16/37/80 | 24 hrs | Bangor Marina |
| Belfast | 16/12/11/10/08 | 24 hrs | Belfast Harbour Radio |
| Carrickfergus Marina | 80/37 | 24 hrs | Carrickfergus Marina |
| Larne | 16/14 | 24 hrs | Larne Harbour |
| Portrush | 16/14 | 24 hrs | Portrush Harbour |
| Coleraine Marina | 16/37 | 24 hrs | Coleraine Marina |
| Londonderry | 16/14 | 24 hrs | Foyle Pilots |

# Appendix 7

## MARINE RESCUE SERVICES

(1)  The Maritime & Coastguard Agency (MCA) – Northern Ireland
(2)  Irish Marine Emergency Services (IMES)
(3)  Royal National Lifeboat Institution (RNLI)


### (1)  THE MARITIME & COASTGUARD AGENCY (MCA) – NORTHERN IRELAND

#### MCA – NEW AGENCY

The Maritime and Coastguard Agency (MCA) was established on 1 April 1998 as an executive agency of the Department of the Environment, Transport and the Regions (DETR). The Agency was created by the merger of the Coastguard Agency (TCA) and the Marine Safety Agency (MSA) and is responsible for carrying out the functions of both organisations.

The primary aim of the Agency, as stated in its Framework Document, is to develop, promote and enforce high standards of marine safety; to minimise loss of life amongst seafarers and coastal users; and to minimise pollution from ships of the sea and coastline within the policy framework set by the Secretary of State.

The primary responsibility of MCA is the initiation and co-ordination of civil maritime search and rescue within the United Kingdom search and rescue region. This includes the mobilisation, organisation and tasking of adequate resources to respond to persons either in distress at sea, or to persons at risk of injury or death on the cliffs or shoreline of the United Kingdom.

The initiation and co-ordination of all incidents on the shoreline or in the waters around Northern Ireland are conducted from Belfast Maritime Rescue Sub-Centre (MRSC).

Belfast MRSC is HM Coastguard's headquarters in Northern Ireland and is located at, Bregenz House, Quay Street Bangor, Co. Down BT20 5ED. Telephone 01247-463933. (In an emergency dial 999 and ask for the Coastguard).

HM Coastguard call on dedicated and additional search and rescue facilities to perform search and rescue operations at sea. These include RNLI lifeboats, RAF and other helicopters, HM Coastguard Auxiliary Coastguard response teams, other emergency services and vessels at sea. Belfast MRSC work closely with the Irish Marine Emergency Service who are responsible for the co-ordination of search and rescue in the Irish search and rescue region.

Belfast MRSC is fully equipped with modern radio, telephone equipment, computer network and emergency planning facilities. It is continuously manned with a minimum watch of 3 Coastguards. Radio coverage on VHF is maintained through links to remote aerial sites situated at; Ramore Head (Portrush), West Torr (near Torr Head), Blackmountain (Belfast), Orlock Head (near Bangor) and Slieve Martin (Carlingford Lough). These aerials cover most of the Northern Ireland coastal waters. A dedicated and continuous distress listening watch is maintained on VHF channel 16.

Stations wishing to make routine (ie non-emergency) contact by VHF radio should call "Belfast Coastguard" on VHF channel 16, they will be requested to move to the primary working frequency VHF Channel 67 (or secondary frequency VHF Ch 73).

For emergency use, 2 aerial sites are fitted with VHF DF (Direction Finding) equipment. These sites are situated at West Torr (Lat. 55° 11.90′N Long. 06° 05.60′W) and Orlock Head (Lat. 54° 40.42′N Long. 05° 34.97′W). The equipment is primarily to obtain bearings of stations in distress. However, where bearing information is needed for safety purposes, it can be requested. Please note that HM Coastguard cannot accept responsibility for any decisions the Master or Skipper of a vessel may make based on this information.

HM Coastguard can call on Auxiliary Coastguard response teams based throughout Northern Ireland. These carry out Cliff, Search and Mud rescue under the co-ordination of MRSC Belfast. They are located in Castlerock, Portrush, Ballycastle, Rathlin Island, Portmuck, Bangor, Portaferry and Newcastle. Initial response teams, which can provide a quick on scene presence but with limited rescue capacity are located at the stations above plus, Red Bay, Larne, Ballywalter, Ardglass and Kilkeel.

Yacht and small craft owners are encouraged to participate in HM Coastguard's Yacht and Boat Safety Scheme. The aims are simple:

- to provide your nearest Rescue Centre with information needed to mount a successful search and rescue operation
- to promote closer links between Coastguards and all small-craft owners and users.

Registration forms can be obtained from MRSC Belfast, marinas and some harbour masters. The registration requests details of a vessel's size, appearance, equipment and sail plans.

## MRSC NORTHERN IRELAND

H.M. Coastguard is the coordinating authority for search and rescue at sea. Its headquarters in Northern Ireland is Belfast Marine Rescue Sub Centre at Bangor, telephone Bangor (01247) 463933. This station is the only one in Northern Ireland maintaining a 24 hour watch. It has remote VHF aerials and can accept VHF calls on Channel 16 from almost anywhere off the Northern Ireland Coast. Having received a call from a yacht they will request it to transfer to Channel 67.

It is suggested that small craft owners and users who sail off Northern Ireland should obtain from their local CG station (or from YCs or marinas in Northern Ireland) a "Safety Scheme Card", fill in details of their craft on it and return it to Orlock Head Station. This helps the CG to identify the vessel if it is reported overdue or in distress.

## (2) IRISH MARINE EMERGENCY SERVICE (IMES)

### Rescue at Sea

Rescue at sea and round the shores of the Irish Republic is the responsibility of the Irish Marine Emergency Service (IMES). In emergency, the Service can best be contacted on VHF radio through the nearest VHF Radio Station on Channel 16 or by dialing 999 and requesting "Marine Rescue".

The IMES maintains two medium range Search and Rescue helicopters, one at Shannon Airport, the other at Dublin Airport, and a network of Coastal Rescue teams around the coast of the Republic. The service, through the Marine Rescue Co-ordination Centre, (MRCC) avails of the services of The Irish Air Corp SAR helicopters, Finner and Waterford Airports, the RNLI, the Irish Naval Service, the Gardai, Coast Radio Stations and other organisations engaged in SAR activities. Close liaison is maintained with the rescue services in Northern Ireland and adjacent countries and yacht safety information is exchanged on a routine basis. A passage surveillance scheme is operated, free of charge, for yachts bound to or from Ireland or round the coast.

For routine information, the IMES can be contacted at IMES HQ, Leeson Lane, Dublin 2, Telephone 01-6785444. (From N. Ireland 003531-6785444.)

## MRSC ORGANISATION

The organisation is based upon 3 Marine Rescue Sub-Centres, located at Dublin, Malin Head and Valentia where a continuous 24 hour radio watch is maintained on marine distress frequencies: 500kHz W/T. 2181kHz R/T and 2187.5kHz DSC at Valentia: 2182kHz R/T and 2187.5kHz DSC at Malin Head: 156.8mhz (Channel 16) at 12 remotely controlled VHF stations located at Dublin, Wicklow Head, Rosslare, Mine Head, Cork, Bantry, Valentia, Shannon, Clifden, Belmullet, Glen Head and Malin Head which together give radio coverage of the entire coastline.

**Dublin MRCC/CRS Communications Control Centre** located at IMES Headquarters, Leeson Lane, will control SAR co-ordination and marine radio communications along the East and Southeast coasts from Carlingford Lough to Youghal: Telephone 01-6620922 (2 lines) Fax 01-6620795 Telex 93039 IMES EI

**Valentia MRCC/CRS Communications Control Centre** located at Valentia Island, Co. Kerry, will control SAR co-ordination and marine radio communications along the South, Southwest and West coasts from Youghal to Slyne Head: Telephone 066-76109 (2 lines) Fax 066-76289, Telex 73968 VALR EI.

**Malin Head MRCC/CRS Communications Control Centre** located at Malin Head, Co. Donegal will control SAR co-ordination and marine radio communications along the West, and Northwest coasts from Slyne Head to Inishowen Head: Telephone 077-70103 (2 lines) Fax 077-70221, Telex 42072 MALR EI.

### IMES Coastal Units

These are maintained by the IMES and staffed by part-time volunteers. There are 50 Stations strategically located around the coast and on call 24 hours a day every day and are provided with fully equipped all-terrain rescue vehicles and area lighting.

Personnel are trained in cliff rescue and local search techniques.
Inshore rescue craft are maintained at several of the stations.
Watch is not kept except when required during an emergency.
Stations are best contacted through the Marine Rescue Co-ordination Centre, which can page all personnel through the IMES marine VHF network.

**Appendix 8 – PRINCIPAL LIGHTS –** *continued*

| Name | Lights in fog | Character and colour | Period secs | Elev m | Range Miles Nom | Fog signal | Type and height of lighthouse |
|---|---|---|---|---|---|---|---|
| South Rock Lamby | On 24 hrs | Fl (3) R | 30 | 12 | 20 | Horn (3) 45s | Red light float Racon (T) RC |
| Donaghadee | | Iso WR | 4 | 17 | W18 R14 | | Wh Tr 16m on S pier |
| Mew Island | On | Fl (4) W | 30 | 37 | 24 | | Bl Tr, white band, 37m Racon (O) |
| Black Head | | Fl W | 3 | 45 | 27 | | Wh Tr 16m |
| Barr Point Larne Hbr. | | | | | | Horn 30s | White House 5m |
| Chaine Tower | | Iso WR | 5 | 23 | 16 | | Grey Tr 24 m |
| Maidens | On 24 hrs | Fl (3) W | 20 | 29 | 24 | | Wh Tr, black band, 23m Racon (M) |
| Auxiliary Lt. | | Fl R | 5 | 15 | 8 | | |
| Rue Point Rathlin Island | | Fl (2) W | 5 | 16 | 14 | | Wh Tr, black bands, 11m |
| Rathlin East Altacarry Head | On 24 hrs | Fl (4) W | 20 | 74 | 26 | | Wh Tr, black band, 27 m Racon (G) |
| Rathlin West Bull Point | On | Fl R | 5 | 62 | 22 | | Lantern at base of white tower 18m |
| Inishowen | On 24 hrs | Fl (2) WRG | 10 | 28 | W18 R14 G14 | Horn (2) 30s | Wh Tr, 2 black bands, 23m |
| Inishtrahull | | Fl (3) W | 15 | 59 | 25 | | Wh Tr 23m Racon |
| Fanad Head | | Fl (5) WR | 20 | 39 | W18 R14 | | Wh Tr 22m |
| Dunree Head | | Fl (2) WR | 5 | 46 | W12 R9 | | House 6m |
| Tory Island | On | Fl (4) | 30 | 40 | 27 | | Bl Tr, white band, 27m Radio Beacon Racon (M) |

# CHAPTER 5 ONLY

| Name | Lights in fog | Character and colour | Period secs | Elev m | Range Miles Nom | Fog signal | Type and height of lighthouse |
|---|---|---|---|---|---|---|---|
| Coningbeg Lt. F | On 24 hrs | Fl.(3)W | 30 | 12 | 24 | Horn (3) 60s | Red hull and tower lantern amidships Racon (M) |
| Hook Head | On | Fl.W | 3 | 46 | 23 | Horn (2) 45s | Wh Tr 2 black bands 35m Racon (K) |
| Dunmore East | | L.Fl.WR | 8 | 13 | W17 R13 | | Stone Tr. 16m on pier. |

# Appendix 9

## PLACES WHERE A YACHT MIGHT BE LEFT UNATTENDED

The following list of places where a yacht may be left unattended or the names of people who are mentioned would give good advice on the subject.

   Also most of the yacht clubs mentioned in Appendix 17 are able to find someone with good local knowledge.

| | |
|---|---|
| Kilmore Quay Marina | Harbour Master 053-29955 |
| Wexford | Harbour Boat Club T. Furlong 053-22039 |
| Arklow | Arklow Marine Services 0402-32126 |
| Wicklow | HM 0404-67455 |
| Dun Laoghaire | Advice from Secretaries of main Yacht Clubs - see list |
| Howth | In Marina, Liam Lalor, Marina Manager 01-8392777 |
| Howth Yacht Club, 01-8322141 | |
| Malahide | Kevin Byrne, Fingall Sailing School 01-8451979 |
| Malahide Marina | Manager, Damian Offer, 01-8454129 |
| Carlingford | Carlingford Marina Manager 042-73492 |
| Ardglass | Ardglass Phennick Cove Marina 01396-841291 |
| Bangor Marina | Manager, Andrew Jaggers, 0247-453297 |
| Portaferry | Portaferry Marina 012477-29598 |
| Cultra | RNIYC 012317-2287 |
| | Boatyard 01232-420841 |
| Carrickfergus Marina | Manager 01960-366666 |
| Carnlough | HM 01574-272677 |
| Ballycastle | Ballycastle Marina 012657-62024 (provisional) |
| Seatons Marina | 01265-832086 |
| Coleraine Marina | 01265-44768 |
| Culmore | Ferrymen |
| Fahan | Lough Swilly YC boatman |
| Ramelton | L. Turner & Son Boat Yard |

# Appendix 10

## SAILING ROUND IRELAND

Ireland is ideal for sailing round. Doing so is difficult enough to be interesting and yet the distance of 681 miles fits well into a cruising holiday of two or three weeks. It would be impossible to explore all the many anchorages in any one year, but one rapidly becomes fascinated by the wonderful scenery and the excellence of the sailing. The numbers circumnavigating increase year by year, and more yachts are now to be found using the west coast anchorages as their base. An increasing number of members of the Irish Cruising Club come from the more remote areas and are always ready to give assistance in every possible way to visiting yachtsmen. A list of port members, with their addresses and telephone numbers, is available from Arthur Orr, Evergreen, 11 Old Holywood Road, Belfast BT4 2HJ, Northern Ireland.

**Time**

Yachts cruising normally, anchoring for the night with only occasional longer passages, seldom take less than 21 days from an Irish port, or a couple of days more from the west of England. It can be done in less time, but this means bypassing a very high proportion of the attractive parts. Anyone who can afford the time could easily spend two months circumnavigating without seeing everything.

**Which way round?**

The majority of boats have gone anticlockwise. Analyses of wind records coast by coast for June and July show a variation of only 3% for clockwise and anticlockwise passages and so in an average year it does not matter from a wind point of view which way you go in these the two most popular months. Allowing for the fact that it is easier to beat on the east coast, where there is less swell than on the west, a clockwise passage in July offers the best statistical chance.

   The chief consideration is your home port or starting point. The west coast is the least known and most interesting and it is a sound principle to begin by heading for whichever end of it is nearest. Some people may prefer to get half way round as quickly as possible and leave the part they want to visit individually, in which it is all too easy to stay longer than intended, until the second half of the cruise.

   Boats from the south of England or the Bristol channel should find clockwise best, but may leave the decision until they see what winds blow as they make the passage up and head for the Tuskar or Fastnet accordingly. For Clyde, Liverpool and Welsh boats the same consideration as for Irish ones would apply.

   The Kenmare Bantry area has always been popular with yachts from Cork and the south of England. Roundstone Kilkieran, and also in good weather Achill Slyne are both magnificent cruising grounds, but unfortunately not places to dally in, unless you have plenty of time, say four weeks at least for an Irish based boat. Aranmore area, also Lough Swilly, are other little known but most attractive places, and yachtmen keen to see a bit of these parts, should go clockwise.

**General**

Some yachts have been round under sail alone, but this is not recommended, for a good engine is of much greater value on the exposed coasts than say in the Irish Sea. On the west coast particularly, a large swell and awful sea can persist long after the gale which caused it has ceased, shaking any wind there is out of the sails and making for miserable conditions aboard a pure sailing vessel.

   Much time can be absorbed in the west getting stores; the nearest town is often a couple of miles or more from the anchorage. The same applies to water and fuel, so ship as much as you can before starting, and top up when opportunity offers.

   Have two good anchors plus a spare, and plenty of chain, warps and fenders. On the west you will be relying almost entirely on natural anchorages, as opposed to largely manmade ones on the east coast. But if you have good enough gear to lie alongside a rough pier in a bit of swell without damaging the boat, it may save a lot of dinghy work and wettings.

   Unless you have time to spare, keep to the islands as much as possible. You will almost invariably be in a much better position to take advantage of the next day's winds if you bring up in the roads at, for example, Gola, Inishkea or Turk, than in the corresponding bays or anchorages of the mainland. These and several others similar provide, more often than not, safe and comfortable anchorages in summer.

## Gales
*Irish Coast Pilot* gives tables for the incidence of gales and these show that both June and July average two force 7 gale days apiece. This ties up with the reports from yachts. In a three week cruise you will almost certainly be held up once, perhaps twice, by gales lasting one or two days, but there is generally warning and nearly everyone manages to get shelter before the blow really develops. To be sure of getting forecasts on the west coast you should have a good set but it is also very important to watch the sky and the barometer. RTE shipping forecasts apply to Irish coastal waters and so are more likely to be accurate for the coastal cruiser than the BBC shipping forecasts which refer to much wider areas of open sea.

## Fog
Ireland as a whole is lucky in this respect and complete days of persistent fog occur on average less than once in ten years. Fog generally only occurs with winds between SE and SW and is much less common on the west coast than elsewhere.

## Sailing Directions
South and West Coasts, the companion to this volume, is published by Irish Cruising Club Publications. It can be obtained from any good chandlery, or from Arthur Orr, Evergreen, 11 Holywood Road, Belfast BT4 2HJ Northern Ireland. In the U.K. it can be obtained from Imray Laurie Norie & Wilson Ltd., Wych House, The Broadway, St. Ives, Huntingdon, Cambridgeshire PE17 4BT.

# Appendix 19

## CONVERSION TABLES

In the first three tables metres are converted to the nearest inch, .25 fathom or yard; in the righthand table feet are converted to the nearest 0.1 metre. Exact equivalents are as follows: 1 metre = 3.28084 feet. 1 foot = 0.3048 metres. For readers unfamiliar with local units: 12 inches = 1 foot. 3 feet = 1 yard. 2 yards = 1 fathom. The Nautical Mile ("M" in the text) is 6,080 feet, about 1,853 metres; it is the average local Sea Mile which is a minute of latitude and therefore variable. The cable is one tenth of a Nautical Mile, approximately 203 yards or 185 metres, usually thought of as 200 yards, 0.75 cable = 139 m. 0.5 cable = 93 m. 0.25 cable = 46 m.

| Metres | Ft. inches | Metres | Fathoms | Metres | Yards | Feet | Metres | Feet | Metres |
|--------|-----------|--------|---------|--------|-------|------|--------|------|--------|
| 0.1 | 4″ | 2 | 1 | 10 | 11 | 1 | 0.3 | 30 | 9.1 |
| 0.2 | 8″ | 3 | 1 | 15 | 16 | 2 | 0.6 | 31 | 9 4 |
| 0.3 | 1′ | 4 | 2.25 | 20 | 22 | 3 | 0.9 | 32 | 9.7 |
| 0.4 | 1′ 4″ | 5 | 2.75 | 25 | 27 | 4 | 1.2 | 33 | 10.1 |
| 0.5 | 1′ 8″ | 6 | 3.25 | 30 | 33 | 5 | 1.5 | 34 | 10.4 |
| 0.6 | 2′ | 7 | 3.75 | 35 | 38 | 6 | 1.8 | 35 | 10.7 |
| 0.7 | 2′ 4″ | 8 | 4.25 | 40 | 44 | 7 | 2.1 | 36 | 11.0 |
| 0.8 | 2′ 7″ | 9 | 5 | 45 | 49 | 8 | 2.4 | 37 | 11.3 |
| 0.9 | 2′ 11″ | 10 | 5.5 | 50 | 55 | 9 | 2.7 | 38 | 11.6 |
| 1.0 | 3′ 3″ | 11 | 6 | 55 | 60 | 10 | 3.0 | 39 | 11.9 |
| 1.1 | 3′ 7″ | 12 | 6.5 | 60 | 66 | 11 | 3.3 | 40 | 12.2 |
| 1.2 | 3′ 11″ | 13 | 7 | 65 | 71 | 12 | 3.7 | 41 | 12.5 |
| 1.3 | 4′ 3″ | 14 | 7.75 | 70 | 77 | 13 | 4.0 | 42 | 12.8 |
| 1.4 | 4′ 7″ | 15 | 8.25 | 75 | 82 | 14 | 4.3 | 43 | 13.1 |
| 1.5 | 4′ 11″ | 16 | 8.75 | 80 | 87 | 15 | 4.6 | 44 | 13.4 |
| 1.6 | 5′ 3″ | 17 | 9.25 | 85 | 93 | 16 | 4.9 | 45 | 13.7 |
| 1.7 | 5′ 7″ | 18 | 9.75 | 90 | 98 | 17 | 5.2 | 46 | 14.0 |
| 1.8 | 5′ 11″ | 19 | 10.5 | 95 | 104 | 18 | 5.5 | 47 | 14.3 |
| 1.9 | 6′ 3″ | 20 | 11 | 100 | 109 | 19 | 5.8 | 48 | 14.6 |
| 2 | 6′ 7″ | 21 | 11.5 | 110 | 120 | 20 | 6.1 | 49 | 14.9 |
| 3 | 9′ 10″ | 22 | 12 | 120 | 131 | 21 | 6.4 | 50 | 15. 2 |
| 4 | 13′ 1″ | 23 | 12.5 | 130 | 142 | 22 | 6.7 | 51 | 15.5 |
| 5 | 16′ 5″ | 24 | 13 | 140 | 153 | 23 | 7.0 | 52 | 15.8 |
| 6 | 19′ 8″ | 25 | 13.75 | 150 | 164 | 24 | 7.3 | 53 | 16.1 |
| 7 | 23′ | 26 | 14.25 | 160 | 175 | 25 | 7.6 | 54 | 16.5 |
| 8 | 26′ 3″ | 27 | 14.75 | 170 | 186 | 26 | 7.9 | 55 | 16.8 |
| 9 | 29′ 6″ | 28 | 15.25 | 180 | 197 | 27 | 8.2 | 56 | 17.1 |
| 10 | 32′ 10″ | 29 | 15.75 | 190 | 208 | 28 | 8.5 | 57 | 17.4 |
| | | 30 | 16.5 | 200 | 219 | 29 | 8.8 | 58 | 17.7 |

# GENERAL INDEX